SEARCHING FOR
BOBBY ORR

STEPHEN BRUNT

TRIUMPH
BOOKS
CHICAGO

ISBN-13: 978-1-57243-902-3
ISBN-10: 1-57243-902-5

Text design: Leah Springate

Printed and bound in the United States of America

2 4 6 8 9 7 5 3

For my mother

Contents

A MEMORY

REG WAS A CONFIRMED BACHELOR. They existed then, without irony, without quotation marks – at least so it seemed. He lived with his mother in a small, square, red brick house on a quiet city street in a humble neighbourhood of a working-class city. There must have been more to him than that, a back story of some sort, but perhaps I was just too young to have heard. What I do remember is that he was tall and rake thin. That he was an exercise buff at a time when that would set him apart from his peers, in the days when only the muscleman Jack LaLanne, doing jumping jacks on the old black and white, represented anything resembling a fitness culture. That he worked for the same people as my father did, performing some vaguely actuarial function on a different floor of the grand old hotel where the company had rented space. That, like so many childless people of a certain age whom I encountered in those years, he had a soft spot for kids.

Years later, they'd find Reg dead in the office, slumped over his desk one afternoon. My father, who though he mostly loved his work had a romantic resistance to the wage slave's life, always thought that was an awful way to go – on the job. The phone rang at home, and when my mother picked up, there was the sound of shock, then silence, which I already recognized as the sure sign of bad news being delivered. I have something sad to tell you, she said. Those first intimations of mortality stick with you.

Beyond his looks and the day he died, what I remember most of Reg was a hockey game, the first one I ever saw in person. It was his idea. He was passionate about the sport in a way that, frankly, my father was not. It was forever unclear how and why that had happened, how a Canadian – or at least an American who lived virtually his entire life in Canada – had resisted the siren song of the national game. The old man could skate a bit, and presumably he had played at some point or another, growing up in the same small Southwestern Ontario tobacco town, Simcoe, that had produced the great Leonard "Red" Kelly. But I never heard him mention it once, and he never cared much whether I could skate and shoot. Even the spectator side of the sport seemed to leave him cold. Football he loved, and he enjoyed the fights, and those I remember the neighbourhood fathers gathering to watch on big, boxy television sets. But the Saturday night ritual that seemed to captivate every other Canadian passed our house over. For us, hockey was more of a sometime thing.

And that's saying something, since in that time, in that country, in that sports world, the opportunities to actually see a game were so limited to begin with. The National Hockey League, on television, was on view only those winter Saturday nights. Baseball came our way just on Saturday afternoons from an American network. There were occasional Canadian Football League games, and on Sundays in the fall the National Football League or the American Football League, the New York Giants, the Cleveland Browns or the Buffalo Bills. Even that, for most of Canada, represented an unbelievably rich smorgasbord. Border towns, or at least those within antenna distance, could add content from three U.S. channels' networks. Most of the vast country, though, was limited to the state broadcaster, the CBC: one station, all the time, beaming the perspective of downtown Toronto from sea to sea, whether the rest of the nation wanted it or not. *Hockey Night in Canada* was its most famous property, but there was other stuff as well: *Don Messer's Jubilee,* the variety show starring our pet, Juliette* and kids' shows – *The Friendly Giant* and *Razzle Dazzle* and *Chez Hélène.* Canada then seemed a quiet, square place. The civil rights marches and the Vietnam War were evening news exotica, the greater cares of the world apparently distant, though for a few fleeting moments my parents did wonder whether they ought to build a fallout shelter in the backyard. To their generation, for whom a world war was a fresh experience, for whom the Depression shaped core values, those placid boom times were a blessing. They were also, it turned out, the calm before a social storm.

What I remember most when it comes to hockey are my father's strong dislikes, one of which was the Toronto-centricity that the rest of the country was forced to endure. Somehow, though he'd spent many hours in the great metropolis visiting his beloved grandfather, the Major, a dramatic, brilliant, florid Englishman prone to extreme financial highs and lows, my father loathed the Toronto Maple Leafs and everything he believed they stood for. It wasn't so much that he was a Habs fan, or a Red Wings fan, or something positive that would fully explain the negative. He just hated the whole notion that the country's beating heart could be found in the yellow brick temple on Carlton Street, that it was the Leafs and then everyone else. (Years later, when the suit-and-tie crowd at the

---

* *Juliette,* a variety show featuring the eponymous chanteuse (last name Sysak, though like Prince, she didn't really need one) from Winnipeg, Manitoba, immediately followed *Hockey Night in Canada* on the CBC from 1954 to 1966. The show that preceded hockey during much of that time – the games came on in progress at 9:00 p.m. and ended by 10:15 p.m. – was *Red River Hoedown,* a country music program. But many a child of that era will remember watching the *Jackie Gleason Show* from 8:00 to 9:00 before switching over to the CBC for hockey. Among baby boomer Canadians, even the commercials associated with *Hockey Night in Canada* evoke strong memories: Murray Westgate as the friendly Imperial Oil dealer, and ads for "The Tea That Dares to Be Known by Good Taste Alone."

Gardens, so knowledgeable, so dignified, took to booing a brilliant young Boston defenceman every time he touched the puck, my father regarded that as definitive proof of the soundness of his anti-Hogtown prejudices.) He also hated Foster Hewitt,* the great icon of Canadian sports broadcasting, the voice of hockey, first on radio and then on television, the man who invented the phrase, "He shoots, he scores!" My father claimed he sounded like a pig.

Not knowing exactly what a pig would sound like doing hockey play-by-play, I thought that still seemed reasonable enough. And as for rooting interests, I admit to considerable confusion. If you

---

* Foster Hewitt, the most famous personality in Canadian broadcasting history, began calling hockey games in 1923. His father, W.A. Hewitt, was the sports editor of *The Toronto Star,* and Hewitt worked there before moving over to the paper's newly established radio station, CFCA, as an announcer/operator in 1922. His first play-by-play assignment was a senior game between the Toronto Argonauts and the Kitchener Greenshirts from the Mutual Street Arena, which he called over the telephone. (The game went into triple overtime, and lasted over three hours). Hewitt began broadcasting Toronto Maple Leafs games when the franchise came into existence in 1927. He was the master of ceremonies for the opening of Maple Leaf Gardens in 1931, and then broadcast the game from his perch in the "gondola," high above the ice. In 1952, Hewitt was the voice of the first hockey game ever televised in Canada, appropriately between the Leafs and the Montreal Canadiens. On what would become known by the 1950s as *Hockey Night in Canada,* Hewitt memorably began each broadcast with the line, "Hello, Canada, and hockey fans in the United States and Newfoundland . . ." (cutting the last part when Newfoundland came into Confederation in 1949). In 1957, he handed over TV play-by-play duties to his son, Bill Hewitt, though he continued doing the Leafs radio broadcasts, as well as hosting between-periods interviews on television and picking the game's three stars. He retired in 1963, but was persuaded to return in 1972 for the Summit Series between Canada and the Soviet Union, where his call of Paul Henderson's winning goal became the most memorable in the country's history, and can still be quoted word for word by those of a certain age. Hewitt was also a successful broadcast entrepreneur, opening his own radio station – CKFH – in 1951. He died in 1985.

lived in English Canada and didn't love the Leafs in the early 1960s, you were out of luck on a couple of fronts: one, they were very good and seemed to win the Stanley Cup pretty much annually; and two, in every way that mattered, there was only one home team. When the games came on television, the first period and part of the second already completed (had to protect the live gate for the team's proprietors), the score mysterious until Foster or his son and successor, Bill Hewitt, delivered the news, it was always the Maple Leafs versus somebody. Of the five available somebodies, you understood that the Habs were also pretty darned good, though awfully French; that the Red Wings were a mere shadow of the great team of the fifties, and that Gordie Howe was already old; that the Black Hawks employed the most glamorous young star in the game, Bobby Hull, and seemed like the vanguard of a new era; that the New York Rangers and especially the Boston Bruins were usually terrible. How you could be usually terrible in a six-team league, how you could go decades without winning a Stanley Cup, was a mystery that flew in the face of all theories of logic and probability, but that's the way it was.

The athletes, not just in hockey but in all sports, were a collection of crewcut heads on bubble-gum cards, the subjects of heroic profiles in the sports pages and the few speciality magazines that turned up in the drugstores. Far-fetched was the notion that an athlete could be part of the nascent 1960s counterculture. That possibility didn't dawn on anyone until Cassius Clay beat Sonny Liston and then told the world he'd rather be called Muhammad Ali. And it wasn't until the arrival of Joe Namath that a sports star possessed the kind of attractive, cutting-edge, sexy danger normally associated with movie stars or musicians. Professional athletes instead represented and reinforced the status quo, whether or not that was true, whether or not that was their choice, whether or not that was who they really were.

In hockey, it wasn't so hard in a six-team league to know the name of every player on every team. The notion that athletes were in any way mercenary, that their loyalties lay anywhere but with the crest on their chest, was an utterly alien concept. The players weren't organized in associations or unions (which greatly facilitated their exploitation by the owners). There were no agents. Those very few who held out for more money at the beginning of a season – never hockey players, though – were regarded as greedy and ungrateful and unaware of the difference between real labour and being paid to play a kids' game.

On the other end of the equation, money was very much the issue, the price of entry to see the heroes in action live and in person. Beyond television, the flesh-and-bones National Hockey League, the real thing, was for me distant and in most ways unimaginable. My town was within easy driving distance of Maple Leaf Gardens, but who had the dough, who had the influential friends necessary to gain access to Saturday night hockey in Toronto? (I didn't see the Leafs play a real live game until I was twenty-one years old, when I moved to the city and could afford to buy my own ticket.) If you said you were going to the hockey game, you meant the local rink, the Forum, an old barn of a place down in the industrial east end, close to the steel mills, where the seats were wooden benches, where pillars obstructed the view, where the local heroes, a junior team affiliated with the Detroit Red Wings, were the biggest game in town. So you might not see Frank Mahovlich, but there was his big, hulking brother, Pete. You might not see Bobby Hull, but there was Dennis, playing for St. Catharines. The Lesser Brothers League. That, plus a host of local heroes whose names I can still remember, guys who today would have enjoyed long, prosperous NHL careers, but who in the six-team days perhaps were invited to one training camp, perhaps plied their trade in a far-flung outpost of the minors and then returned to day jobs, dreaming of what might have been.

So when kind Reg suggested to the old man that it was time he took his son to a hockey game, that's what he meant. Sure, he's awfully young, but he'd get a kick out of it. It's an afternoon tilt; the tickets are cheap. A boys' day out. What a great and wonderful surprise.

It gets blurry here, even as one of those memories that, as the years pass, you desperately hope to preserve, or to resurrect. There were plenty of other games afterwards, but only the one became part of family lore, the time that Reg took you to the rink, the time that you saw you-know-who. (I have seen my own kids' first inklings of nostalgia, understanding the part that parental construction and family mythology play in the process. So much of what we remember is what we are told we must.) But what has stuck, what I think is my own, are the colours of that afternoon, which in a world of black-and-white television were vivid beyond my imagining. That kind of great sensory overload that strikes me still, walking into a sporting event. Not just the visuals, but the arena smell, though in the new, antiseptic NHL buildings, they seem to have finally managed to mask it, the funk of sweat and popcorn, the blue haze of cigarette smoke in the corridors, the chill coming off the artificial rink, the sound of skates carving the ice, a tinny public address announcer, standing for the anthem. The ritual, the costumes, which to a future exceptionally dedicated altar boy would always seem so much like Catholic mass.

There is an image, also, of a kid player, who to me certainly looked like a full-grown man. Every time he stepped on the ice, which was often that day, I was told to keep an eye on number 2, playing for the visiting Oshawa Generals, a Boston Bruins farm team whose uniforms bore a variation on the spoked logo that has been reproduced by many a bored student doodling on school notebooks. So many hockey players are blessed, or cursed, to carry boys' names for their entire lives, as least those that, unlike Wayne, or Mario, could be easily reduced. Howe would never become Gordon, even when he was a playing grandfather. Hull was never Robert, or even Bob. It was and is a game of Gordies and Mickeys and Dannys. And Bobbys. Orr: blond, crewcut Bobby, who could take the puck behind his own net and skate through and past and around the other team. Bobby, who in the days when a young country seemed to be waking from a long nap, when a minor professional sport began to shake off the cobwebs and look to new horizons, embodied the idea that it didn't have to be as it had always been. A defenceman could take off, could improvise, could be so good that they'd let him defy every bit of conventional coaching wisdom. A skinny teenager could play among hardened, violent, resentful men, and survive. A sixties guy – at least when he finally let his hair grow past his ears – could take the place of heroes who in their square, upright Canadianness, looked like your buddy's dad who worked down at the plant.

Remember, Reg said. Remember who it was you saw today. Remember so you can tell your own kids someday. Remember. For forty years, I have tried my best.

Chapter One

PARRY SOUND

ON THE RIVER, HE COULD SKATE FOREVER. No barrier but the banks and the horizon, the ice stretching far out into the bay. Soon enough, the cold seemed to disappear, even for the boy who always insisted on lacing up barefoot – it just felt better, more natural, that way. Take the puck, and try to hold it. Keep away. Offer it up, then pull it back, tuck it behind the blade, make it disappear. Sleight of hand, sleight of feet. Learn to keep your head up, your eyes forward, feel the puck on your stick, don't look down. Speed up, change direction, the motion natural, deceptive, economical, graceful. No churning legs or laboured strides, even on beat-up, second-hand skates. He is smaller than the rest, a skinny kid, scrawny, no meat on his bones at all. But they can't get near him, even though it looks as if he isn't working hard, as if he is shifting through the gears in automatic – one speed, then another, then another. Size and muscle are of no use, without corners, without ends, without limits. There are no coaches standing by, waiting to impose their will. No parents shouting at the side. No drills, no repetition, but rather every rush is an improvisation, a jazz solo, a flight of the imagination. And when the boy is clear of

9

them all, or alone by choice, when all he faces is open ice, the other sounds of his world disappear, the intermittent hum of small-town traffic, the rumble of distant factories, the angry shouts at home. Just the scrape and gouge of metal on ice, the rhythmic tap of rubber on wood, on, on forever. Pick a direction and keep on going, and eventually there's no one in the way.

Why people settled here is no mystery, though in the middle of many a brutal winter they must have wondered. Parry Sound, Ontario, stands by a natural harbour on a deep, cold, dangerous lake, a shelter for sailors on the shores of Georgian Bay at the mouth of the Seguin River. The earliest known residents were the Hurons, who fished and camped in summer before being driven out by the Iroquois, but surely there were others before them. "Shining Shore," the Iroquois named it – Wausakwasene. When the Europeans arrived, those who passed by here were among the very first and most famous to set foot in what would become central Canada, traders and explorers and adventurers and sailors, Étienne Brulé and Samuel de Champlain, Robert de LaSalle sailing his *Griffon*, Alexander Henry, doomed Sir John Franklin. The place got its name, a tribute to the Arctic explorer Sir William Edward Parry, from an English surveyor, Capt. Henry Bagwell, charged by the Crown with the task of mapping Georgian Bay. Soon after arrived the lumbermen, to fell and exploit the endless forest. The first sawmill opened in 1857, and with it naturally came the town's first industrialists. In 1897, a railway was cut through the forest, and within ten years the town was connected to the great transcontinental line, with a trestle constructed over the Seguin linking what would become known as Belevedere Hill and Tower Hill, an engineering marvel and local landmark, the longest east of the Rockies. Industries would come and go, and from the moment the countryside became accessible, tourists began to arrive, marking Parry Sound forever. Here was the wilderness within easy reach of the big cities, the Great North Woods, though not really so far north at all, not far past the point of demarcation where the flat agricultural plain of Southern Ontario gives way to the rocks and trees of the

Canadian Shield. Even Teddy Roosevelt, that connoisseur of the exotic, dropped by in 1908 to sample the accessible wilderness. He was just one in a long, unbroken line of "summer people" stretching back more than a century who became one-half of the town's great divide. The other half, the full-timers, scratched out a living, survived the dark winters and then watched their town come alive with cottagers and vacationers during the long days and brief weeks of summer. The visitors had money and leisure time, and inevitably it was their business, and not the resources, not the factories, that provided the town's economic pulse.

The only fundamental difference between Parry Sound now and the town in the 1960s, the 1950s and before is a diminished sense of isolation. Then the great urban mass along the shore of Lake Ontario, the most densely populated place in Canada, was a half-day's train journey away, or a three- or four-hour drive on lousy roads. It is half that now, not quite commuting distance, but not far off, and on this ever-shrinking planet, no one could disappear here, no great talent could be hidden away, and no one could feel that they were out in the bush alone. Eventually, the line of development creeping north from Toronto might reach this far. Eventually, Parry Sound might not feel like such a separate, different place. As of now, though, it retains its unique identity; it is still "Parry Hoot" (the old nickname left over from a wilder past for the part of the town that wasn't dry) and always – as the big sign out on the highway has proclaimed for more than thirty years – The Home of Bobby Orr.

"I may change my thinking a bit later in life, but right now my idea of the good life is to make my home in Parry Sound and raise a family here," Bobby said to an interviewer early in his NHL career – though of course he was speaking in the fairy-tale language of the sports hero, though of course it wouldn't quite work out that way. "I like the slow pace of life up here and I like the outdoors. I don't really like the big cities – with all the people rushing around. Some people thrive on it, but it isn't my idea of living. The life in Parry Sound represents Canada to me. What goes on in [Boston] is more American. It is all right if you like it but it's not for me."

Why people played hockey here, at least to a Canadian, is self-evident as well. This place and so many rural outposts like it are an essential element of the great national myth, the fantasy of one nation united around a puck. The truth is, most of us don't live out in the country, don't live in little towns, don't have homes within easy walking distance of a frozen river or bay or pond or slough where naturally, come winter, it's time to grab a stick and put on the skates and play the game of our ancestors. Most of us live in big cities not so distinct from big cities in the United States, in Western Europe, in Australia. Most of us would have to drive many miles on multi-lane highways through dense traffic to find a patch of natural ice (and that only if the winter was cold enough to sustain it). Many of us came from other places, far away, where hockey isn't bred in the bone. Many of us never play hockey at all. Most of us have little real experience of a place like Saskatchewan* – the shinny Holy Land (at least in English Canada), birthplace of Max Bentley and Gordie Howe and Wendel Clark – which, for all its vast open spaces, is home to fewer than a million people, about a quarter of the population of Metropolitan Toronto.

Which is the real Canada? Well, that's not the point. The Canada of our imagination, the Canada that Canadians imagine while trying to pin down their elusive national identity, is somewhere just like Floral or Parry Sound or Brantford. When we look in the mirror, we want to see tough, decent people, honest workers, deferential, polite, grateful for what they have, willing

---

* Perhaps because it is vast, rural, under populated and very cold in the winter, the province of Saskatchewan has produced more great hockey players on a per capita basis than any other region of Canada. Among the many other National Hockey League players to hail from the province, spanning all eras, all positions and all styles, are: Sid Abel; Bobby Baun; Johnny Bower; Bernie Federko; Theoren Fleury; Emile Francis; Clark Gillies; Glenn Hall; Terry Harper; Elmer Lach; Keith Magnuson; Bert Olmstead; Wade Redden; Dave "the Hammer" Schultz; Eddie Shore; Bryan Trottier; Ed Van Impe; Doug Wickenheiser.

to stand obediently in line, team players but unafraid to go into the corners, elbows high when it serves the collective good. We are hockey players the way Americans are, in their own very different mythology, Wild West gunslingers (independent and God-fearing and wary of authority, their individual rights held sacred above all).

The game of hockey, for Canadians, seems organic. It emerges out of the trees and rocks and ice, out of the long winter months, the rare, precious daylight, out of facing down nature, surviving and embracing whatever it can throw at us, enduring to spring. Hockey players, the best hockey players, those who go on to star in the National Hockey League – an American-based entertainment conglomerate, though Canadians can still pretend that it is their own, that it isn't just another business designed to sell tickets and beer and gasoline – come from all kinds of different places: here, the United States, Europe, the former Soviet Union. But so many of them, so many of the greatest stars of the game, seem to have come from a place just like Parry Sound. They seem to have emerged from a frozen river, from a backyard rink, to have found the source of their genius somehow in the landscape. Howie Morenz, Maurice Richard, Gordie Howe and Bobby Orr and Wayne Gretzky, spun out of the elements, out of the land.

They had a way of walking, the Orr men did. Not quite a swagger, but more the bowlegged air of supreme physical confidence that is the exclusive domain of cowboys and athletes. As though they could feel the muscle, feel the electric impulses that make the fibre twitch, even while just standing there, shooting the breeze, doing nothing Herculean in particular. In a small town, there are always twin hierarchies. Wealth is one, or more accurately class, to be far richer than average or far poorer, to live in the big house or to live on the struggling side of town. In Parry Sound, there were Townies and Harbour Bums, the village's physical divide mirroring the economic. Those who lived high on Belevedere Hill literally and figuratively looked down on those who made their homes by the water and the railway tracks. The other great

ordering system is sport, in Canada always hockey. Of so many
it is said that he can – he could – really play the game, he was a
pro, or he could have been a pro but for circumstances, he had a
taste of the big time, he's the best ever seen around these parts.
There is no similar scale for measuring the local poets, philoso-
phers, artists and rock stars; invariably, they're the outcasts until
they go away and have their genius confirmed somewhere else. In
real time, in the here and now, it's money and hockey. And the
Orrs, who constantly fought to scrape by, who were Harbour
Bums, who lived almost on top of the tracks, sure could play the
game. Their men were something to look at, too, or so the women
(quietly) said.

The old boy, the patriarch, Robert Orr, had come to Canada
from Ballymena, Ireland, as a young man in the early days of the
twentieth century. He had been a soccer player of some repute,
a professional, they said, though who knows what that really
meant, other than as a possible genetic explanation for what his
grandson would later achieve. He earned an extremely modest
living working for the railway and in a local garage, and the family never climbed beyond what in Parry Sound was the norm,
what today would be described as the working poor. His sons,
born in Canada, residents of the still-isolated near north, naturally
took up the national game. They were damn good at it, and they
played with a certain style, an élan. Especially Doug, a natural,
gifted athlete – in 1939, he was named the outstanding competi-
tor at the Parry Sound High School track meet – who could skate
like hell. Just about everyone figured he could have been a
hockey pro if he'd put his mind to it. He didn't play much
defence, he didn't like to check, but he sure could fly and he sure
could score. The Boston Bruins took a look at him in 1942, when
he was eighteen years old, and one of his buddies and linemates,
Pete Horeck, a scrappy little undersized forward, made it all the
way to the NHL, where he scored twenty goals in a season a couple
of times for the Chicago Black Hawks. But it was only a six-team
league. Only a handful of jobs came open every winter. The
minors, where one could be lost and forgotten for a whole host

of reasons beside talent or the lack thereof, were distant and dingy and the money earned there was nothing to celebrate, even for a boy from Parry Sound. It was hockey, and that beat working in a mill or back on the farm, but still it was no shortcut to wealth and glory. The Atlantic City Seagulls – that's where Horeck started, and that's where the Bruins wanted to send Doug. "I could skate as well as Pete Horeck," he boasted years later, "if I do say so myself." Doug Orr assessed his options, looked at what life held in store and joined the Canadian Navy instead, serving on Corvettes as they escorted merchant ships across the North Atlantic corridor during the Second World War. He came home to Parry Sound, settled down with Arva Steele, whom he'd married just before shipping out, and began the business of producing and raising a family. Doug was an easygoing kind of guy. Funny. Content with his lot. He was hired to pack dynamite into crates at the Canadian Industries Limited factory and thought that was just fine.

Old Robert Orr drank a bit. That was the first thing that came to mind when one of the locals was asked to describe him, always uttered with a wry smile. He was some kind of boozer. And Doug liked to tip a few back himself. It certainly wasn't unusual. In so many of the working-class homes in Parry Sound, the men put in their time during the week, working in the local factories, then on Friday and Saturday night, they'd cut loose, hard. The boys hit the town, hit the local beverage rooms, a man's world. They'd get lit up, they'd laugh, they'd fight, they'd flirt if there were women around. Repeat the scene in the thousands, and you'd have a pretty fair picture of small-town Canadian life in the 1950s. Not paradise, certainly, since there were plenty of dark secrets, since there was no exit, since in some of those modest frame houses, behind closed doors, the drinking and the anger and the struggle for economic survival could turn violent and ugly. But people stuck together in those days, in those places. They rarely split. They toughed it out. They got by. And, if necessary, they turned a blind eye. In a small town you do that, you learn to get along for the sake of appearance, you learn to keep your opinion to yourself. Life's too short.

Arva Steele's family came from Callendar, Ontario, near North Bay, famous as the home of the Dionne Quintuplets.* Arva was a serious woman who, especially to those who didn't know her well, could seem severe, aloof. Arva held a job for years waiting tables in the Brunswick Hotel coffee shop and kept her own home functioning, her kids fed and clothed and cared for as well. She was fair-minded, but other people's children sometimes found her a bit intimidating. You sure as heck didn't want Mrs. Orr mad at you. Once, a pal remembers, he and Bobby spent a day fishing for pickerel on the Seguin. (Angling was Orr's second passion as a boy, as an adult, and remains so now. It is fundamentally different from hockey, a game that can be ordered and controlled to a large degree – though both pursuits require a larger awareness and patience. In the end, the fisherman lives by fortune and chance and the occasional intersection of knowledge, technique and dumb luck). The fish weren't biting, but in the clear water they could see one lunker, ten pounds or more, hanging beside a rock, and so they decided to try and catch it by any means available. Their old men had taught them to fish, and their old men weren't averse to snagging dinner occasionally, to temporarily suspending fishing's strict, self-imposed ethics in order to secure the great aquatic delicacy. The boys lowered a big, weighted, bare three-pronged hook, and eventually

---

* The Dionne Quintuplets – Annette, Cecile, Yvonne, Marie and Emilie – were born in the hamlet of Corbeil, Ontario, just outside of Callendar, on May 28, 1934. The five were taken from their poor parents and made wards of the province of Ontario as infants, ostensibly for their own good, and then were exhibited at a hospital/theme park dubbed "Quintland" set up across the road from the family home. Between 1934 and 1943, 3 million people came to view what was, in essence, a government-sponsored freak show. The exploitation continued as the quints appeared in three movies during the 1930s, and their images were used to endorse various commercial products. In 1998, the three surviving Dionne sisters were awarded $4 million in compensation from the Ontario government.

Bobby managed to sink it into the pickerel's belly flesh and haul his catch to shore. He'd bring it home, he'd be the provider, the mighty hunter. Bobby wrapped the fish in his brand new hockey jacket to protect it on the proud walk back to the family home. On the porch, his mother was waiting, and watched as he unveiled his prize. She didn't react quite the way he'd anticipated – something about the jacket, the fish, the scales and the slime ruining a perfectly good expensive-enough piece of clothing that in the Orr family economy could not be easily replaced. Arva hollered at him, scaring Bobby's little pal half to death. "You put that fish back where you found it, now!" And so the carcass was consigned to the Seguin.

The Orr children had been born in quick succession. Patricia. Ronnie. Bobby. Penny. Doug Jr. Bobby's birth, on March 20, 1948, was complicated. He was a sick baby, and for a little while there was even a question whether he'd make it. His grandmother Elsie Orr worked as a nurse at St. Joseph's Hospital, where he was born. In later years, long after old Robert Orr was gone, Grandma Orr's house would become a second home for Bobby, a place where he could escape for a while, where he'd be fussed over, a warm, welcoming, loving refuge. Years later, Elsie Orr would beam while telling anyone who asked that her grandson, the National Hockey League star, paid all her expenses, made sure she had everything she needed, would accept nothing less than the best for her.

When the down-at-the-heels duplex on River Road became just too small for all those kids, the Orr family moved to a bigger, ramshackle place on Great North Road, at the base of Tower Hill. Across the street was a railway siding. Just beyond that was the Seguin. Still, it was a step up. The house would remain a local landmark long after Bobby had moved his parents to much nicer digs high on the hill. At a parade in the local hero's honour, someone fashioned a giant hockey stick that was carried through the streets like Jesus' cross. When the festivities ended, they dragged it over to Great North Road and leaned it against the side of the Orrs' house. New owners just left it there, where it remained for years. It was easier than putting up a sign.

The Orr boys – the extended clan that included Bobby and his many cousins – were the kind of kids you messed with at your own peril. Boys fought all the time then, and the Orrs fought particularly well, with a mean streak. They'd hurt you without a second thought, and if you took on one and happened to beat him, you'd wind up challenging them all.

Later, as it became apparent that he was a natural, gifted athlete, competing and succeeding against older kids, Bobby was automatically looked to for schoolyard leadership, and though he appeared very young he seemed somehow more mature than his years. He was challenged to fight constantly – just as he would later be challenged by the toughest players in every rink – but rarely by the same foe more than once. Orr seemed small, always, the origin of his strength a bit of a mystery, but he had a way of grabbing a bigger kid and wrestling him to his back. They called it the Parry Sound Flop, and it worked nearly every time. He would attempt any sport but do it his way, stubbornly, independently, often in an unorthodox manner, and more often than not successfully. And always to win, though he wasn't boastful, but rather quietly intense in his competitiveness. In a schoolyard baseball game, another sport in which Bobby stood out, a friend, playing catcher, remembers Orr standing on third base, tagging up and then tearing toward home on a fly ball. The kid catcher tried his best to block the plate. Orr ran right through him, sending the catcher flying, leaving him flat on his back, gasping for air. The run scored. And Bobby never looked back. Never turned around. Never wondered whether the other kid was all right – and when they connected later, never mentioned the collision. He just sat down on the bench and waited for the game to resume.

Bobby was by all accounts a diligent, if unremarkable student, physically extraordinary, intellectually ordinary. The old teachers don't like to talk about things like marks, their sense of professionalism still strong years into retirement, but they make it clear in conversation that he was certainly no troublemaker, that they never had to worry about him, that he tried hard and he barely got by. Hard work was never the issue. As a child, he was already learning the relationship between toil and reward, not just in school, not just in the garage, banging shot after shot into a piece of tin that Doug had set up for him, but in real, paying jobs, providing a bit of pocket money where none would have been available, helping the family out. In grade school, he stayed behind after classes and helped the janitor on his cleaning rounds for a few cents a shift. Later, he worked during the summer as a bellhop at the fancy hotel up on Belevedere Hill.

Ronnie Orr was the closest to Bobby, a year older – and in the Orr family, while the women might well have been the bedrock, the men and the boys were always in the forefront. (The youngest boy, Doug Jr., grew up in an entirely different world, aware from his earliest days that his brother was a hockey star and that by extension his family was special). By Grade 8, Ronnie and Bobby were in the same class. Everyone talks about how different they were then. Bobby loved to hang out with his father, loved the outdoors, was driven and serious as well as physically gifted, had a volatile temper, though it only occasionally broke through, was willing to work at a challenge hour after hour until it was conquered. Ronnie preferred his mother's company. He liked to stay close to home. He still lives in Parry Sound – for years he ran a clothing store, and now he runs a meat shop – and so the locals are diplomatic, and they differentiate between Ronnie then and Ronnie now. Now, they say, he reminds them an awful lot of Bobby, which in town is the highest compliment anyone can earn. Then, they say, he was a bit soft, a bit lazy, a bit of a whiner. Though you have to wonder how much hockey has to do with that. Ronnie was a talented player, everyone agrees – maybe even Bobby's equal, at least when it came to natural gifts. But he never really wanted it. He never really cared. That was Bobby's thing – and his dad's thing. As a teenager, Ronnie Orr walked away from the game altogether, even as his brother was approaching stardom, aside from occasionally serving as a stick boy. He didn't play again until lacing up with a bunch of old-timer pals in an adult rec league, where he seemed to have a ball.

In the summer of 1970, after the Bruins won their first Stanley Cup of the modern era, Parry Sound held a Bobby Orr Day, what may have been the biggest event there since the day the railway arrived. It was all Bobby, all the time. His every move was charted, his praises were sung by all, and everyone was thrilled to see the famous friends he'd brought along to his old hometown. One ambitious reporter sought out his older brother and asked him about his own life, his own career. Ronnie's words, even now, seem impossibly poignant. "I guess I couldn't have been too keen [on hockey]," he said. "Now I regret it – deeply. I still play in an inter-mediate league here, but I wonder, will always wonder, what might have been."[1]

Bobby Orr's first skates came from Gene Fernier, a family friend who worked for the Canadian Pacific Railway. The Orrs certainly didn't have the money to buy new. Bobby was four years old when his dad first pulled the laces tight for him. He teetered onto the frozen Seguin and immediately fell down. "The skates could have done me more good," he liked to joke, "if I wore them someplace other than my feet." The skates were several sizes too big, so the toes were stuffed with paper. It was two years before he grew out of them. When Orr first held a hockey stick in his hands, it was mostly to keep from falling down. Bobby was fourteen, on the brink of hockey stardom and on the verge of leaving Parry Sound for good, before he'd have a pair of new skates to call his own.

He looked like every other hockey-playing kid, at least in the beginning. Some of his pals the same age had already been playing for a year by the time Orr first took up the game. There was no eureka moment then, no instant when the boy genius suddenly sat down at a piano and banged out a sonata. But Doug Orr, whose night shifts at the dynamite plant left him time during the day to watch his son, thought he saw something there, a flash of natural talent, plus an unmistakable diligence – the kid never wanted to come off the ice. Arva didn't see it. Neither did anyone else. But Doug was seduced by the same fantasy that ensnares so many deluded Canadian hockey dads, especially those whose own dreams of glory were somehow aborted. To his credit, he wasn't pushy about it. He wasn't particularly demanding. He wasn't a stage parent. He wasn't even kindly Walter Gretzky, plotting his son's hockey ascendance while watching him skate through drills on the famous backyard rink. "He was more interested," says a crusty old teammate of his, an old coach, "in getting drunk." But it turned out that Doug was no dreamer, that he was sober and clear-eyed about what he was watching. Soon the boys of Parry Sound understood too, though without any true sense of perspective. They would chase and follow and lag behind and be left measuring their own failings, believing that the little blond boy was merely the best kid hockey player in a small Canadian town. The larger truth took a while to dawn.

Chapter Two

BUCKO

H E IS A STOCK CHARACTER of the Canadian town: the patron of the shinny arts. A man – they're invariably men – of considerable means, a local business leader, someone with a little time and a little disposable income on his hands, selflessly dedicated to improving the state of the game. They coach and manage, or they inspire others to do so. They spread around a little cash where it is most needed, to help a poor kid buy a new pair of skates, to bring in a ringer from elsewhere to play with the local heroes, to pay for room and board and the odd case of beer. Jobs found. Sponsorships secured. Troubles swept away. They make sure there's gas for the bus and new uniforms for the rep teams. When there's a shortfall, when there's a problem, when there's something that needs fixing, they are the first to be summoned. Eventually, folks naturally start calling them "Mr. Hockey," a title more grand there, more grand here than Your Honour, Your Worship, Your Royal Highness, Your Holiness.

In Parry Sound, the honorific, it seems, will forever be attached to the late Alex Eagar. He arrived in town in the Depression year 1933 with a bit of money to invest, bought a modest tourist establishment called the Mansion House and renamed it the Brunswick Hotel (later, in a nod to changing times, he added a modern veneer by dubbing it a "motor inn"). Eagar built the business into a thriving one, made a small-town fortune, and after his wife, Leona, died too young in 1943, turned his attentions other than those dedicated to his business almost exclusively to hockey and eventually to the minor game, which in the years after the war wasn't much organized at all. Eagar himself managed intermediate and Junior C teams in the early 1950s, the Brunswicks and Shamrocks, representing the elite local level of the sport, where he enjoyed great success. But still, he felt that grassroots development was suffering, that the kids weren't getting the proper training. No one, in those days, was talking about summer hockey schools and scientific methods and weightlifting and power skating and cross-training and teaching children how to play the left-wing lock. It was more about having fun than about preparing for wildly unlikely fantasy jobs as professionals. The local youths, though, could still benefit from exposure to someone who might at least show them how to play the right way, the National Hockey League way, and there was no one in town with that kind of pedigree.

There was, however, someone nearby, someone at loose ends, someone in another summer town called Sundridge, fifty miles to the east. Wilfred Kennedy "Bucko" McDonald was an imposing figure, a big man with a huge barrel chest and a voice that seemed to fill a room. That last trait came in especially handy during his second career, as the Member of Parliament for the riding of Parry Sound-Muskoka, though, truth be told, during his twelve years in high office he hardly said a word – or at least a word that was recorded in Hansard. Bucko was in his own way another stock character, the local sports hero who finds a way to ride and exploit his fame for the rest of his life. (McDonald got the nickname after getting involved in a childhood wrestling match and being told, "You'll be a real bucko" – a character – "one day." It apparently beat being called Wilfred). He was born in Fergus, Ontario, some distance to the west and south, an anomalous Canadian burg where the dominant local game wasn't hockey at all but the other official national sport, lacrosse. "It's just what happens when you're born in a community where one particular sport seems to be part of the heritage and is popular above all other sports," he would explain late in life. "There is a time when something becomes very much a part of your existence, and you become noted for it." McDonald took up the game as a ten-year-old, won a Mann Cup* national championship as an amateur in 1931 and by age twenty-one was playing in a nascent, fragile, ultimately doomed professional lacrosse league for a team owned by Conn Smythe** and based out of Maple Leaf Gardens in Toronto. He had hardly skated to that point in his life, and hadn't played organized hockey at all, preferring to concentrate on his first love. But Smythe, who also owned the hockey Leafs and their home rink, liked the look of the big, strong kid. When the lacrosse league

---

* McDonald was a member of the 1931 Brampton Excelsiors team that won the Mann Cup. The trophy, donated by the railway contractor Sir David Mann in 1901, was originally a challenge cup, but would later be awarded to the winner of a playoff between the champions of the Western Lacrosse Association and the Ontario Lacrosse Association. Until 1935, the games were played outdoors – "field lacrosse." After that, they were played indoors – "box lacrosse."

**Conn Smythe, a graduate of the University of Toronto, first found hockey success coaching the Varsity Grads to the 1926–27 Allan Cup. A year later, the same team of U of T alumni, minus Smythe, travelled to St. Moritz, where they won a gold medal in the second Winter Olympic Games. Smythe also helped put together the New York Rangers team that would win the Stanley Cup in 1928, but following a dispute with the team's management in 1926 decided to buy the Toronto St. Pats franchise, which he renamed the Maple Leafs, for $160,000. The building of the magnificent Maple Leaf Gardens during the Depression years was regarded as one of the great triumphs of Canadian capitalism. In 1962, Smythe sold the arena and the team to his son Stafford, along with partners Harold Ballard and John Bassett Sr. (Bassett was bought out in 1970, and Ballard assumed full control after Stafford Smythe's death in 1971.) Conn Smythe, who fought in both world wars, gave up his last link to the team, a directorship in Maple Leaf Gardens, in 1966, when a man he regarded as a draft dodger, Muhammad Ali, fought George Chuvalo there. Conn Smythe died in 1980.

finally succumbed to fan disinterest, McDonald would have been happy to return to play as an amateur while keeping his job at a flower farm in nearby Brampton. But he was barred from his beloved sport for three years because he had dared to commit the sin of accepting a paycheque. "I was a lacrosse player, not a hockey player," he told *The Toronto Star*'s Jim Proudfoot decades later. "I became a hockey player late in life, out of sheer necessity. This was the Depression, remember. You took whatever job you could find."[2] Smythe, on a whim and a long-shot hope, invited him to attend the Maple Leafs training camp in 1933. No harm in at least taking a look. "Mr. Smythe thought, without my saying so, that I was a pretty good hockey player. I had told him that I could be a good player if I got the chance, and that's the attitude I took into training camp." However unorthodox his background, McDonald's size and strength and athletic ability piqued the interest of the Leafs brass, but not enough to immediately earn him a spot with the big club. He was sent instead to the Buffalo Bisons of the International-American Hockey League. Over the Christmas season in 1934, McDonald's contract was purchased by Detroit's minor-league affiliate, the Olympics, and he would be summoned to play the final fifteen games of the 1934–35 NHL season with the Red Wings. In 1936, he became part of hockey history, playing in the longest game ever, the marathon playoff battle between the Wings and the Montreal Maroons that stretched into a sixth period of overtime and ended finally at 2:25 in the morning on a goal by Modere "Mud" Bruneteau, whose only claim to immortality would be as the answer to a hockey trivia question. McDonald had his own favourite statistic from that night and early morning: during the course of what amounted to nearly three regulation games, he knocked thirty-seven Maroons to the ice. "The reason somebody kept track was that this oil dealer from Detroit had offered me $5 for every knockdown. We agreed on a limit of $200, so I didn't quite make it. But he did pay me $185, which was a lot of money in the 1930s. Of course he never dreamed I'd have so many chances to collect. Also, the ice got slushy as the evening wore on, so the Maroons became easier to hit."[3] That was near the beginning of a big-league career that would stretch for the better part of eleven seasons and include three Stanley Cups. McDonald was known for his solid physical style of play, for being a rock on the Red Wings, Leafs and New York Rangers defence, for being an all-star and obviously for being a great open-ice bodychecker. But despite that reputation for toughness, McDonald was also regarded as a gentleman on and off the ice. In his final season in the NHL, he played forty games for the Rangers and recorded not a single minute in penalties. He didn't pick up a fighting major during his entire professional career. Bucko played it plenty tough, but it seems he never felt the need or the necessity to raise his fists.

On his retirement from the professional game following a final season in the minors, McDonald all but stumbled into politics. Back in the flower trade, he'd met a fellow who vacationed in Sundridge, and in the early 1930s he accepted an invitation to set up a minor lacrosse league for the town. McDonald loved the place, moved there, married and never really left. In 1945, his father-in-law, Willard Lang, was seeking the local federal Liberal nomination, and McDonald accompanied him to lend support. With the party meeting deadlocked without a candidate, and Lang having lost interest and lost votes, the assembly turned to the local hockey celebrity and asked him if he'd carry the Liberal torch. McDonald was naive enough to accept (it wasn't so much different from becoming a professional hockey player without experience), and thanks in no small part to his celebrity status he won the election that followed. "I always played square with them during my career in sports, and I'm not going to be any different in this one. I'm not a politician, and the fact I've been elected to Parliament isn't going to stop me from being a friend of the people," Bucko said. "I'm through with sport. From now on I'm directing my energies to looking after the welfare of my constituents."[4] Though he might have made little impact in Parliamentary debates, he did at least develop a reputation for delivering projects and public money to his riding. McDonald held the seat twice more before retiring undefeated prior to the election of 1957 (getting out just before the John Diefenbaker sweep of 1958, when the riding went

Conservative).* After politics, McDonald broke his vow and went back to sports when he was hired as a head coach in Rochester, New York. That stint, with the Americans of the American Hockey League, ended disastrously. Only fifteen games into the season, with a record of 4–10–1 and the team mired in last place, McDonald was fired. He returned home in November 1958, undoubtedly humbled, at loose ends. That's where Alex Eagar found him.

Bobby Orr played his first year of organized hockey as a five-year-old, in the minor squirt division, just a year after he first teetered on skates. The locals remember two things about him then. That he was tiny and apparently frail. And that soon enough he could skate faster than anyone his own age, not to mention many kids far older, whether in the heat of a game or in a staged race around the circumference of the rink (at least he could until the day he and a buddy found their way to the skate sharpening machine in the arena and decided to grind their own blades – their operating theory being the more sparks produced, the better. It might have been the only time in his life that Orr found himself unable to keep up with the pack). His stride even

---

* John Diefenbaker was an Ontario-born, Saskatchewan-raised populist who in 1957 became the first Conservative prime minister of Canada since 1935. A year later, he led his party to the largest parliamentary majority in Canadian history, the "Dief Sweep," winning 208 of 265 seats. "Dief the Chief," as he was known, was famous for being a thorn in the side of American president John Kennedy, refusing the United States' request to base nuclear warheads on Canadian soil. In 1962, Diefenbaker's government was reduced to a minority, and a year after that, he lost to the Liberal party led by Lester Pearson. (It was Pearson who famously said in 1947 that Canada was more than "a few frozen farmers and trappers huddled in igloos around the North Pole emerging periodically to produce wheat, hockey players and quintuplets.") While still PM, Diefenbaker presided over the ground-breaking for the Hockey Hall of Fame in Toronto. "There is nothing greater than hockey to bring about national unity and a closer relationship between the United States and Canada," he said. (Hockey Hall of Fame website.)

then seemed effortless, not a windmill of short, quick strides, but deceptively fast like the relaxed motion of a big man, a Frank Mahovlich or a Mario Lemieux. Time after time, players would move in to check him, underestimating his speed, only to be startled as Orr sailed by, untouched.

By the time he'd turned nine, Orr was a local standout and had fully dedicated himself to hockey. But he was hardly hailed as the game's second coming. During those early years of minor hockey – really, until he left Parry Sound for the Oshawa Generals and was anointed a star on a larger stage – Orr was regarded merely as the best of the local crop, as an athletically gifted Parry Sound kid from an athletically gifted family. That he might be more, that he might be the greatest player who had ever lived was simply beyond the realm of comprehension. (Except in hindsight. It seems now that anyone who ever shared the ice with Orr claims to have immediately understood his destiny.) He was talented, but he was small, and there had been other talented boy players before him, including a handful of local lads who made it all the way to the National Hockey League. There were others who might have been just as good, but didn't want it as badly, didn't work as hard, or got a steady job or got a girl pregnant, and so they wound up somewhere else. Bobby Orr surely fitted somewhere in that spectrum, but who knew, really, what it meant to be the best eleven-year-old hockey player in a town of six thousand people? The kids played on weekends, they practised a couple of times a week, they were on the ice officially in the winter months maybe four days out of seven (plus pond hockey, plus road hockey . . .), but no one was fixated on "development," on identifying professional prospects, on isolating the very best and pushing them forward. There was none of the hothouse pseudo-science that would seduce young hockey players and especially their parents in the decades to come. For the kids then and there, damn the cliché, it was still a game.

McDonald arrived in town to great fanfare with his big-league pedigree, lured by Alex Eagar, who, by directing a few dollars his way, made the move worthwhile. But Bucko's coaching style initially came as a bit of a shock. It seemed less modelled on the fierce men who stood behind NHL benches, barking at the pros, and more a reflection of his own studious, analytical approach to learning the game. Though he had failed miserably coaching in Rochester, his method seemed to work with the young boys of Parry Sound. He didn't treat hockey-playing children as though they were hockey-playing adults. He didn't act as though hockey was all that should matter in their lives. Rather, he delivered his advice to Bobby Orr and to all the others with the tone and concern and affection of the ideal hockey dad. He rarely raised his voice during practices or games. If a player made a mistake, he'd be pulled aside and corrected. No intimidation or humiliation. His players didn't live in perpetual dread of screwing up. McDonald was a teacher of the patient, pleasant sort. He got his message across without playing the ogre.

Still, for all that civility, hockey when played to win can be a nasty, elemental game. When the Parry Sound teams ventured afar, and the opposition came to understand how valuable the little blond, crewcut kid was to their cause, they did what all hockey teams, all sports teams, have done from the earliest days of competition: they singled him out, they tried to neutralize him, they tried to remove the threat through tactics, through hard work and if necessary through force. Orr, because he seemed so physically vulnerable, and because he was scoring goals and setting up goals at will, became an obvious target. When teams couldn't find a way to beat him on the ice, they tried to do it by any means necessary. He was hit and hacked and hooked and challenged to fight. Anything, within the rules or otherwise, that might slow him down. For Orr, it would become a constant of his hockey life until the day he was forced to retire.

McDonald well understood what was happening. He'd seen it all in the NHL, during an era when it was a rough, tough place where players were expected to fend for themselves, to enforce their own eye-for-an-eye moral code, to be their own law and order. Whatever the rule book said, in the end no one was going to come to your rescue. So he pulled Orr aside at a practice following one particularly brutal game and gave him a piece of advice that would stick with him all the way to Boston: if somebody hits you, Bucko said, make sure you haul off and hit him right back. Don't ever back down. Don't let him think he's won. McDonald might not have been a fighter, but he had learned to look after himself, learned how not to be pushed around. He understood that, if Orr was to thrive at a higher level, he would have to prove again and again that he couldn't be intimidated.

During Orr's rookie season in the NHL, Terry Harper, the veteran defenceman for the Montreal Canadiens, a player with a mean streak, stared him down and dared him to drop the gloves and fight. Let's see what the golden boy is made of. Let's see what the star, the kid with the fat contract, does when he's face to face with a real hockey man. Orr stood his ground, he dropped his gloves, he punched like hell, he gave as good as he got. Maybe it was a draw. Maybe you could award Orr a close decision. In either case, a message went around the league that the new kid with the Bruins could fight back when pressed, that he hit hard, that he had stones – though naturally that didn't stop the challenges from each team's tough guy in turn. Hearing about the fight with Harper, Bobby's old Parry Sound buddies figured that Bucko's words must have been playing in his head even as he was pounding away. That was McDonald's second great contribution to the building of Bobby Orr. The first was even more fundamental.

Not much had changed strategically in hockey since they eliminated the seventh skater – the rover – back in 1911, or at least since they first permitted the forward pass in 1929. There was a simple alignment from the goaltender out, two defencemen, three forwards – one a centre, one on each wing. Left-handed shots normally played on the left side, right-handed shots on the right side. It was the job of the centreman to take faceoffs, to lead the attack, to score goals, to work with his wingers, who had both an attacking and checking role. At the back, the defencemen defended. They stayed home. They would move forward on the power play, firing the puck in from the opposing blue line, but primarily their role was to make sure no man got past them. Very, very occasionally, some had been skilled enough, been fast enough skaters, to join in the attack, to advance the puck and then get back to their position on time. Eddie Shore, the great Bruin of the 1920s and 1930s, was known for his ability to take the puck and carry it from his own end of the ice into the opposition zone, for exploiting previously unheard of offensive possibilities as a defenceman. Shore scored twelve goals in his rookie NHL season in 1927 – an astounding, earth-shaking number then, by one calculation the equivalent of thirty-five goals in the modern game. By the 1930–31 season, he had pushed that tally to fifteen. Famously, Shore perfected the trick of rushing the puck, firing it intentionally off the boards behind the opposition net, then picking up the rebound and banging it past a startled goaltender. He did all that, revolutionizing the possibilities of his position, and then turned out to be a one-off: none of those who followed him possessed the necessary skills or chutzpah to play defence like that, and no coaches were willing to risk it with a lesser talent. Thirty years after his retirement, old-timers would still be saying that they'd never seen a defenceman quite like Eddie Shore, and they were right. Doug Harvey, perhaps the closest thing to it, and the game's other great innovator at the position, was more of a playmaker than a pure scorer. He amassed 540 points in 1,113 NHL games, including a high of 50 in one season, but Harvey never scored more than nine goals in any hockey year. He was a smooth skater who kept the puck in front of him, someone who could slow down or speed up the tempo of a game, as Orr later would, simply by subtly altering his own tempo. Harvey saw the ice the way a great soccer midfielder sees the pitch, distributing the puck to those who knew what to do with it. Francis "King" Clancy saw Shore, Harvey and Orr play, close up, from the perspective of player, coach and finally a kind of owner's sidekick during the Harold Ballard era of the Toronto Maple Leafs. "I think Orr is a ringer for Shore when Eddie first broke into the National Hockey League," he once said. "Bobby isn't as old or as heavy-set as Eddie was when he came from the western wheat fields, but he has the same kind of poise out there. Shore was the greatest defenceman of his era and Harvey of his. However, it took Harvey almost ten years to get the savvy that Orr showed from his first game with Boston. Right now, I would still take Shore over Orr, but Bobby may pass him eventually. Shore had one weakness that Orr does not. You could get the better of his temper and goad him into stupid penalties."[5]

That fact is that Shore and Harvey, in the context of their eras, were freaks. Whatever their genius allowed them to achieve, they produced no true heirs. The prototype for the position remained the same: a big, strong, tough guy who could check, who could skate backwards, who could deliver a hit in open ice and pin opposing forwards against the boards. If he scored the odd goal, it was regarded as a bonus. That set of presumptions naturally filtered down from the National Hockey League all the way to the dividing-up of squirts and tykes and peewees in backwoods Canadian towns. In all kid sports, positions tend to be fixed early, and snap judgments are made based on some pretty obvious surface criteria. (Take a look at any group of professional football quarterbacks: somewhere, way back, the tallest, handsomest kids were the ones handed the ball.) In hockey, the fastest of their peer group, the best skaters, the ones who can handle the puck and shoot it the hardest, are made forwards so they can score plenty of goals. Smaller boys tend be stuck up front as well, where they won't be in as much danger of getting pushed around. Those who are bigger, and especially a bit round, who might not be the strongest skaters, automatically look like goaltenders in a coach's eyes: in a worst-case scenario, at least they'll cover ground, and maybe the puck will hit them. The biggest, the strongest but not necessarily the fastest, those who are the first to master the tricky art of skating backwards, become defencemen automatically. Things change, bodies and skills change, nothing is graved in stone. But talk to most National Hockey League players, and you'll find out that they've played the same position nearly since they put on skates — that long ago, someone told them what they were.

Looking at Bobby Orr, Bucko McDonald should have drawn a simple, logical conclusion. A kid built like that, with those skills, had to be a forward. He was never going to outmuscle anyone, but he could skate around and through and past an entire team, at his age level, and even at a level up. He could carry the puck, he could shoot and he could pass and he could score. Slot him in as a winger, as a centre, and he'd dominate the game up front, and his lack of physical presence wouldn't be too much of a handicap. Doug Orr thought that as well. It had, after all, been his position, and, as he'd tell anyone who didn't remember, he was quite the player. "There's no doubt about it. I gave Bucko some arguments," Doug said years later. "I had nothing against his playing defence – except that I wanted him to be a forward. Why? Well, I was a forward myself."[6]

As a nine- and ten-year-old, Orr in fact played for a time on the wing. But then McDonald arrived, and he saw something else, something different, something that no one had really seen before in the whole history of the game, and it's hard not to believe that his own unusual introduction to the sport allowed him to be somehow free of ancient prejudices. He had learned about hockey not as a boy but as an adult. He wasn't steeped in the game's orthodoxy from an early age. It wasn't second nature; it was learned. He had to figure it out for himself. And when he saw Bobby Orr, scrawny, skilled, a natural skater, a stickhandler, a scorer – everything that Bucko McDonald wasn't – he still saw a defenceman, but not a defenceman the likes of which the game had ever known. He put him at the back, he gave him his position, and then when Orr began to modify, to improvise, to make it his own, McDonald chose not to try to rein him in. He opted not to tether him. He never once said, Stay home, stay where you belong, play the game the way it's always been played, remember that your only job is to prevent goals, not to score them or to set them up. He never said, Just who do you think you are? Eddie Shore? He thought that defence was the perfect position not for a plodder but for a player with a creative streak, who could take advantage of seeing the whole game unfold in front of him. So when Orr rushed the puck and left his position, when he led the team's offence, when he skated deep into the opposing zone and then had to scamper back to cover his position, McDonald didn't tell him he had made a mistake. He didn't tell him that he might get away with that stuff playing against kids in Parry Sound, but that it wouldn't work against older, better, more sophisticated opponents down the road. He didn't use his own big-league experience as a measuring stick. "I used to tell Doug the kid was in his natural position when he played defence. You didn't have to be a genius to see that – honest. I don't think Doug agreed, but he accepted my decision. You'd say it worked out all right, I guess."[7] Perhaps not a genius. But the decision required both a level of confidence and a lack of overriding ego, resisting the temptation to play the all-knowing former pro. It took guts to let Bobby Orr go.

Those who played beside Orr on defence, even in those very early years, learned the happy truth that would become apparent to a whole series of NHL defencemen years later. Bob Cardy, who was on some of those minor teams, says, "I just stayed home and watched. Stayed back at centre ice and stayed out of trouble."

Sure, you could cover for him when you thought he had gone too far, when you thought he was way out of position, but he'd surprise you by getting back, racing all the way down the ice and making the play that covered for his absence. Those instincts were original, innate, beyond any coaching. "Bucko taught me almost everything I know," Orr said once, which was a humble overstatement, to be sure. But at least Bucko, hearing the prodigy play beautiful music by ear, didn't drag him back and force him to work on his scales.

In 1960, a minor hockey team from Winnipeg was scheduled to pass through Parry Sound on the Canadian Pacific's great cross-continental train, the Canadian, en route to the first edition of what would become a famous annual peewee tournament in Quebec City, the Stanley Cup of boys' hockey.* Parry Sound had

---

* The Quebec International Pee-Wee Hockey Tournament, the world's biggest minor hockey tournament, began in 1960 and features teams from throughout North America. Among the National Hockey League stars who participated as eleven- and twelve-year olds were Wayne Gretzky, Mario Lemieux, Eric Lindros, Brad Park, Guy Lafleur, Marcel Dionne and Gilbert Perreault.

a pretty decent group of peewees itself that year, but there was no way they'd be heading east. The cash just wasn't there. Even an ordinary trip to a town up the road required pounding on doors to beg for gas money. Instead, an exhibition game was arranged, a tune-up for the Winnipeg team, a chance to get off the train and stretch their legs and show their stuff to the locals. It was a big event during one of those long, cold quiet winters in Parry Sound. The arrival of the sleeper cars carrying the Winnipeg players had a bit of the feel of a royal tour, and by game time the old arena was packed. In local minor hockey lore, it is remembered as a classic, a thriller, with the home team led by Orr eventually coming out on top, 4–3. The train pulled out the next morning, and the Parry Sound boys went back to their lives. Only much later did they learn that Winnipeg had gone on to the Quebec City tournament and won it all.

The following spring, the Parry Sound peewees played for the provincial championship for towns of similar size, the title game held in Napanee, near Kingston. Orr was there, of course, the best player on the ice, though in the end his team lost. He was forced to leave the game early after being hit in the face and suffering what seemed to be a broken nose. One teammate's father was a doctor, and he did his best to staunch the bleeding. He was also the one to drive Bobby on to his next game, since the Orr family didn't own a car. As had been the case in Parry Sound for most of his hockey life, Orr was part of two teams, one for his own age group, and one for the next. Just as he was the star for the peewees, he was also the star for the bantams as they tried to win their own provincial championship, this time up the road in Gananoque. The Parry Sound kids lost again, with Orr on the ice for fifty-eight minutes, busted-up nose and all – he spent the other two minutes in the penalty box – skating around the older, bigger kids with relative ease. Except at that game, someone noticed.

Movie stars in legend are discovered sitting on drugstore stools, their natural glamour enough to knock a talent scout dead. Hockey players in Canada rarely enjoy that element of surprise. Today, the best of them have an official bio and an agent on call and maybe an endorsement deal ready to sign before they're drafted as eighteen-year-olds into the pros. Back then, they'd be known in a different way; they'd be spotted by some local bird dog, who would tell someone higher up the hockey chain of command, who would have a connection to a National Hockey League scout, who would then decide whether to try to land the prospect for his team. Signed to a contract at age fourteen, a player would be effectively locked to one franchise for the remainder of his professional life. The best Ontario kids would tend to shun all other offers if the glamorous Toronto Maple Leafs came calling, having been seduced by the cult of Foster Hewitt and perhaps by the promise of a fine religious education at St. Michael's College, where the Leafs' top hockey prospects studied and played. After the Leafs, the Detroit Red Wings had some cachet, a holdover from their great success in the 1950s. In French Canada, it was understood that the Montreal Canadiens, Les Glorieux, had the first choice of anyone they fancied, a birthright born of culture and history and hockey politics.

There were only six teams in all, but there was also only one vast, underpopulated country representing the known hockey world. What were the chances that a great, original player could emerge unknown from a town a few hours' drive from Maple Leaf Gardens? What were the chances that he could fall into the lap of a bunch of no-hopers? Easier to find the next Lana Turner demurely sipping a soda somewhere.

Chapter Three

SIGNED

ITT'S A GODDAMN BORING DANGEROUS DRIVE, Kingston to
Sault Ste. Marie by bus, in the dead of winter, in a hockey
league of faint hope, even without taking the scenic route,
without crawling through the construction on Highway 69 and then
stopping for dinner at a hotel in the middle of nowhere while the
boss makes house calls. That's it. No more of this bullshit. Ask the
old man what the hell's going on. You've been around. You know
the ropes. You're the captain. It's your job. You tell that bastard. No
more detours. No more house calls. Whatever he's getting on the
side, he can get it on his own time.

The captain takes the lead, but with deference. These are
hockey players who know their place, and this is 1961, before athletes in any sport dreamed that they had rights and privileges and
power. The authority of the men at the top to prolong or end a
career is absolute. In the Eastern Professional Hockey League,
designed as a bridge between the juniors and the big time, far
from the bright lights, far from the glamour (as it turns out, not
far from extinction, destined to be shifted south soon enough
and reborn in places where they've never seen the game), one

false move and you're back home pumping gas, or worse. Still, there are a few dreamers among them. Some are young and fresh, and a few will make it all the way to the National Hockey League – "Whitey" Stapleton's on the team, and so are J. P. Parise and Bruce Gamble. Mostly, though, they're guys who would rather do this than get on with their real lives, at least for now. The captain, Harry Sinden, stands out as a little bit different from his team-mates, not a future star but still a hockey lifer in the making. Playing in the NHL was for him long ago out of the question. Only six teams there, only the best 120 players in the world (or at least in North America, the known hockey world). Sinden was a decent journeyman defenceman who had ridden his limited hockey talents and second-rate skating just about as far as they would go. He won an Allan Cup with the Whitby Dunlops back when that really meant something, the height of amateur hockey in Canada. The Dunnies were rewarded with a trip overseas, to Oslo, where they won a world championship for Canada in 1958. Two years later, Sinden was part of the Canadian team that won a silver medal in the Olympics in Squaw Valley, California. (The Americans won the gold. And how the heck did that happen?) But the pinnacle of his career, as measured in the only hierarchy that really mattered, was a single game in the American Hockey League, one big step below the NHL, and that had happened a while ago. Sinden had to be persuaded to finally turn full-time pro and move to Kingston. He was twenty-seven years old, had a wife and three kids and a good job with General Motors, but still, here was the chance to make a buck playing hockey, maybe inching up the ladder, and wasn't that every kid's dream? Now he's the captain of the Kingston Frontenacs, a year away from becoming a player coach, stuck in the lowest reaches of the Boston Bruins organization – and the Boston Bruins were then stuck in the lowest reaches of the six-team league.

So there will be no boat-rocking here. Sinden knocks on Wren Blair's door a little sheepishly, even though he'd known him since they were both with the Dunnies, and it was Blair who had brought him here. Wren is a busy guy, the coach and general manager of the Frontenacs, running another team for the Bruins on the side, and he also considers himself a fine judge of hockey talent, though he feels as though he isn't getting quite the credit he deserves from his masters back in Boston.

It is evening, so he's surprised to see Sinden. Usually the boys are out having a few beers by now. When he first started coaching, Blair tried being a hardass, tried banning them from the bars and beverage rooms, but that didn't work, so he decided to take a new tack, to treat them like men. So far, so good. No one has been arrested yet. He hands Sinden a beer from his personal stash and grabs one for himself. It takes Sinden a while to summon up the courage to get to the point, to get past the hockey small talk. Then, finally, he steels himself sufficiently to do the captain's duty.

"Wren, the boys want me to ask you something. When we go to Sudbury, we used to drive through Smiths Falls and North Bay and then straight north. Now we're going back through Toronto and up Highway 69 and all over the goddamn place. We're eating at a hotel in Parry Sound, and then you disappear. The guys on the team are asking me to ask you what the hell is going on."

"I don't have to tell you nothing, Harry. It's none of your goddamn business."

Sinden makes his case, says he wants to learn how you run a hockey team, how you make decisions. He needs to know things about buses and highways and pit stops and the rest, as if all of that really mattered. It could come in handy someday.

"Okay," Blair relents, falling before dubious reason, and then begins his story. "There is a boy . . ."

He spins a tale that might as well be the Canadian hockey ur-myth, about a golden child, a genius, a prodigy, a shinny Mozart born of the rocks and the trees and the water of near–Northern Ontario, fully formed, original, perhaps the greatest player who has ever been born. And just maybe he'll ignore the Maple Leafs and the mighty Habs, he'll turn down the Wings and Hawks and Rangers, he'll sign over his playing life instead to the sad-sack Bruins and lead them, finally, to the Promised Land. He is up there in Parry Sound, and Blair is courting him, buttering up the family, keeping in touch, trying to get the inside track. That's what the mysterious side trips, the detours, the dinners are all about.

"Shit," Harry says. "That's all? That's it? We thought you had a broad."

One day Harry will tell Wren, That kid you found in Parry Sound – he's going to win me a Stanley Cup. And there you are, stuck out in the wilderness in Minnesota with a sad expansion team. You'll never get a sniff. As though Blair didn't know it.

The night it happened, the night the kid scored the winning goal and then flew through the air like a hockey angel, Harry phoned Wren to remind him. It was two in the morning, and Wren figured that Harry was pissed to the gills.

Wren. It was some kind of a name for a bird dog. As though Mom and Dad knew his destiny. He was more than just that, though, more than one of those who are forever locked in the scouting life, who spend years driving too far and too fast over death-trap winter roads, drinking bad coffee in small-town rinks, smooth-talking the moms and especially the dads, telling them that their kid is special, that he's got a real shot, whether or not that's entirely true, just so long as they'll sign on the dotted line. Blair was also an operator, a hustler, an entrepreneur, a promoter and to no small degree a self-promoter, a guy who'd wind up running a junior team here and a minor pro team there before finally getting his big break when the NHL made its great leap forward. He'd take hockey to the hinterlands then, but at least they knew the game a bit in Minneapolis – St. Paul. It wasn't like the poor schmucks who had to peddle shinny to beach bums in California. Blair was a big talker, a large personality, a wearer of loud sports jackets, a hockey Music Man. Wren Blair, by the early 1960s, looked a whole lot like the future.

But as that decade began, he was still locked in the sport's cob-webbed past, a mid-level functionary in a bad, tight, dead-end organization, working for bosses who would never get it right on their own. The man who owned the Boston Bruins, Weston Adams, was an old-fashioned capitalist gentleman, though also a bit of a dinosaur, and a penny-pincher. The Bruins hockey men, Harold "Baldy" Cotton and Hap Emms and Milt Schmidt and Lynn Patrick, were all skilled and savvy in their own right but with their own agendas, and in some cases perhaps a bit past their prime. In an era before the amateur draft, before teams were rewarded for their ineptitude with the first choice of graduating juniors, they were forced by Boston's circumstances to scrounge for leftovers, to go after the kids already passed over by the glamour teams, hoping to luck into late bloomers, and do it all on the cheap. It was a rare kid outside of Boston who dreamed of suiting up for the B's, and since the NHL's players were all Canadians, the team's local allure didn't do them a whole lot of good. The scouts Baldy and Blair could beat the bushes for talent but understood that they were operating always with a handicap. To succeed, they'd have to get lucky, and sometimes they'd have to make an end run around their own bosses. Eventually, Blair dreamed, the old guard would be gone and maybe he'd get his shot at running the big team, and running the big team right, but even back then, with expansion just beyond the horizon, he knew he'd probably have to find his break elsewhere.

Still, you did the job you were paid to do, and this was one more hockey scout's day, probably pointless, in the midst of a long, cold Canadian winter. In the spring of 1961, the Eastern Ontario bantam championship was being contested in Gananoque. The Bruins brain trust had gathered to watch Kingston in the playoffs and to hold an organizational get-together – Adams and Patrick; Milt Schmidt, the assistant general manager; Phil Watson, who was going to coach the team; Cotton, the chief scout; Scotty Monroe, who ran Boston's junior franchise in Saskatchewan; and Emms, who owned and operated their affiliated Ontario junior team, the Barrie Flyers. Blair suggested that the whole lot of them come along on a scouting trip to the Gananoque rink. There were a couple of kids on the home team, one named Doug Higgins and especially another flashy young player named Rick Eaton, who might have potential and who weren't yet spoken for. They'd all have a look, they'd compare notes afterwards, and then they'd have a few beers. The opposition, not that it mattered much, was a bantam team from up north, from Parry Sound, that as far as Blair knew contained no prospects of note.

Patrick watched the game from behind the screen at one end of the rink. The son of one of the great figures in early professional hockey history, Lester Patrick, he had played in the league and had run the Boston franchise for Adams since 1954, including a short stint as both the GM and head coach. Blair stood by himself along the side. The other members of the Bruins hierarchy staked out their own places. Better to watch independently than to be swayed by the group dynamic. Blair noted Higgins, and Eaton, and he noted another player as well, a tiny kid wearing number 2 for Parry Sound. He was the smallest boy on either team but still managed to dominate with his speed and his stickhandling. There wasn't a program, so there wasn't any way of knowing who the Parry Sound kid might be. Eventually, Blair left his post and walked down to where Patrick was standing. He just wanted to make sure his eyes weren't deceiving him. "Forget those Gananoque kids," he said to Patrick. "There's a kid on that Parry Sound team that's unbelievable. Do you see the same thing I do?"

"That little kid, number 2?"

"Yeah, that's the one."

"Jesus, isn't he something."

When the game ended, Blair headed for the Parry Sound dressing room. He recognized the old pro Bucko McDonald holding court out in the corridor, talking to a couple of the locals. He waited his turn and then popped the question.

"Bucko, who was that kid on your team, number 2?"

McDonald seemed to rise another six inches in height in that moment, to puff out his massive chest and to put on the great orator's voice that he hadn't bothered to exercise much during his quiet tenure in Parliament.

"Wren, his name is Robert Gordon Orr," he said, stretching out the name for maximum effect. "I wouldn't worry about him if I were you, because he's going to be signed by the Detroit Red Wings."

Blair immediately did a few quick calculations in his head. Bucko must have been bird-dogging for his old team. And maybe the kid really was locked up, maybe he had been signed, sealed and delivered to the Wings. Still, best not to seem too interested, too excited. That was rule one for any buyer. Make them think you're ready to walk away.

"Oh hell, he's not that good," Blair said. "I was just curious to find out his name. Never seen him before."

Blair needed the name because he knew he'd be driving to Parry Sound the next day, headed straight for the boy's parents. They were always the key. And maybe the kid would turn out to be just too small, or spoken for, or fatally flawed in a way that wasn't apparent in this one game. But he sure looked special, and if that was the case, Blair knew there was no time to waste. Maybe the Leafs or Habs could take their time, could play hard to get. But not the Boston Bruins.

Blair realized when he arrived at the family home on Great North Road the next afternoon to begin the courting of Bobby Orr that he had at least one small advantage: no other team had yet really shown its cards. It turned out, though, that Orr's existence would soon enough become an open secret. The Toronto Maple Leafs, the team Bobby Orr and nearly everyone else in his town had grown up worshipping, had even been informed in writing that a young star was playing within their de facto home turf. In the spring of 1960, an old army pal of Leafs coach Punch Imlach sent a letter from Parry Sound to the grand arena on Carlton Street. Anthony Gilchrist had coached Orr as a boy before Bucko McDonald took over. Orr's peewee team had played a game at Maple Leaf Gardens not long before, and the Toronto coach, even while only half paying attention to the game, couldn't help noticing their best player.

"You will no doubt remember a fair-haired, crew-cut lad who was in the group," Gilchrist wrote to Imlach. "You sized him up and made a remark that he was a hockey player. Well, he sure has the earmarks of a combination of Howe and Harvey. His name is Bobby Orr, age 12, and he plays defence on the peewee all-stars for the town team. . . ."

"His team is in the minor hockey playoffs and they play in Barrie this coming Wednesday, March 30, then back here in Parry Sound on Saturday, April 2. It might pay to have one of your men look him over in Barrie and place him on your list before Hap Emms sees him, or I feel sure it will be too late."

The Leafs, though, could barely stifle an organizational yawn. Gilchrist eventually received a reply that was short on enthusiasm and read a whole lot like a hockey form letter.

April 7, 1960
Mr. A. A. Gilchrist
Box 1072,
Parry Sound, Ontario

Dear Mr. Gilchrist:

Your letter addressed to Punch was handed over to me.

I would like to take this opportunity to thank you for recommending Bob Orr to our organization but the boy is a little too young to be put on any list for protection. I will keep his name on file and when he gets to be fourteen or fifteen we will contact him and if he is good enough I would recommend a hockey scholarship for him here in Toronto.

In regard to Emms placing him on any list, the Pro Clubs cannot put a boy on the list until he is eighteen years old and the only way a Junior Club can protect him is that they would have to move him to Barrie and put him on the Sponsored list, and at the present time I do not think anybody would move a twelve-year-old boy.

I appreciate your interest in the Maple Leaf Hockey Club and hope we can win that Stanley Cup. I hope that some day Bob Orr will be playing for the Maple Leafs.

Yours very truly,
R. E. Davidson
Chief Scout

(Years later, R. E. "Bob" Davidson explained it this way: "When Orr came to our attention we had the Metro League operating in Toronto, and I was already in some trouble because of all the boys we had brought in. You have to remember at the time Orr was still in public school. Maybe if I had pressed I could have gotten him here. I guess I'll never know. Oshawa needed players. They were able to arrange for him to stay home in Parry Sound and commute for the games, and that's how he got there.")[8]

Not that Blair knew it at the time, but another potential suitor for Orr had been in the rink in Gananoque and had witnessed exactly the same miracles he had seen. William Peachey, a Parry Sound old-timer, a lawyer who was a long-time friend of Frank Selke, the man who ran the Montreal Canadiens, had sent a letter to his old pal, telling him about the local boy wonder Bobby Orr, suggesting that the Habs might want to take a look. Selke passed the note along to his general manager, Sam Pollock, and Pollock in turn relayed the tip to the club's head scout for eastern North America, a bright young up-and-comer named Scotty Bowman. He was in the rink that day, looking at Higgins and Eaton, whom everybody was chasing, but also keeping half an eye on the little kid from Parry Sound. Bowman's travelling companion that day was the owner of the boarding house where he resided in Ottawa – an address that was also favoured by many of the players from the Ottawa Rough Riders of the Canadian Football League. It was the landlord who first stated the obvious: "Why don't you forget about those two," he said to Bowman, "and just concentrate on number 2 for Parry Sound?"

"He was dominating," Bowman remembers now. "But he was very small – much smaller than all of the other guys. He could really skate and fly around. I'd never seen a guy that good at that young age."

Bowman followed the scouting trip with a visit to the Orr home in Parry Sound, more of a social call, as he remembers it, because the Habs had nothing to offer beyond their storied history. The franchise was not in the practice of doling out signing bonuses then, nor would it have committed to a kid still in grade school. Doug Orr made clear his wishes (or at least Arva's wishes) that Bobby wasn't about to leave home, and so Scotty left it at that. If later on the

Orrs were interested and Bobby was prepared to join the Junior Canadiens in Montreal, well, then, they'd have a serious chat.

That didn't mean, though, that Orr was out of bounds for everyone. Teams were free to sign a player at age fourteen to one of their affiliated junior clubs, which, while not a binding professional contract, would effectively tie him to one organization. But there was still the question of a boy that age and that small leaving home, leaving family and friends behind and entering a league where he'd be playing against young men. The Bruins certainly couldn't afford to be as cavalier and dismissive as the Leafs had been and were more than willing look to beyond Orr's age and his size in a way that the Habs were not. So Blair continued his regular visits to Parry Sound. He arrived firm in the belief that, like any working-class Canadian family, the Orrs, on hearing that one of their sons might be chosen for the country's highest sports/cultural calling, would be flattered and excited and at least a tiny bit gullible. Unlike future hockey parents, they wouldn't automatically assess their options – they wouldn't have lawyers and agents to advise them; they wouldn't be able to use the possibility of attending an American university on scholarship as a bargaining chip. To become a professional hockey player, there was only one route, there were only six possible options, and there was precious little leverage available.

Blair was the first salesman to really get his foot in the Orrs' door. Like any good peddler, he knew that his initial task was to pick up on the marital dynamic, to figure out who really called the shots in the family, to understand what they wanted, what they needed, whether they'd be suckers for flattery or would run and hide from anything that smelled of BS. Had to do it quickly, too, and set the proper tone. First impressions and all.

Arva Orr was the only one home when he arrived that first afternoon. Bobby was still in school. Blair asked if he could wait for the boy, and she told him she thought that was all right. He felt welcome enough but still chose to bide his time outside on the porch. The mother was friendly and straightforward, to a point, but wary as well. When Bobby came home, Blair was careful not to scare him off, not to overwhelm him with a hard sell. They talked quietly – well, mostly it was Blair talking and Bobby listening, shy in the presence of the stranger. Wren said he'd been at the game in Gananoque, that he'd seen him play, that he was impressed, that he thought Bobby had the potential someday to make it all the way to the National Hockey League and that he'd like him to do that with the Boston Bruins. Simple as that. This was about building trust, building a relationship, long-term. Bobby was naturally deferential; he listened politely. Blair made his point and made his exit, promising to stay in touch.

The visits came regularly after that. Blair had other duties for the Bruins, scouting young players, keeping track of prospects, operating the Frontenacs. But at every available opportunity, he'd make the detour to Parry Sound, leave the team during its pre-game meal at Alex Eagar's Brunswick Hotel and drop in on the Orr household. There was nothing formal about the meetings. Just a quick chat, the requisite inquiries about everyone's health, talk about Bobby and hockey and how things were going. Usually he'd arrive with a small token – some equipment, or books about hockey, or that most prized gift, tickets for a Leafs game in Toronto. Blair understood the socializing as part of the job, and he understood also that he wasn't alone, that the secret was out. Other teams would soon enough be beating a path to the very same door.

During those trips, Blair began to pick up on the rhythms and realities of the Orr family. They had enough money to feed and house themselves but beyond that were clearly just scraping by. The father was an easygoing chap, an avid fisherman, a fellow who liked to hoist a few, who didn't always see eye to eye with the missus. He fancied himself a hockey player and could imagine nothing better than his son someday playing in the National Hockey League. Doug Orr was in every respect a pretty standard hockey dad, who probably wouldn't present a whole lot of obstacles. But still, he needed to be sold on Blair, and especially to be sold on the Bruins, now that it was clear Bobby could sign with any team in the league. The scout figured he had a small advantage because he'd been first on the scene, because he'd been persistent, because he had slowly, carefully built a bond with Bobby and his family.

Just to help firm things up, he had also persuaded the Bruins to cut a deal with the Parry Sound minor hockey organization, as was standard practice in those days. In return for a generous donation – the Bruins handed over a thousand bucks, about twice the going rate – the town's hockey fathers would identify their best prospects and subtly point them in the direction of Boston.

That wouldn't lock up Orr retroactively, though. He was still free to choose his own path. So Blair followed with a pitch to Doug, and to Bobby, that he hoped might overcome any remaining doubts. Yes, he acknowledged, the Boston Bruins were at that moment a terrible team. Yes, they lacked the glamour and star power of the Leafs or the Habs. But what did that mean for a bright young hockey player on the rise? It meant that they represented the quickest ticket to the bright lights. If Bobby Orr's dream was to play in the NHL, he might have to wait years to achieve that in Toronto or Montreal or Detroit, where they were stacked with talent and he'd have to take his place in line. In Boston, though, he would instantly be on the fast track to the bigs. He might never have to play a game in the minor leagues.

Arva Orr, Blair understood from the start, was a harder case who would not be so easily swayed by the hockey talk. She was clearly the guts and brains of the family, the selfless hard worker, the one who held it all together. She was a bit more suspicious of Blair and his motives. Most of all, she was protective of her son (protective of all her children is what she'd have said, always going to great lengths to remind everyone that Bobby, golden Bobby, was merely one of five, all of them equal in her eyes). She wasn't going to let this kid out of her sight, out of her home, until she was absolutely certain it was the best thing for him, until she knew he'd be well looked after. For her, there was certainly no rush to make a decision. Out of a hockey uniform, her son was still just a boy.

Bobby himself was quiet and shy, a small-town kid in the usual ways, but exceptionally confident too, Blair soon realized. He was serious and dedicated to the idea of becoming a professional hockey player, a little restless, always in a hurry, which meant he might be more inclined to listen to the Bruins' pitch. He worked at building up his skinny frame by lifting weights, practised the game for hours without complaint but wasn't much of a scholar. At school he was average, or a bit below, but plugged away to keep his marks above 60 per cent. Bobby certainly wasn't spoiled, he was no prima donna, and he had learned early in life the value and necessity of hard work. Looking around the modest house, Blair saw also that Bobby had grown up with only the basic creature comforts. The Orrs didn't own a car, and the family home seemed in dire need of repair.

"Mr. Blair," Arva said during one of his visits. "Do you have any idea what they want to stucco this old house?"

"No idea."

"They want $800. Can you believe that?"

Wren nodded sympathetically and filed that one away for later.

While he was courting the Orrs and serving his primary employers, Blair was at the same time taking the opportunity to work his own angle on the side. Oshawa, Ontario, was then about an hour's drive beyond of the last vestiges of Metropolitan Toronto's suburban sprawl. As the Canadian base of General Motors, it was a thriving company town. It had also been a good market for junior hockey, populous enough and separate enough, far enough away from the closest outpost of the big-league brand. But the first Generals franchise had died, apparently forever, in 1953, when the Oshawa rink burned to the ground and there wasn't the money to rebuild. Blair hatched a plan, backed by local movers and shakers including the lawyer Terry Kelly,* to bring junior hockey back to town and to build a new arena. Then, as now, owning a junior franchise could be a rather lucrative proposition. Behind the veneer of community service, the bottom line was that you could charge whatever the market would bear for tickets, you could sell plenty of popcorn and

---

* In addition to being a powerful figure in Oshawa sports circles and a former director of Maple Leaf Gardens, lawyer Terry Kelly – who was dubbed "super-fan" by *Toronto Star* sports writer Jim Kernaghan in the 1960s – is famous for travelling the world at his own expense to watch a wide variety of sporting events. Among other things, he has attended every World Cup soccer final since 1966.

soda pop, and you didn't have to pay the players more than a bare-bones living allowance. In the era before the amateur draft, when junior teams were sponsored by NHL clubs, that supply of nearly free labour was delivered to your doorstep in the form of the organization's best teenage prospects. As business models go, it was tough to beat.

The Boston Bruins already had a junior team in the elite Ontario Hockey Association – the Barrie Flyers, who became the Niagara Falls Flyers in 1960 when their volatile owner/operator Emms decided to move the franchise to the honeymoon capital of the world. Hap would sacrifice his first-born before allowing another Boston-sponsored team into the OHA. Sharing the wealth would do him no good at all. But Blair knew there was soon going to be an alternative. Plans were afoot, the brainchild of the Maple Leafs president, Stafford Smythe, to start a new junior league featuring only teams from in and around the city of Toronto, including what would become the Leafs number-one junior affiliate, the Marlboros. Oshawa fell just outside the intended geographic boundaries. But if Smythe could be persuaded to expand his sights just a little, and if they could relaunch the Generals with the game's next great star as the featured attraction, building that new arena – and filling all of its seats – didn't seem far-fetched at all.

So Blair began employing his considerable persuasive abilities on two fronts, apparently separate but linked in his own grand plan. Put together a new junior organization in Oshawa, of which he would become the president and general manager. And sign Bobby Orr to become the foundation of that team. To make the last piece fall into place, he would also have to convince Adams and Patrick that they should not just split their sponsorship and put some start-up money into Oshawa but give him, rather than Emms, the right to sign Orr. After coming up with an ownership structure that allowed the Bruins to control 51 per cent of the Generals for $50,000, and having sold the NHL team on the idea that two farm clubs were better than one (as both Toronto and Montreal already understood), Blair persuaded the Boston ownership to make Orr the property of the Oshawa Generals if and when he signed. No one bothered to tell Emms about the arrangement. He'd find out soon enough.

On March 20, 1962, Bobby Orr turned fourteen years old, making him eligible to play junior hockey in the upcoming 1962–63 season. By that spring, Blair had worked his way into the hearts of the Orr family sufficiently that he could ask them to allow Bobby to make the long train trip to Niagara Falls for a junior tryout camp. Young players would gather there to train and compete against each other in a series of scrimmages, and those who made the grade would be divided between the Flyers and the reborn Oshawa Generals (presuming they were willing to commit their hockey lives to Boston). It would turn out to be an august group, featuring future pillars of the Bruins, Stanley Cup champions like Wayne Cashman and Derek Sanderson, and other players, like the goaltender Bernie Parent, who would find stardom elsewhere. Orr was the featured attraction, in stature a boy even among other boys but still obviously a special talent. Emms couldn't help licking his chops, thinking of what he'd look like in a Flyers uniform. When Patrick pulled him aside and explained the deal that had been cut to send Orr to Oshawa, Emms exploded. His already low opinion of Wren Blair dropped a couple of notches.

The camp was to wrap up just before the beginning of Labour Day weekend, the traditional symbolic finale of the Canadian summer. Throughout the scrimmages, Orr had looked every inch the future of the Boston franchise. Sensing the importance of the moment, the owner of the team, Weston Adams, decided that it was time to intervene personally, to bring his own unique touch to the ongoing dialogue with the family. Having the head man deal with them personally was sure to impress them, he figured. Blair could step aside now, his job done. "I'll talk to Orr," Adams said. "You stay out of it." Blair departed unhappily, seeing his prize prospect delivered into other hands.

The conversation apparently did not go well. The Orrs, who had grown used to Blair, were intimidated or offended or simply scared off by Adams' hard sales pitch. Bobby was particularly uncomfortable. "All I want to do is get out of here," he told Doug, who had come to pick him up after the camp. Father and son left quickly for Parry Sound without signing anything and apparently repelled by the whole idea. Adams, it seemed, had blown it.

The next day, he was on the phone to Blair.

"What are you doing this weekend?" he asked

"I'm taking my family and heading for the cottage in Haliburton."

"No you're not. You're going to Parry Sound. I think we're going to lose that young man. Call me as soon as you've got an answer."

Blair wasn't thrilled at sacrificing his holiday weekend, and he was angry that Adams had elbowed him aside at the climactic moment. But he was enough of a hockey pragmatist, enough of a company man, to swallow his pride and change his plans. He called his brother and asked if he and his wife could look after the kids. Then Blair, with his wife, Elma, riding shotgun, began the familiar trek to Great North Road.

The scene inside the Orr house certainly wasn't encouraging. Arva was polite enough and welcomed Blair in, but there was no sign of Doug anywhere. The parents had just concluded one hell of a spat, and Doug had walked out to find some peace, quiet, fraternal companionship and libation. It wasn't hard to understand the source of the disagreement: it hadn't changed since day one, and Arva wasn't shy about once again making her feelings known. Bobby was too young to leave home. He was only fourteen years old. He wasn't even out of public school. Oshawa was a long way away. Maybe they could talk again in a year, when Bobby would be settled in high school. But not now.

Bobby was there as well, sitting silently to one side, angry – he had the Orr temper, slow boil, violent release – but was careful not to let loose in the presence of his mother. He wanted to sign, he wanted to play for Oshawa, and he wanted to play in the National Hockey League as soon as possible. But he understood very well who was the boss. When his mother told him it was time to go to bed, he shuffled upstairs immediately, unhappy but compliant. In the back of his mind, Blair took note of that: a kid who obeyed authority, who was quick to follow orders. How much better could it get?

As it grew late, with Doug still absent, Arva suggested that Blair come back the next day to continue the conversation. So the Bruins hadn't completely blown it yet. The next day, when Wren came back, Doug was there, and the domestic front seemed a little bit less tense.

Wren pulled Doug aside and whispered, "Where the hell were you last night?"

"She was giving me a hard time. I got mad, then went out and got drunk. The hangover is killing me now."

They returned one more time to the kitchen table, Doug and Bobby and Wren, who laid out the terms of the deal. Arva chose to stand back, alone, in the living room. The first step was for Bobby to sign a "C-Form"* with the Oshawa Generals, Blair explained. He knew that Arva didn't want her son leaving home, and they didn't want to disturb his schooling in Parry Sound any more than necessary. So the team was willing to enter into a unique arrangement, letting Bobby skip practices during the week

---

* The C-Form was one of three documents National Hockey League teams used to secure the services of teenage players in the days before the universal amateur draft. Unlike the A-Form, which committed a player only to attending a tryout at training camp, and the B-Form, which gave the team the option of signing a player in return for a bonus payment, the C-Form was close to a de facto professional contract, linking a player to one team, potentially for his entire career. It was used to tie up the best, most talented pro prospects. In return for a bonus, the team was given the right to summon a player at any time during the following year and sign him to a standard professional contract, with the terms already laid out in the agreement. If that option wasn't exercised during the first year, it could be renewed annually by the team. Players couldn't legally sign a C-Form until they were eighteen years old, but parents could sign on their children's behalf. The potential for abuse – teenage players having their playing rights signed away by their gullible parents for a relative pittance – was obvious, the first stage in an economic system that exploited NHL players for decades.

and then come south to play games on weekends. There would be a lot of winter driving involved, but he'd at least be able to remain at home, under his mother's watchful eye. The Generals would pay Bobby the usual small weekly stipend available to junior players. And in addition, in return for signing and effectively committing his professional hockey rights to the Boston Bruins, Orr would be given a most generous bonus: $10,000. In professional hockey, that figure was unprecedented.

Doug picked up the paper that had Blair's notes on it and carried it into the living room, where his wife was waiting. "Arva, this looks pretty good to me. I'm going to take it over to Joe and have him look at it." Joe was their lawyer. He was playing golf that day. Doug could meet him at the course.

"Can I borrow your car, Wren?"

Wren's wife, Elma, had been patiently waiting outside in the passenger seat. She came in long enough for Doug to drive to the golf course, get a quick legal opinion and then return home.

"Joe says it looks pretty darn good," Doug said.

Arva was still resisting, so Blair, remembering an earlier conversation, upped the ante.

"Mrs. Orr, if he signs with us, we'll pay to stucco this house."

She wasn't buying it.

"Now don't you start doing that with me. You're trying to get me to waver. He's too young to leave home."

Sensing the moment, Blair then came through with his closer.

"If you let Bobby sign," he said, "I'll buy you a new car."

The boy was sitting silently on the woodpile in the kitchen, listening to all this, listening to his parents argue, listening to his future being decided. He was a good kid, an obedient kid, but headstrong, too, sure of himself. And all he wanted to do was play hockey.

Doug glanced over at him.

"What do you want to do, Buck?"

"You know what I want to do," Bobby said.

"Then get up to the table here and sign this card."

And there, Bobby Orr put pen to paper.

—

Elma Blair was sitting outside in the car waiting for her husband when he bolted out the door of the Orr family home. He had the car started and moving before he said a word. You'd have thought he'd just robbed a bank. He was breathless.

"How'd you make out?" Elma asked, breaking the silence.

"I finally got him signed."

"Where are we going?"

"To Huntsville."

"What's the hurry?"

"I'm afraid his mother is going to find a car and hunt us down, grab this card away from me if we don't get the hell out of here right now."

So they drove, not stopping until Huntsville, where Wren got on the first pay phone he saw and, as ordered, called his boss, Adams. "I've got him, Weston. I've got him signed."

"Great. Great. How much did it cost?"

"Ten grand."

Adams paused on the other end of the line. Sure, the kid was the saviour. Sure he was going to single-handedly revive his franchise and fill up those empty seats in the Boston Garden. But $10,000 was a lot of money for a kid hockey player, especially coming from someone so used to counting every nickel.

"Do you know where Lynn is?" Adams asked.

Blair was under explicit orders from the general manager never to divulge his whereabouts to the owner under any circumstances. "He drives me nuts," Patrick explained.

"I have no idea." A white lie, that.

"Well, you'd better get hold of him somehow. Get him right away and get him to send those people a cheque for $10,000. American."

The Canadian dollar then was worth more than the U.S. greenback – just a few cents more, but Adams figured the kid's family, country rubes, wouldn't know the difference.

And Wren thought to himself, though he didn't dare express it, You cheap son of a bitch.

He hung up and got right on the line to Patrick. Of course he knew where he was. "We've got the kid," he said.

And Patrick, who would be fired by Adams before Orr ever played a game with the Bruins, who would be long gone when the team finally became a winner, all but jumped for joy. "To hell with Weston," he said. "You send that cheque in Canadian money."

Who knows if Adams ever noticed. But in any case, it seems he never asked.

Not so long afterwards, Blair, still flying high from his career achievement, happened to be at Maple Leaf Gardens to watch a game. He was pulled aside and summoned to appear in the office of Stafford Smythe, who could be a prick at the best of times. Immediately, Blair understood that this wasn't one of Smythe's better days.

"Don't think you're so fucking smart about signing Orr," Smythe barked.

"I never said I was smart," Blair answered.

"We had him signed long before you did," Smythe said.

Well, that was interesting. "If that's the case, Staff," Blair wondered, "how come Orr isn't wearing a Leafs uniform right now?"

"Because my people were too goddamn stupid," Smythe said.

Chapter Four

A WHOLE NEW GAME

C HANGE WAS ON THE WAY, radical, fundamental change, not that they would have seen it beyond the horizon in Parry Sound any more than they would have seen the Beatles coming. Never mind the societal stuff, never mind the stirrings of defiance in the 1950s, the musings of Beat poets, the rebellion against post-war conformity brewing in big cities so far away. That shock wave wouldn't reach the hinterland for years, when the first local boy grew his hair past his ears and rode out the ridicule, when the first hometown kid was busted carrying a joint, when somebody protested against something or simply stood up and told their parents they were misinformed. That would all happen eventually, but long after a seismic shift that would strike every one of those small-town Canadians exactly where they lived. One of the signposts of their conservative, ordered universe, the six-team hockey solar system, the Saturday night Church of Foster Hewitt, unchanged for so many decades, was about to be turned on its head. Not because some hockey visionary made it so, not because of anything endemic to the game. Larger forces were at work, social and economic and demographic and political. Professional sports would be dragged kicking and screaming along, with hockey at the rear, its heels dug in, the very last to go.

In 1958, Walter O'Malley had uprooted his baseball Dodgers from their ancestral home in Brooklyn, breaking many a Flatbush heart in the process, and moved them across the country to Los Angeles, where he would build a beautiful new stadium in ever-sunny Chavez Ravine. That same year the New York Giants also headed west, abandoning the Polo Grounds in Manhattan for San Francisco, the town that had given birth to Joe DiMaggio. Both teams followed in the wake of a shifting population and its shifting wealth. All signs pointed to California, and those baseball owners wanted to be the first at the trough. They had begun to understand not just the opportunities involved in a booming, virgin market, but also the possibility that television, still a primitive vehicle for delivering their product to a mass audience and attracting sponsors, could become a source of significant revenues. They'd have the whole West Coast, the whole Pacific time zone, all to themselves, rather than fighting with the omnipotent Yankees for a piece of the action in New York City. The new ease of transcontinental air travel would overcome previously insurmountable distances between games. History, tradition, community loyalty all fell by the wayside in the pursuit of the almighty buck. That wasn't to suggest that professional sport had only suddenly become a bottom-line business; such had been its true nature for many decades. But in moments like this, when the commercial foundation was laid bare, it became that much more difficult for the passionate fan to suspend disbelief, to pretend that it was all just a game.

As it happened, 1958 was also the year the New York Giants and Baltimore Colts played for the National Football League championship in what would be described (especially through the propaganda machineries of the NFL itself) as the greatest game ever played. Whatever its true aesthetic value, what it was, really, was the first time that the sport had broken through as a significant mass audience event, thanks entirely to television. Football, it turned out, was as perfectly suited to the booming medium as was *I Love Lucy*. The possibility of multiple cameras shooting a rectangular field made football games simpler to produce than a baseball telecast. More important, the game stopped and started on a predictable basis. After each play, lasting a few seconds, the players regrouped and huddled before the next burst of action began. There were breaks between quarters and a long interval at halftime. All that dead time was perfect for filling with endless analysis of what had preceded, augmented – when the technology evolved – by instant replays. Announcers had plenty of opportunity to entertain, to enliven even the dullest game and to extol the virtues of the league and the athletes, to shill for the product. And when none of that was happening, there remained ample dead air to be filled with commercials, which soon enough would become the economic engine of the professional football business and of all professional sport. In 1960, at the urging of their bright young commissioner, Pete Rozelle, the NFL owners agreed that they would share what were then modest national television revenues equally among all franchises, a huge concession from the New York Giants' owner, Wellington Mara, who had a monopoly in what was by far the country's largest market. That momentous decision would become the philosophical underpinning of the most lucrative sports business on the planet, a moment of visionary corporate socialism.

Both baseball and football were also spurred on in this revolution by the threatened emergence of rival leagues. The challenge presented by the upstart American Football League helped move the NFL owners into their revenue-sharing scheme (and eventually forced them into merger). In baseball, talk of a new loop to be called the Continental League (pushed by, among others, a Canadian radio tycoon by the name of Jack Kent Cooke, who hoped to put a team in Toronto, where he owned the Maple Leafs of the International League), which was designed to take advantage of the owners' innate conservatism and long-time reluctance to expand beyond the traditional markets, forced the Major Leagues to add four new franchises to help stave off the threat: the New York Mets, the Los Angeles Angels, the Houston Colt .45s (later the Astros) and a new incarnation of the Washington Senators to replace the team that had moved to Minneapolis.

Between the day the Dodgers left Brooklyn in 1958 and the playing of the first Super Bowl game in 1967, pitting the NFL champion against the champion of the rival American Football League in an event wholly created for television, the landscape of professional sport in North America was entirely redrawn. It extended from coast to coast, east to west. It had evolved from a gate-driven enterprise to one increasingly at the mercy of television networks for its most significant source of income. The sports business had entered into a cycle of phenomenal growth and would achieve a level of societal importance unseen since the 1920s, arguably unseen ever in the history of mankind. There was clearly a need to be filled for some sort of collective passion, and the spectacle of professional sport, empty but ordered in a way that made it seem plenty meaningful, was just the ticket.

And then there was hockey.

The truth is that the National Hockey League, in its earliest incarnation, was far ahead of the curve – forty years ahead, to be precise. But the timing of the ambitious expansion of the first incarnation of the NHL south of the border was all bad. The prosperity of the pre-Crash 1920s had kicked off the initial Golden Age of pro sport in the United States. That decade's star athletes would transcend their games to become larger, cultural icons: Babe Ruth in baseball, "Big Bill" Tilden in tennis, Red Grange in college football, Jack Dempsey, the heavyweight boxing champion of the world. Crowds increased, athlete salaries increased, the boom times seemed without boundaries. Spectator sport filled the empty hours of a society suddenly blessed with more discretionary income, suddenly faced with new leisure time to kill. Entrepreneurs who had made their fortunes in other pursuits were eager to plough their profits into professional franchises, eager to ride the wave, eager to attach themselves to something so sexy, so glamorous, so much fun, dreaming that they might absorb some of those qualities by association. (And yes, that should all sound extremely familiar.)

This sports landscape, though, was entirely different from that which would evolve in the second half of the twentieth century. Baseball was far and away the most successful of the team games, firmly established during the late 1800s as the self-anointed National Pastime, undiminished by the Black Sox game-fixing scandal of 1919, granted a special exemption from the monopoly-busting aspects of American anti-trust law. It was a big business that produced the first great outdoor stadiums and would make fine use of the new medium of commercial radio. Technically, it was a regional product: the St. Louis Cardinals and Browns were the only big-league team located west (just barely) of the Mississippi River. There were no clubs in the Deep South or on the Pacific Coast, and most of the action took place in a narrow corridor extending from Boston to Washington, D.C. But there were minor-league outposts everywhere, and the big teams – especially Ruth's New York Yankees – enjoyed a national following, largely thanks to the mythmaking powers of the first great generation of celebrity American sports-writers such as Grantland Rice and Damon Runyon.

Other team sports lagged far behind. Basketball was a game that kids played for recreation at the local YMCA. The professional National Basketball Association was still decades away. College football, dominated by the Army team and by Knute Rockne's Notre Dame Irish, was the subject of much sports-page hyperbole, but the games were few and far between. Meanwhile, professional football, in the form of the fledgling National Football League, struggled for survival, with teams stuck in tiny backwaters like Canton, Ohio, and Green Bay, Wisconsin.

Professional hockey was significantly more advanced and would become entrenched in the big cities of the Northeast long before any other winter sport. Its growth was driven by the construction of mag-nificent new venues. The grand arenas (beginning with New York's original Madison Square Garden) had several uses: for boxing and wrestling matches, both of which drew huge, enthusiastic audiences attracted by the stars of the day; for distance running and six-day bicycle races, both popular fads; for evangelists and band concerts and anything else that might bring in a crowd. Once the technical hurdle of artificial ice was overcome, hockey was a natural tenant, though its allure for audiences outside its passionate, Canadian base was still an open question.

The National Hockey League, formed out of the remnants of previous leagues, was established in 1917, with two teams in Montreal – the Wanderers and the Canadiens – and single franchises in Quebec, Ottawa and Toronto. The intent then was to peddle the game exclusively to those who had grown up with it, who had played it, who understood it as part of their tribal identity: Canadians. In those early years, there was plenty of shuffling of franchises. Quebec didn't actually operate that first season, or the next. The Wanderers were gone after their rink burned down in 1918. In 1920, the Quebec team became the Hamilton Tigers. But despite that apparent instability, there were also signs early on that the game had legs. People would turn out in numbers and fill the buildings, thrilled to watch a sport so fast and so savage. There was money to be made.

Among those smitten during the early years of the NHL was a man named Charles Adams, who had been born in Northern Vermont, not far from the Quebec border, and who had made his fortune in Boston, an area where amateur ice hockey already had a uniquely engaged following in the United States. Adams' fortune was amassed in the grocery business, which was lucrative, stable and a little bit boring. Soon, though, he began to invest in ventures that clearly were more stimulating to his imagination. Adams for a time owned the Boston Braves of baseball's National League and for years was the proprietor of the Suffolk Downs race course.

His hockey epiphany, legend has it, came while he was watching a Stanley Cup playoff game in Montreal; he became so caught up in the action and the atmosphere that he immediately fell in love with the sport and decided that he had to bring the professional game to Boston. There was also, however, a more pragmatic explanation for his sudden devotion, at least when it came to taking risks with his own money. A scandal had recently shaken fan confidence in the amateur game in Boston when it was revealed that players were being paid under the table, but there was still an audience there, one that was sophisticated in the sport. The time was ripe,

Adams figured, with the amateurs in disarray, to ride into Boston with professional hockey, to bring the fans the highest form of the game and eventually to build his own arena.

Persuading the National Hockey League's governors wouldn't be so simple, though. They were the Canadian guardians of a Canadian sport; they'd be loath to risk what they had developed at home by taking a wild leap into a foreign land. They would assess and reassess how moving into the United States would affect their business model, whether in the long run it would help them or hurt them.

Or at least they would do all of that until 1924, when Adams presented them with a cheque for $15,000, the exorbitant price of an expansion franchise. When that vast sum of money was placed on the table, the league fathers' response could be summed up in two words: welcome aboard. The Boston franchise – nicknamed the Bruins by a secretary working for the man hired to build Adams' hockey operation, Art Ross – became the first American-based team in the NHL. With the club struggling on the ice during its first two seasons, and with plans afoot to build his own grand building in Boston, Adams made a further investment, paying the Patrick brothers, Lester and Frank (father and uncle of Lynn Patrick), for the rights to players in their Western Hockey League, then a dying West Coast rival to the NHL. Included in the package was Eddie Shore, the great skater and scorer who had revolutionized the defenceman's position. With the new talent on board, with Shore established as a local box office attraction, Boston immediately became competitive. The Boston Garden (with half a million dollars of Adams' money sunk into the building project) was opened in 1927, and two years later, the Bruins captured their first Stanley Cup. (They were not, however, the first American team to win the trophy. Before it became the de facto championship of the NHL, it was a challenge cup, and not the property of any one league. In 1917, the Seattle Metropolitans of the Pacific Coast Hockey Association had captured the Stanley Cup by challenging and defeating the NHL champion Montreal Canadiens.)

So here was the new model. Sell expansion franchises for profit. Take the game to fresh markets. Hustle hockey tickets even to those who might never have been on skates before. Set off an arena construction boom. Turn the National Hockey League, just a little more than a decade into its existence, into a true big-league sport, second only to baseball in North America. In the booming economy of the mid-1920s, all that and much more seemed possible. There were no obvious limits to growth.

The Montreal Maroons were the first new team added after the Bruins, but after that the league's sights turned entirely to the United States. In 1925, the Hamilton Tigers (whose players had gone on strike rather than play for the Stanley Cup) became the New York Americans. That same year, a new franchise was added in Pittsburgh, owned in part by the boxing champion Benny Leonard. In 1926, the New York Rangers, Detroit Red Wings and Chicago Black Hawks came into being, transforming the NHL into a ten-franchise, cross-border, major-league sports business, entrenched in the United States' biggest, richest markets. And that seemed like only the beginning.

Instead, it was the peak, as big and important as professional hockey would be for more than forty years. In 1929 came the Crash, and in its wake the Great Depression. Suddenly, the business of hockey, and especially the NHL's expansion shell game, didn't seem quite so attractive. While baseball survived the greatest economic crisis of the century intact, and other entertainment businesses (the movies, especially) thrived even in the darkest days, the NHL, without deep roots in many of its markets, entered a period of instability, followed by precipitous decline. In 1930, the Pittsburgh franchise was shifted to Philadelphia and shortly thereafter closed shop. Ottawa disappeared for a year in 1931, reappeared in 1932, two years later moved on to St. Louis and folded finally in 1935. Next to fall were the Montreal Maroons, in 1938. In 1941, the New York Americans were renamed the Brooklyn Americans before being consigned to history a year later.

The ten-team league had shrunk to a six-team league. Professional hockey had been rendered down to its essence, to its core market, to the places where the game had grown roots. The NHL had survived, just barely. And the men who controlled the remaining teams then, who would control the remaining teams for many years thereafter – the Norris family in Detroit and Chicago, Conn Smythe in Toronto, Charles Adams (and after his death in 1947, his son Weston) in Boston – would be deeply affected by the near collapse of the league. Their little business would have to putter along just as it was. There would be no more grand schemes. There would be no more pretensions of grandeur. The limits of the professional hockey universe were clearly defined. The business was driven by bums in seats. Institutional conservatism became deeply ingrained. And even while enjoying the new prosperity in the years following the Second World War, even watching as professional basketball debuted, as other sports flirted with the idea of stretching their wings, the NHL's governors were unmoved. They understood from experience everything that could go wrong.

That attitude persisted well into the 1950s, when the Cleveland businessman Jim Hendy came to the league with a completely sound proposal for adding a seventh team in his city and was rebuffed. Hendy's American Hockey League club, the Barons, had been a huge success at the box office and had been powerful enough on the ice that at one point they'd toyed with the idea of launching a challenge against the NHL champion for the Stanley Cup. Cleveland was geographically in the right place, easily accessible from the other cities, the hockey market was firmly established, and most important Hendy had access to plenty of money. But during a special meeting at the Royal York Hotel in Toronto, the governors gave him the cold shoulder: the rink in Cleveland was a bit small, they argued, and they didn't like the fact that his major investor came from a faraway locale – Detroit. (Three decades or so later, when Phil Esposito cobbled together an expansion franchise in Tampa, Florida, backed by mysterious investors in Japan, the NHL expressed no such qualms, just as long as the cheque didn't bounce.) The message was clear: they just weren't interested in expanding anywhere, anytime. Those memories of past failures were still too fresh in the minds of the old men who ran the game.

—

At just about the same time as Bobby Orr was being courted by the Boston Bruins, soon after the Dodgers and Giants were being made to feel at home in California and the NFL was establishing itself as the smartest, most progressive operation in professional sport, stirrings of change were also beginning to be felt in the National Hockey League. All of the same forces at play in other professional sports were pushing the NHL as well, including at least the hint of possible competition – a minor professional loop, again called the Western Hockey League, had expanded its operations to California, which suggested a flanking operation that might set the stage for bigger things. But what finally spurred the NHL to act was the arrival of new blood at the ownership level, as those who had lived through the dark days of the Depression finally gave way to a new breed of sports businessmen who were free of those deep, historically rooted fears, who saw what was happening around them and who, especially, felt that there was all kinds of money to be made, grand fortunes that the passing generation could never have imagined. Bill Jennings, the young president of the New York Rangers, was one of those prime movers. So too were the new proprietors of the Toronto Maple Leafs empire: Conn Smythe's son, Stafford, and his business partners, Harold Ballard and John Bassett. "If the right people come to us with five million and the right kind of plans [for expansion]," said Ballard, showing his true colours from the start, "we'll listen."[9]

In September 1960, the Leafs and Weston Adams' Boston Bruins played a pair of pre-season exhibition games in Los Angeles, a way of damping down any big-league pretensions the WHL might still harbour and of testing the waters in an exotic locale. Hockey in Hollywood, hockey amid the palm trees, hockey where the natives wouldn't know one end of a stick from the other. "Every successful pass and the lightest body check were cheered to the rafters," Jim Proudfoot of *The Toronto Daily Star* wrote, in an article for *The Hockey News,* of the strange scene.[10] The two games drew crowds of 9,861 and 10,742 paying customers respectively, attendance that impressed two members of the ancient NHL power structure who made the trip: the league's president, Clarence Campbell, and Conn Smythe, who, though he had handed over day-to-day operation of the hockey team to his son, still held on to the chairmanship of Maple Leaf Gardens. "This is a hockey gold mine," the elder Smythe said. "But there's a lot of work to be done before we can put an NHL team in this city. I'd like to be a young man starting out in this town with this arena and with people as hungry for hockey as these folks."[11]

Pockets of resistance remained, but it proved futile. Some of the old-order owners wondered what was really in it for them. Would any new revenues really be worth splitting up their pie into several more slices? And where would the players come from? Wasn't the talent stretched a little thin already? (Not to mention the fact that after an initial draft to stock any new teams, expansion would also have to be coupled with a universal draft of juniors, ending the teams' ability to monopolize and control talent within their orbit, a blow especially to the Leafs and Canadiens). "There aren't enough players," Conn Smythe cautioned. "Too many clubs are now short of good players. Take [Gordie] Howe away from Detroit and they have nothing."[12] Hockey had to remember what it was, where it had come from; it couldn't afford to take risks, the conservatives argued – not even in a time of great prosperity, with the league approaching historic highs in attendance and ticket revenues.

Most of that Chicken Little talk fell on deaf ears. Stafford Smythe was talking about establishing teams not just from coast to coast but perhaps in European cities as well. Jennings didn't see any insurmountable barriers to hockey's global expansion. At the first league meetings dealing with the subject, there were all kinds of scenarios suggested, and there were signs of all kinds of outside interest, coupled with all kinds of fresh money. A new team in Vancouver looked like a lock. Jack Kent Cooke had moved to Los Angeles (in part because he had failed to secure a Major League Baseball franchise for Toronto) and was building a new arena there with the NHL and the NBA in mind. There were modern buildings in place or in the planning stages for every potential new market except for St. Louis. Bing Crosby – Bing Crosby! – was part of the group that wanted to put an NHL team in San Francisco. "We want them strong enough to provide a big-league show when they come into our rinks," Stafford Smythe opined. "We're in the entertainment business and can't afford to have 'weak sisters' for partners. So it is up to us to profit by the mistakes that baseball made in stocking its new teams for expansion. The National Football League did a much better job; maybe we can improve on that."[13] Four years max, he figured, and the new franchises would be on a competitive par with the Original Six.

"It is a known fact that the American television networks have bypassed the National Hockey League as a major TV attraction only until the league has a coast-to-coast operation, particularly in the West Coast area of San Francisco and Los Angeles, where hockey is growing," wrote Ken McKenzie, publisher of Canada's traditional bible of the sport, *The Hockey News*.[14]

All that excitement, that momentum, leading where? To the big time, baby. To America. To television, and inevitably to the creation of a hockey-mad continent. Step right up, boys. It'll cost you $10,000 – non-refundable – just to have a conversation. It'll cost you another two million bucks (Ballard's $5 million price tag proved to be his own personal pipedream) if we decide you're worthy of a franchise. Soon enough, that's going to look like the bargain of the century, because hockey represents the bright future of professional sport. The Americans in the South and the West don't know that yet, because they've never seen it, because it wasn't on television, because they don't understand the nuances of the game. But educate them (maybe a cartoon character could do it. Peter Puck!), teach them, expose them to all of that speed, that power, that excitement, and they'll instantly be seduced.

The players, heroes in Canada now, will become like movie stars. And among them will naturally emerge the face of the big-league NHL, the embodiment of the sport's new generation. Rocket Richard is done. Gordie Howe is just a shadow of himself. He can't have too many years left before he calls it quits. The kid in Chicago, Bobby Hull, has plenty of pizzazz and that wicked shot, but he's really a 1950s kind of guy. This evolving game will need a different kind of look, a fresh-faced boy any Canadian mom and dad would be proud to call their son, but contemporary, too, so the kids will "dig" him. And maybe a little sex appeal wouldn't hurt. Not like the football player, Joe Namath. That's too sleazy, too dangerous, a bit too suggestive of actual hot, sweaty physical congress for the hockey crowd. The NHL model would be more the guy who would make the perfect pal, the perfect boyfriend. There should be a little bit of yesterday about him, a hint of old-fashioned small-town Canadian values, a little bit of now, and especially a touch of tomorrow. And the selling point, beyond all that, will be that he is the greatest hockey player in the world. They might not know a thing about the game in vast sections of America, but that idea – come out to see the best who plays, perhaps the best who has ever played – would have selling power even among the shinny philistines.

Chapter Five

THE LITTLEST GENERAL

THE SEGMENT OPENS WITH A STATIC SHOT, the familiar label from a bottle of Molson's Canadian lager beer filling the television screen. Then cut to Ward Cornell, staring straight into the camera with his dark baggy eyes, his hair as shiny and slick as patent leather. You don't see faces like that on television anymore, but then, for all of those years, there seemed nothing odd about it, the look, the voice not of an actor but of an ordinary man. On Saturday nights, for so many Canadians, it was also the familiar, reassuring look of home.

"All across Canada we're finishing up a very exciting week of minor hockey. Our two guests tonight, our first two guests, are a couple of gentlemen who played a little bit of minor hockey, and now they're in Junior A. You've read a great deal about them, if you haven't seen them. Bobby Orr of Oshawa is on my immediate left. Wayne Carleton of the Marlboros on my far left."

It is between periods, intermission at Maple Leaf Gardens. In a studio near the dressing rooms, not much bigger than a closet, two huge cameras stand facing the host, hunched over in his chair, leaning forward like a kindly doctor quizzing a nervous patient.

Carleton – "Swoop," they'll nickname him – has pale blue eyes, striking even in black and white, and blotchy teenage skin. He is wearing a Marlies team blazer, the crest embroidered on the left breast, over a light-coloured vest. Next to him sits a younger-looking boy with a blond brush cut, wearing a light-coloured suit with vest, hands folded tightly together, knees wide apart, dark eyes staring down, only occasionally daring a darting glance at the camera. He wears a tie and a high white collar – Don Cherry high. His pants look uncomfortably tight, stretched over his thighs, bunched up around the crotch.

This is most of Canada's first glimpse of Bobby Orr.

"Actually, boys, you didn't play minor hockey very long, did you? Wayne?"

"No, Ward . . ."

Carleton calls the TV star by name, by his first name, as though they're equals, co-adults, lifelong pals. He seems absolutely at home, comfortable, confident, laying out his short hockey history before arriving in Toronto. Like Orr, he's a Northern Ontario boy. Carleton comes from Sudbury. But in the moments that follow, they seem worlds apart.

"How old are you, Bobby?"

"I'm fifteen now."

"Where's your home?"

"Up in Parry Sound."

"And now you're living in Oshawa?"

"Yes."

Cornell asks them about how they came to be scouted by the teams of the National Hockey League. "Yes, I talked with them all," Carleton says, almost a swagger there. "Chiefly Montreal. Scotty Bowman with Montreal. I was satisfied with Toronto."

Satisfied. With the Toronto Maple Leafs. With – as far as the English side of the *Hockey Night in Canada* universe is concerned – God's own team. Satisfied.

"How about you, Bobby?"

"Wren Blair scouted me for the Bruins organization when I was playing in a bantam game down in Gananoque."

"Did you have other scouts around too?"

"Yes. Scotty Bowman from Montreal and Jim Skinner from Detroit."

"Why did you decide to choose Boston?"

"I think that Boston is building their team now. And I'd just like to be a part of their building."

Both teenagers agreed that they didn't really feel so much pressure to sign with any one team, that they could make their own choices, that no one forces you to make that decision. Then they're asked about their hockey influences.

"Bobby, have you tried to pattern yourself after anyone in particular in the National Hockey League?"

"I play defence myself, and I like to watch all the defencemen. I like to watch Tim Horton for Toronto, and I really think a lot of Terry Harper in Montreal."

"Well, that's an interesting decision. You've taken a youngster, a rookie. What do you like about [Horton's] style?"

Orr smiles for the first time during the interview.

"I don't know – I just like the way he plays."

"You like his moves?"

"Yes."

The conversation turns to school, to academics. It is one of hockey's dirty little secrets, and will forever remain so, that the boys in junior hockey rarely finish high school, that they are full-time quasi-professionals before they reach the age of majority. Carleton, though, is in the final stretch, in Grade 13 at North Toronto Collegiate.

"Well, I'd say being in Grade 13 at age seventeen is pretty good," Cornell says. "Do you hope to go on with your education?"

"Yes, I do, Ward."

"What about you, Bob – school and hockey?"

"I'm in Grade 9 in Oshawa Collegiate, and I just think it's up to the boy himself if he's going to get his schooling. It can be done."

"You plan to go on with your education?"

"Yes, I do."

"And, boys, your ambition in terms of hockey?"

"I hope to play pro someday."

"Bobby?"

"Someday I'd really like to play pro."

This was modesty, and not the false modesty that professional athletes would soon perfect for use in just these situations, with the cameras rolling. Bobby Orr was plenty confident in his hockey ability, but not yet so confident about his place in the wider world.

Even among his peers, he seemed a boy among boys, small, slight, a fringe of close-cropped blond hair on his head and hardly another tuft anywhere else on his body. The first day of camp they lined up and performed a kind of roll call, each member of the reborn Oshawa Generals, a ragtag crew that first season, young and green, calling out their name and position. There were only two kids with any kind of Junior A experience among them, a couple of others from Junior B, a whole bunch new to this level, some of them locals added to the mix as much to send a hometown message as for their hockey assets. The Gens wouldn't even be playing in Oshawa to start – their home rinks would be Maple Leaf Gardens and for a short time the tiny Bowmanville arena, until the new Civic Centre was finished. (At the Gardens, when they first took the ice, the PA announcer intoned, "Please welcome – after a ten-year absence – the Oshawa Generals.") Wren Blair, wearing the hat of the entrepreneur now, understood that he had to start sowing the seeds. These kids would mature together, develop together as a team. They would become the clean, correct beacons of hockey-playing youth, soon enough hailed as local heroes, re-establishing the Generals in the town's imagination, creating a true home team. They wouldn't be winners right away, but all of the other ingredients would be in place, the look, the attitude. And he knew that, with the boy Bobby Orr, he had his marquee attraction, a star who would eventually lead the club to glory and profitability. In the meantime, Blair would run a very tight ship.

When the call-outs worked down to his place in line, the littlest General was initially afraid to pipe up among his new peers. "Orr," he finally squeaked. "Defence."

And the other guys couldn't help laughing, even having heard the stories that a boy genius was lurking in their midst. That kid, all 125 pounds of him, sure didn't fit anyone's idea of how a blueliner was supposed to look. Playing defence meant being big, tough, prepared to bodycheck, prepared to fight when necessary. This young fellow, whatever his abilities, looked as if he belonged back in the bantams, looked as if, when faced with one of the nineteen- or twenty-year-olds who played in the juniors, he might just run back home to Mom.

The truth was, unlike the rest of them, who were adapting to life on their own, he hadn't really left home yet, which was Arva Orr's one small victory. Doug Orr would have been willing to do pretty much anything to advance his son's hockey career, and Bobby himself surely wouldn't have objected. But if this fourteen-year-old was going to risk playing among men for the entertainment of others, his mother was going to at least protect him off the ice. Once pre-season training camp was over, he headed straight back to Parry Sound, and all week long, he'd sleep in his own bed, continue attending Grade 8 and practise with the local intermediate team. (A boon for the folks running the show back in Parry Sound, who charged outside teams to come in for mid-week exhibition games and then sold tickets to watch the local boy-hero in action, ignoring Blair's orders to protect him from any undue risk.) Somehow, they'd get him south for games and get him home afterwards. Doug Orr still hadn't quite managed to buy the car Blair had paid for as part of the signing bonus, so unless he could bum a ride, others did the driving. Ken Johnson, the school principal, was one of the chauffeurs. He was taking a course at the University of Toronto on weekends and would drop Bobby off at the Carlton streetcar for the ride to Maple Leaf Gardens. Johnson knew the Orr family well and had many dealings with Arva, as the parent who handled all school matters. He always noticed how meticulously dressed the quiet, serious boy in the back seat was. Other times, Mike Kolisnek provided the transportation. He was a minor hockey coach and former playing teammate of Doug's who was working on a construction project at Queen's University in Kingston and could drop Bobby in Oshawa en route. Kolisnek noticed something else about the boy, what he interpreted as a kind of melancholy. He wondered if perhaps all wasn't well on the home front.

Because he didn't live in Oshawa that first season, because he came and went and was only a part of the team on game days, Orr was slow to feel that he truly belonged – and at first he faced undercurrents of resentment from the others, who didn't like the fact that he could skip practices and was apparently free from the curfews and rules that dictated their lives away from the rink. He was shy, understandably more comfortable with the sixteen-year-olds than with the older players. He didn't say much, kept his thoughts to himself, spoke only when spoken to and then with "yes, sirs" and "no, sirs." On the ice, he initially struggled through the first few games, trying to adjust to the new tempo, to the physical size and strength of the opposition, to a skill level far higher than anything he had experienced before. Orr was remarkable for a fourteen-year-old, but at first not so remarkable, or so spectacular, in the context of big-time junior hockey.

But there was something else there from the beginning, qualities the other players still find difficult to describe more than forty years later, difficult to explain in the familiar hockey language. If he wasn't the biggest, the strongest, the fastest, if his shot wasn't the hardest, what made Bobby Orr so good? What skills defined his game? They speak of his talent now as though speaking of something nearly mystical.

Wherever he was on the ice, the puck just seemed to come to him, as though directed by a higher force. And when he carried it, when he was stickhandling, Orr never needed to look down. He could somehow feel the puck there on his stick blade – a blade with just a tiny single strip of black tape wrapped around it, and no one had ever seen that before. (Orr explained to the team's sceptical old trainer Stan Waylett that he thought his stick felt lighter that way. "I guess it's all in my head," he said. Who knew that years later, in the stripper's trade, a "Bobby Orr" would be a way of describing how the girls on stage trimmed their pubic hair, with just one strip down the middle.) Orr didn't need the reassurance of glancing ice-ward. He was like Pele or Maradona with a soccer ball at their feet. With his eyes always up, scanning the rink, he could see the play unfold around him, he could anticipate, he could direct the game, he could orchestrate the action, he could speed up or slow down the tempo simply by the way he chose to proceed – or at least he could once his confidence at each new level grew.

Orr's skating ability was remarkable but not startling at first glance. He wasn't even the fastest player on the team, never mind in the league. He was no Yvan Cournoyer, then playing for the Junior Canadiens, so obviously waterbug quick. But Orr seemed to have five or six different speeds, different gears, each of which he could achieve without any obvious extra effort. When he acceler-ated, there were no little stutter steps to get going, just the same smooth, graceful motion. For his opposition, even for his team-mates in practice, the first temptation was to maul the little kid physically, to beat him up, to hit him and slow him down, to scare him, the traditional hockey approach to neutralizing greater talent with brute physical force. But with Orr, at least in terms of landing a clean, open ice check, that proved to be nearly impossible. Players would run at him on the forecheck, anticipating that he'd be at one point in space, only to miss badly as he sped away. Eventually, as his reputation grew, Orr could skate into the neutral zone and the other team would seem to back away and grant him the open ice, as though they were afraid of being embarrassed. Of course, some teams tried to play the intimidation game more directly, by mugging Orr and grabbing him and hooking him and hacking him and sending their goons forward to challenge him to fight. Then they learned something else. When pushed, Bobby Orr could handle himself just fine with his fists and seemed to relish a fight, showing flashes of the Orr temper as he lay on a beating. "It's not really a good practice if they see you're going to turn and run," he said. "I never run the other way, but sometimes I would like to. During the season I had a few scraps, but they're part of the game. The older guys take a run at you as part of breaking in. They would take runs at me, and if I had a chance I would come right back at them. That's what makes it a great game."[15] (In later years, physically slight NHL stars like Wayne Gretzky would have goons by their side to do the fighting for them.) During his first season in junior, the Generals played an exhibition game in Parry Sound against the Junior B Shamrocks, who then had Bobby's older brother, Ronnie, as part of their lineup. A huge brawl broke out, players squared off around the ice, and the Orr brothers found themselves standing face to face. They did what hockey players, brothers or not, are supposed to do in such circumstances. They fought. And Bobby dropped Ron flat on his back.

So he could skate, he could stickhandle, he could fight when he had to. He could shoot without looking at the net, without tipping a goaltender as to what was coming. His slapshot came without a big windup and was deadly accurate. Skating backwards, defending, he was all but unbeatable one-on-one. He could poke-check the puck away, or muscle a forward into the boards. In front of his own net, stronger on his feet than his skinny frame would suggest, he wouldn't be moved. But there was more. He seemed to know things about his teammates, as hockey players, as people, that they didn't necessarily know about themselves. Orr understood the assets and liabilities of those around him and made instant decisions, taking all of that into account. He played to the others' strengths, covered their weaknesses; he anticipated their moves and set them up to succeed. A gifted offensive forward would know both that if he broke free, a lead pass was coming, and that if he abandoned his defensive responsibilities in pursuit of a goal, Orr would be there to cover for him. As he grew more secure in his own game, as he felt comfortable carrying the puck himself, regularly rushing the length of the ice, they saw that, if anything, he was too unselfish, that he passed when he didn't have to, that he seemed to take more pleasure when someone else scored than when he scored himself. If caught up ice, he'd scramble back furiously, often returning to his own zone in time to make a defensive play. And Orr's goals were greeted with a subdued, head-down, almost sheepish non-celebration. It was an age long before the great self-congratulatory displays became common-place, but even in that more modest time, Bobby Orr's seemed especially self-effacing.

No one had taught him to play like that, and certainly no one was going to teach him much here. Doug Williams was the coach that first year, a local schoolteacher and a bit of a hothead who had played for Wren Blair's Whitby Dunlops. The Metro Junior League in the 1962–63 season featured teams from a narrow geo-graphic area: Whitby and Brampton, like Oshawa on the near out-skirts of the big city, the Marlboros, Knob Hill Farms and the Neil McNeil Maroons from within Toronto. Weekends they'd play doubleheaders at the Gardens, and on most Tuesday nights, the Generals would make an appearance at their temporary home rink in Bowmanville, a tiny place, intimidating to visiting teams, where the fans sat so close that they could grab a player skating by. There weren't even proper dressing rooms. The Generals were forced to gather at the Kinsmen Hall in Oshawa, where their crummy, mostly second-hand equipment (old Whitby Dunlops' leftovers) was kept, damp and mouldering, in the basement. They'd dress there, climb on a bus for Bowmanville, then bus back after the game. The coaching the players received was by current standards primitive. They'd skate and scrimmage, run through a few two-on-ones and three-on-twos, get yelled at as they were seen to be loafing and yelled at during and after games they lost. There was precious little science to it, and certainly no one was going to tell Bobby Orr how to play his game. They just let him go. That first season, the Generals weren't competitive with the better teams in the league, finishing out of the playoffs. Orr ended his first year of junior hockey with six goals, fifteen assists, and forty-five penalty minutes in thirty-four games and was selected to the league's second all-star team. He also found time to graduate from the eighth grade.

In September 1963, arriving in time to begin high school before his second season with the Generals, Bobby Orr left Parry Sound for good and moved to Oshawa. The Metro League had folded, and the Generals had been absorbed into the larger, far tougher Ontario Hockey Association. Orr was now fifteen years old. Junior hockey players, at least those who came from elsewhere, were traditionally placed in the homes of locals, folks who liked hockey, or liked hockey players, or simply hoped to make a few bucks. Out of the tiny stipend the players were paid by the team – $50 or $60 a week – a significant portion was turned over for room and board. But there was more to the billeting arrangement than simple food and shelter. Each boy, each young man, was put under the care of people who would make sure he got to school on weekday mornings, make sure he was home by curfew, make sure he was well fed and cared for and kept under control. That last part was key, especially in the way that Wren Blair ran his hockey team. He wanted to know where every player was every hour of every day. He didn't want any unpleasant surprises.

In his first year as a boarder, Bobby Orr was placed with Bob and Bernice (everybody called her Bernie) Ellesmere, who owned a big ramshackle nine-bedroom house at 263 Nassau Street in Oshawa. Bob drove a truck for a living, and Bernie ran a beauty parlour. They took in junior hockey players for the fun of it and for the small amount of money it provided. A boy named Mike Dubeau came first, and then the team asked if they could handle one more, and so Orr arrived. Eventually they'd have as many as seven Generals staying under their roof at the same time. Before the season began, Bobby started classes in Grade 9 at R. S. McLaughlin Collegiate. "Bobby was always on the go," Bob Ellesmere once said when asked about his most famous tenant. "He could never sit still. I don't remember a single time that he'd sit in the living room and watch a television program from start to finish. Except maybe a hockey game."[16]

After just one season with the Ellesmeres, Bobby moved to a different place, a comfortable, modern red brick ranch-style house owned by Jack and Cora Wild, where he was one of two players bunking in the basement. He remained there for the duration of his junior career. The Wilds didn't have children of their own, and Cora remembers now that it was Stan Waylett, the Generals' trainer, who suggested the idea to Jack. "I think I can arrange to get a couple of good ones for you," he said. Bobby arrived with another boy, Jimmy Whittaker, and just as soon as they'd set their bags down, the Wilds outlined the first and most important house rules: no matter what happened, the couple wouldn't lie for them. Whatever the team said, that was the way it would be. The boys thought about it for a second and then said that would be fine. In the early years, before the drinking age dropped from twenty-one to eighteen, before the players started to develop an attitude, to act like pros, the Wilds would never have much of a problem with their Generals. The kids' lives were so regimented, the team retained such tight control, that there wasn't really much opportunity to get into trouble. The players were intimidated by, and respectful of, authority. And Orr, particularly, was so quiet, so self-disciplined, that he never created much of a headache.

The routine during the hockey season rarely varied. On weekdays, the players got up and walked to school. Some of them, after playing a game the night before, especially if it was on the road and especially if the bus didn't return until after midnight, might be sorely tempted to sleep in. But if they did, there was a call from the school at nine o'clock to find out where they were. "Bobby always went to school," Cora remembers, "but the teachers said the odd time he went to sleep sitting at the desk." Just as in grade school, Orr wasn't much of a student (though his Grade 9 average was reportedly a more than respectable 71.3 per cent). His formal education would end after Grade 11, in any case, when he left to play for Bruins, and with effort he managed to get that far. "He did what he had to do," Cora Wild recalls, "but he didn't overdo it. He did his homework and he'd pass. That was, I guess, the main thing."

After school, on any day when there was no game scheduled, the Generals went directly to practice. Then they returned to their billets, ate their dinner and did their homework. Maybe there was time to watch a little television after that, or play some Ping-Pong, or do their laundry. And every night, the call would come from the team, making sure that the players were safely behind closed doors. Curfew was ten-thirty – nine o'clock on the nights before game days or during exams. A first curfew violation brought a reprimand. A second, a letter home to the parents. A third meant an automatic suspension. "The odd night, if they didn't phone, the kids used to laugh," Cora Wild says. "They thought, This was the night we could have stayed out."

On Saturdays, when the Generals played in the evening, the routine changed. Bobby would get up early, walk into town to have his hair cut and then return home for a nap. Eventually, the neighbourhood kids, realizing that they had an honest-to-God Oshawa General in their midst, started to bang on the door in the afternoon, asking if Bobby could come out and play road hockey with them. The first time, Cora sent them away, told them to be quiet because Bobby was sleeping. When he found out afterwards, he told her to make sure to wake him up if they came back. After that, the Saturday afternoon ball hockey game became part of his weekly ritual.

The Orr family visited their son regularly at the Wilds', Doug and Arva, often with a brother or sister in tow. Arva especially wanted to check with Cora about how her son was faring, though she tried to make sure that Bobby didn't think she was fretting. The women's conversations remained discreet. She'd pull Cora aside and make sure Bobby was doing what he was supposed to be doing – if he wasn't, she'd set him straight right away. Arva would habitually poke through Bobby's dresser to see if he'd been wearing the clothes she'd sent along to Oshawa. If not, she'd take out the stuff that wasn't getting much use and pass it along to Jimmy Whittaker.

Clothing was always important to Bobby. He wanted to look right, to be in style, to fit in. Once, Cora Wild thought she'd help him out a bit by washing his blue jeans for him, then pressing them with a nice sharp crease. Bobby didn't have the heart to tell her that the other kids would get a huge laugh out of that. He left particularly early for school that morning, wearing his ironed jeans and carrying an extra bundle along with his books. Before school started, he snuck in and changed – then changed back after practice, just before returning home to the Wilds', so that Cora's feelings wouldn't be hurt.

—

Doug Orr didn't seem to worry about his son's well-being nearly as much as his wife did, and the fact is, there really wasn't much to worry about. Wren Blair saw to that. His boys, his Generals, were going to be an example for others to follow. Out in public, they'd always be dressed to the nines – at very least in a sharp team jacket, but more often in a suit and tie (the players received a clothing allowance), and for a time sporting a mandatory fedora. They weren't supposed to drive their own cars, they weren't supposed to drop out of school, and when Bobby and Jimmy Whittaker decided to hitch-hike to Parry Sound when they had a few days off from hockey, they quickly found out that they weren't supposed to do that, either.

Oshawa was a small, quiet company town, rooted in the 1950s past rather than the 1960s present, but still there were many of the same temptations available that any other teenager might encounter. Not drugs – no one remembers the issue ever coming up. But there was booze, though players lived in fear that even a single casual beer would be reported to the boss. And there were cigarettes. Only a few players would dare take a drink or grab a smoke – and only in a situation where they knew everyone in the room could be trusted. (Ian Young, who became a star goaltender with the Generals, remembers once walking through a local beverage room – in the front door and straight out the back without pausing – just to see what it looked like, just to feel that he'd actually been inside a bar. Even then, he was scared to death that someone might have recognized him and reported him to Blair.) No one on that team can remember seeing Bobby Orr touch a drop of alcohol (though in his last junior seasons he would discreetly have a beer when he was sure no one was watching), or with a cigarette in his hand. The consequences of getting caught, for all of them, were simply too grave. If Blair turned against them, their entire hockey lives, their chance of someday suiting up in the National Hockey League, could come tumbling down in an instant. His power, and by extension the Boston Bruins' power over their lives, was absolute.

There were girls, though. They'd hover around the rink after games. Puck bunnies. The players were stars, they were celebrities, their every move was covered in the local paper as though they were the Maple Leafs. And they were young and handsome, many of them exotic out-of-towners, and soon enough maybe they'd be playing on television in the National Hockey League – not movie stars, but close enough for Oshawa. A few of the guys had official girlfriends – though given their tight schedules, and curfews, and the pittance they were paid for playing, there wasn't much time for conventional dating.

"Girls," Blair said in a magazine interview in 1965, were the "cause of the greatest casualty list of them all" among his charges. "They bug hockey players. They hang around after a game, waiting for the players to come out, hoping for a pickup. They'd like nothing better than to hook a guy, especially in junior, where these kids are as big with the teenage crowd as the Beatles. . . . Hockey players are Canada's glamour boys. They get a kind of Hollywood adulation, particularly in the small and medium-size towns where junior hockey flourishes. In the small papers they get more space than Mike Pearson, particularly young Orr, who because of his extreme youth has been getting incredible publicity for three years now. I mean, imagine playing Junior A hockey at 14 – that alone is enough to attract wide attention. So I've drummed it into him over and over that it is his job to be level-headed enough to handle it." (Said Bobby, "I try not to read about myself. So many people have told me not to get a swelled head that I'm scared to read the stuff.")[17]

As his fame grew, as the stories circulated about Bobby Orr being the next can't-miss hockey star, the new Gordie Howe, the second coming of Bobby Hull, he naturally became a bit of an Oshawa sex symbol. He had that clean-cut, little-boy look, but he was strong and he was tough, and humble too, not like some of them who were a bit stuck on themselves. Bobby had his shy, aw-shucks smile, and, increasingly, his previously skinny frame was carrying obvious muscle. He was a fantasy boyfriend, someone you could take home to Mom and Dad, the non-threatening teen idol. But the girls understood that behind those little-boy looks, behind that shy smile, was an appeal definitely less than innocent.

Orr didn't do much about it, though he certainly enjoyed the attention. Aside from the girls he might talk to at school, his love life didn't amount to a lot. At night, sitting in the Wilds' living room watching television, he'd see the cars cruising up and down the street, girls just hoping to catch a glimpse of him in the window. They were too shy to actually come to the door or even to honk their horns. Bobby would get Jack or Cora to turn the lights out so they could watch without being watched, and he'd laugh at the passing parade.

During his second and third seasons with the Generals, Orr became more comfortable with his place on the team. He still wasn't an obvious leader, but no longer was he the kid outsider. In the dressing room, he'd talk quietly to the others, cooling himself between periods by pressing an ice cube against the veins in his wrist. He wasn't a speech maker or a screamer. If he got mad, it was normally in frustration at his own performance. Orr also began to feel secure enough to let his sense of humour show around others. He especially delighted in playing practical jokes. A coach who sent him out to fetch a hamburger received a bun with a slice of cardboard in place of the meat. Another coach blew his whistle in practice, only to find out that it had been filled with corn syrup.

The team itself was improving very slowly. Partway through Orr's second season, the first for the Generals in the much tougher OHA, Doug Williams blew a gasket over a referee's call during a game and was thrown out of the rink. He stepped down as coach shortly after that (the story was that the school board didn't much like one of its educators behaving that way). Blair took over behind the bench temporarily, then a fellow named Jim Cherry (no relation to Don) was elevated from the Junior B Whitby Dunlops to become head coach. Not much changed, really. The teaching was still rudimentary, and the players knew they'd still be yelled at in the dressing room by Blair whenever they lost.

On the second-last night of the regular season, Orr scored three goals to break Jacques Laperrière's record of twenty-nine in a season (set when he was nineteen years old) by a junior defenceman. For the first time, he was named a first team Junior A All-Star. The Generals made it into the playoffs but were beaten in six games by a St. Catharines team that included Dennis Hull, future team-mates Ken Hodge and Fred Stanfield and Orr's personal nemesis, a goon named Chuck Kelly, who had been chasing him down all season long.

Early in the following season, in December 1964, the Generals finally moved into their new home, the Civic Centre, where a capacity crowd of 4,109 packed the place, and the pre-game speeches had to be postponed until the second intermission because a traffic jam kept the fans from arriving on time. The Generals would again be beaten in the first round of the playoffs – this time by the Niagara Falls Flyers, who went on to win the Memorial Cup. Orr broke his own scoring record, getting his thirty-first goal in February, but still lost the league's most valuable player award, the Red Tilson Trophy, to André Lacroix, the scoring star of the Peterborough Petes. Lacroix would win it the next season as well. In four years of junior hockey, during which he established himself as the game's next great player, Bobby Orr would never be judged the best junior in Ontario.

Doug and Arva watched all of the Oshawa home games from their regular seats a couple of rows behind the Generals' bench, where they sat near the team's unofficial historian and biggest fan, the legendary Babe Brown. Or at least Arva would watch there, holding her breath when it seemed as though her son was hit, occa-sionally letting loose with some emotion, happy or angry. "I try to let on I'm not with her," Bobby's sister Pat said in 1965 about the times she accompanied her parents to the games. "Let's just say she's unrestrained."[18] Doug, the hockey dad, was too nervous to stay in one place as he watched. He'd wander the corridors of the arena and often wind up under the stands, talking to the guy who drove the Zamboni, even as the play was going on.

In February 1965, Orr was again thrust into the national spotlight, this time as the subject of a cover story in the then-biweekly news magazine *Maclean's*. The black-and-white photo on the front of the mag showed a crew-cut Orr in action for the Generals against the Hamilton Red Wings. "How hockey's hottest 16-year-old is groomed for stardom," the cutline read. Inside, in his always elegant prose, the great sportswriter Trent Frayne explained to the country just who this magical sixteen-year-old was. "Briefly, Bobby Orr is the finest professional hockey prospect in Canada today, and Boston owns title to his services. Bobby Orr possesses the potential to become the finest offensive defenceman since Doug Harvey, the former nonpareil of the Montreal Canadiens. Bobby Orr is a swift, powerful skater with instant acceleration, instinctive anticipation, a quick accurate shot, remarkable composure, an unrelenting ambition, a solemn dedication, humility, modesty, and a fondness for his parents and his brothers and sisters that often turns his eyes moist. Put simply, Bobby Orr is too good to be true. But there he is."[19]

In fact, there's not an awful lot of Orr himself in the story: he was still far too shy to provide even a decent quote. Instead, Blair took centre stage and clearly relished it, filling Frayne in on the difficult lives of famous hockey players. "You'd be surprised how many hero-worshippers there are," Blair opined. "Even in big businesses in big cities there are guys who pander to athletes just to be seen in their company. They wine and dine a good athlete, wanting to be seen by their friends with a celebrity. Sure, it's a free ride for the athlete but he'll wind up a lush if he doesn't learn to handle fair-weather friends."

The other star of the piece is Bobby's older sister, Pat, who talks about her brother and her family like someone who hasn't yet learned to treat all interviewers with suspicion. "We're a nutty family," she told Frayne. "We've all got wild tempers but we're soft as mush, too. Every time Bobby phones, I cry and I can hear him start to blubber, too. I always cry when I see him. Dad thinks we're nuts."[20]

In the summers, Orr would return to Parry Sound, where he'd spend a lot of time fishing, reconnecting with old friends and earning a few extra bucks. He worked in his uncle's butcher shop one year, and another summer made $35 a week at a local clothing store, most of which he handed right back to the owners to build his wardrobe ("What a Beau Brummel!" Pat chirped). To keep in shape, he lifted barbells and every day ran a two-mile circuit, twice around the harbour. Bobby had precious few responsibilities around the house, and certainly no curfews, because Arva figured he worked hard enough for the Generals during the winter. On one of those lazy summer days, Bobby and Doug and Mike Kolisnek drove out to a nearby summer camp in which the great Gordie Howe had become involved. Nothing as slick as the place Bobby would one day open himself in partnership with Mike Walton. More of the traditional, familiar kids' retreat in the great north woods, but with the name of the greatest hockey player to that point in history attached. Bobby's junior career was progressing, his stardom was established, his progress to the National Hockey League, never really in doubt, was all but assured. And Doug had slowly begun to realize that Wren Blair wasn't a neutral party in the equation, that he wasn't his son's advocate, that he was the Boston Bruins' and represented only the owner's interests. They had already signed away Bobby's rights to the franchise, and there wasn't any other big-league hockey option, so their leverage was limited. But Bobby couldn't sign a professional contract with the Bruins before he turned eighteen years old, and until then he retained at least a tiny say in his future.

Why not ask Gordie how to handle things from here? Doug figured. Who would know the territory better than the sport's reigning superstar?

What the Orrs didn't know then, what few knew until many years later, was the degree to which Howe had been used by the Red Wings ownership, that he had once settled for a new hockey jacket in lieu of a bonus following a great season, that he wasn't even the highest-paid player on his own team, that he had been scared off participating in the first, doomed players' union, that his small-town Saskatchewan innocence had been turned against him time and time again. Gordie Howe had been played for a sucker, as so many others had been. Their fear of being forced out of the hockey life, their false belief that the game itself was extremely fragile, their awareness of the owners' absolute power to make or ruin careers had turned them into pawns, unable to fully participate in the success of a cozy, profitable six-team monopoly.

Howe didn't tell the folks from Parry Sound all of that because he still didn't really know all of that himself. Only years later would it dawn on him the degree to which he had been exploited. But his message to the rising star and his father probably wouldn't have changed in any case.

Get all the money you can, up front, he told them. Don't trade off cash in pocket for empty promises. You might be around for three years, or five, or ten, but whenever it ends, it ends absolutely. You're finished. And what are you going to do then? What's your next job? What have you been prepared for, other than playing hockey?

Take the money and run, son, Gordie said. Take every nickel you can get.

Chapter Six

THE EAGLE

W HAT HE MUST HAVE LOOKED LIKE standing there, young and smart and slick and sophisticated, all balls and bravado, funny as hell, the future incarnate. Here was Al Eagleson in tiny Parry Sound in the year 1964, making a speech in honour of the new Ontario Juvenile Fastball Champions, congratulating the kids, patting them on the head, telling a few jokes, talking about his good pals who played for the Toronto Maple Leafs, telling everyone how badly treated they were by the evil, greedy owners, knocking 'em dead. They knew him a little bit there, or at least they did just down the road in MacTier, where Al had worked one summer running the local rec programs a decade back. Maybe all of that potential was already obvious in the teenager. But this was something else again, a great, full-speed-ahead force of nature. If you were a betting man, you'd drop a few dollars on Al Eagleson to win without a second thought. He was a lawyer, a graduate of the University of Toronto, a partner in a thriving practice and had become a major player in the Ontario Progressive Conservatives, the de facto one-party rulers of Canada's wealthiest, smuggest region, who had been in power since Adam cast his first vote. Eagleson had already lost a long-shot federal election running for the Tories (taking on the hockey-playing Member of Parliament Red Kelly, no less) and then bounced back from that defeat inside a year to win the provincial Lakeshore riding. In the Ontario legislature, though consigned to the government's distant back benches, Eagleson became briefly famous as part of a small group of like-minded loudmouths known for the quality and ferocity of the barbs they would fling during debate – the "Chicago gang," they called them, which tells you a lot about how early 1960s Ontarians viewed big-city Americans. He seemed destined for greater things, maybe to be premier, or even prime minister, if he could ever smooth those rough edges and cut down the cursing a bit. And if politics wasn't his future, if the law began to bore him, there was always the sports business to fall back on. Eagleson had played a bit of lacrosse as a young man, once a growth spurt lifted him out of pipsqueak adolescence, and was famously ruthless and competitive. Later, he had become a friend and financial adviser to several of the Leafs, the brightest stars in the Canadian sports firmament. He seemed connected to everybody and everything that mattered. He was tapped into money and power and influence and celebrity. He was the kind of guy who, one way or another, by charm or force or manipulation or intimidation or all of the above, could get things done.

From the audience in Parry Sound, Doug Orr listened along with his boy Bobby, who had played shortstop the previous summer for that championship fastball team. Doug thought this Eagleson fellow looked a bit familiar, then remembered that he'd played against him in an old-timers game organized by Bing Blanchard, that Al had a reputation as a feisty prick on the diamond, that he was a whiz at stealing bases and that he'd do anything to win. In his head, he began to make connections more radical at the time than he could possibly have understood. Things weren't going so well between the Orrs and the Boston Bruins. The people who ran the team were starting to act as if they owned the boy, as if he was chattel. Maybe this big talker who seemed to know a whole lot about how the hockey business worked could help out. Maybe this Eagleson fellow could create a little leverage with Wren Blair in Oshawa. Maybe he could say the right, necessary things, and say them in a way that a simple guy from Parry Sound could never manage. Weston Adams and the rest of the boys in Boston might treat the Orrs like backwoods hicks, but they sure couldn't look down their noses at this guy.

Doug didn't know how alike they really were, how Al's urban, old-money, old-power veneer was cover for a background not at all dissimilar from his own. Eagleson's parents had been working-class immigrants from Ballymena in Northern Ireland, the very same place where old Robert Orr had grown up. Al's father worked in a tire factory, where he was also a union steward. The Eaglesons had moved around from St. Catharines, where Al was born, to Guelph and finally to New Toronto, a suburb full of strivers on the western fringes of the city, far from the Rosedale monied classes, from the WASP Family Compact who had for so long run the place as their own. No one paid Al's way into Upper Canada College, or into any other private school. No one put in a good word for him. No one gave him a break he didn't earn, or handed him his first job. In the sports world, his entrée was an old lacrosse buddy from the neighbourhood, Bob Pulford, who wound up playing hockey for the Maple Leafs and introduced Al around the dressing room. Not that Eagleson was intimidated by anything or anyone. Not that he knew his place. Talking about him later, someone brought up the character Duddy Kravitz. Ethnically, it was all wrong, of course, but otherwise, you could see their point. They were both hustlers. They could both play the angles. They'd both seize any advantage, even if it hurt people, even if it pissed people off. Al Eagleson had smarts and boundless ambition, and if he harboured any self-doubt, it was kept well hidden. He was going to rule, if not the world, at least a world. In 1964, he just didn't quite know which one it would be.

Doug Orr introduced himself, and Eagleson didn't know who in the hell he was, though he managed to keep that camouflaged behind his smile. Then Doug mentioned his kid, the hockey star,

the marquee attraction of the Oshawa Generals, the future star of
the Boston Bruins. News travelled differently in those days. There
weren't any all-sports channels. Everything in hockey below the
NHL was pretty much a local concern. And Al Eagleson was only
peripherally in the hockey business and certainly didn't go all the
way out to Oshawa to watch the juniors. Still, he was intrigued by
the story, intrigued by the possibilities. One thing he had learned
from "Pully" Pulford, and from the other Leafs with whom he
had become close enough, Bob Baun and Billy Harris and that
oddball, high-strung eccentric with a mind of his own, Carl
Brewer,* was just how badly Canada's heroes were being treated
by their employers. Even though the rinks were full every night,
even though the radio and television audiences were enormous,
precious little of the cash being generated was trickling down to
those who made up the product itself. The stars of the biggest,

---

* A true iconoclast in a sport that makes a fetish of conformity, Brewer amused,
confounded and enraged owners, general managers, coaches, opponents and
teammates alike. In the end, he turned his energies full-time to the effort to restore
NHL players' pensions and to topple Alan Eagleson, and there achieved more
than he ever had during his fitfully brilliant career on the ice. Brewer's playing
days wound down in typically atypical fashion – he played one season for the
Toronto Toros of the World Hockey Association, was an assistant coach for
Finland at the 1976 Canada Cup, and then returned to play twenty games for the
Toronto Maple Leafs in the 1979–80 season at the behest of his old nemesis, Punch
Imlach, who had been rehired by Harold Ballard. After leaving hockey for good,
Brewer and his companion, Susan Foster, fought the long, hard and often lonely
fight that culminated in a court victory awarding the retired players $40 million
in pension money from the NHL owners. He was also one of those – along with
Orr and the Massachusetts-based reporter Russ Conway – who hounded
Eagleson, eventually sending him to jail. While many of the old players were initially afraid of rocking the boat, and of taking on a figure as powerful as Eagleson,
Brewer knew no such fear, and revelled in the fight. By the time of his death in
2001, the outsider and eccentric was widely regarded as a hero, at least among
those who had played the game.

wealthiest, most important professional sports franchise in Canada were being paid the same kind of salary a successful office worker might expect (all the while funding a pension plan entirely out of their own paycheques). And if they didn't like that? If they fought back? If they rebelled? Well, how about a trip down to the minor leagues, where conditions and the money were considerably worse? How about being blacklisted from the league entirely? Players were handed a contract and expected to sign it without much discussion. (They weren't even offered a copy to call their own.) There was no such thing as a sports agent, and no one hired a lawyer, because that would be seen as uppity, and the team owners would simply refuse to deal with one, in any case. Never mind that, from the lawyer's point of view, the salaries in the NHL were so low that it would hardly be worth the effort, working for a tiny percentage of nothing.

Eagleson, purely for fun, purely out of goodwill, organized an "investment club," where the players, helped out by a few of his more powerful pals, could at least try to put a bit of their money to work. But the larger cause intrigued him, the unfairness of it all, and the possibility that a good lawyer, who wasn't afraid of a little confrontation, could maybe make a difference. He couldn't have imagined a career in it – he had all of those other irons in the fire, and anyway there was no apparent fortune to be made here. But if it was another reason to hang around with hockey players, to have a little of that celebrity rub off, well, that would be fine, too.

He listened to Doug Orr and learned all about the boy's predicament. Bobby had effectively signed his hockey-playing life away to the Bruins as a fourteen-year-old, but he wasn't yet old enough to sign a pro contract. He was emerging as a star for the Generals, who were in the process of building their new rink. Wren Blair and the others looked as if they would soon be making all kinds of money off his back, and yet Orr was receiving only the same sixty bucks a week that every other player got. That didn't seem right, somehow. It didn't seem fair. But when asked by Doug whether he could up the stipend just a little bit, Blair was unmoved. Maybe Eagleson could go in and have a talk with him. Maybe he could take some of that big-city lawyerese to the table. Maybe, to start with, he could get Bobby another ten bucks a week. It sure wouldn't hurt. Eagleson agreed to meet the kid, to talk to the Generals, to do whatever he could do. When Doug Orr asked what it would cost, Eagleson told him that this one would be on the house. Over the next couple of years, as he became the Orrs' adviser, as he set the stage for Bobby's entry into the NHL, Eagleson didn't charge the family a cent. This wasn't about billable hours, at least right now. This was about building the future – for Bobby and especially for himself.

It's not as though there was a role model, a ready job description for somebody with a law degree and a bunch of athlete friends who thought there had to be some way to make a living on the perimeter of professional sports. Oh, there had been sports agents, or something like them, way back when, during the golden age of the 1920s, the first time athletes made more money than presidents of the United States and no one much complained about it. Jack Dempsey's wildly lucrative career as heavyweight boxing champion of the world – which in his prime didn't include a whole lot of actual fighting – was directed by his genius manager, Doc Kearns, though he wasn't technically an agent, as the term would come to be understood. Charles "Cash and Carry" Pyle was, however. He was the man responsible for the deal that paid Red Grange $3,000 a game to play for the Chicago Bears in the early days of the National Football League (even forty years later that was half a season's wages for an NHL player). He also had the bright idea of turning the great French tennis star Suzanne Lenglen professional after she won five Wimbledon titles in a row, signing her for a $50,000 bonus. Then came the Depression, for most athletes and most sports the end of the boom times. The need for agents disappeared with the Crash.

All the professional leagues operated as monopolies, all of them controlled their athletes through the reserve clause or the C-Form or some other kind of de facto lifetime contract, and the notion of organizing players like labourers seemed ridiculously far-fetched. It wasn't until the early 1960s, right around the time that Al Eagleson first met Bobby Orr, that the earliest intimations of a coming free market for playing talent began. In the spring of 1964, a pitcher with the Boston Red Sox named Earl Wilson was having trouble negotiating a new deal with the team, helped not at all by the fact that he had absolutely no leverage. He had once called a local criminal lawyer named Bob Woolf, seeking advice after a traffic accident. They hit it off, and he figured that maybe Woolf could help him once again. He did, though at a distant arm's length so as not be too provocative – Wilson did his own negotiating, calling the lawyer on the phone every so often for advice. Soon enough, Woolf would abandon the rest of his law practice, move full-time into athlete representation, make a star of a handsome, flashy kid named Derek Sanderson and build a company that, many years later, would be bought by a retired athlete-turned-agent by the name of Bobby Orr.

But there were other factors as well. It wasn't just that athletes had suddenly become emboldened, or that lawyers had suddenly become clever. And there was plenty of resistance. A famous story from the early days of sports agenting has Jim Ringo, centre with the Green Bay Packers, arriving at coach Vince Lombardi's office to negotiate a deal for the upcoming season, with an adviser in tow. Lombardi excused himself briefly, walked to another room, then returned to inform Ringo's agent that if he wanted to talk contract, he perhaps ought to get in touch with the Philadelphia Eagles, because he had just traded Ringo there by telephone.

What forced the hand of Lombardi and others was the emergence of rival leagues (most notably, the American Football League) to provide an alternative market for players, Curt Flood's brave legal challenge to baseball's reserve clause and the beginnings of organized sports labour, a movement in which Eagleson would eventually play a significant role.

In the meantime, before the dawn of free agency, the pioneers in the sports agent business had to work hard to find a pressure point, to find an angle they could use on their clients' behalf. In the case of Joe Namath, the quarterback from the University of Alabama who graduated in 1965, the sources of his negotiating power were all external. Professional football was on the verge of passing baseball as the premier television sport in the United States. The AFL, formed as a rival for the long-established NFL, was struggling to find its feet and needed a marketable attraction, a player who was clearly good enough for the established, best league in the world but chose to come to them. It helped as well that Namath was good-looking and charismatic, that he seemed like the poster boy for a decade in which nearly anything would go. That's why the New York Jets were willing to pay him $400,000 a season – an astronomical sum, more than any other professional athlete earned at the time. Both Namath's talent and the Idea of Namath held special value for the franchise and for the league.

Athletes in other sports didn't yet have the luxury of bidding wars spurred on by rival leagues. Their one big hammer in negotiations – the only one, really – was the threat to withhold services, to simply walk away from the professional athlete's life. Most players, if they tried that, would be told by team owners to go right ahead, to see how they liked the real world and real work. But the stars had something else on their side. They could inspire the paying customers, who desperately wanted their favourite team to win, and who had to believe that the owners wanted the same thing. The most famous use of the holdout strategy came in the spring of 1966, when Sandy Koufax and Don Drysdale, who made up a brilliant half of the Los Angeles Dodgers' starting rotation, decided to work together in negotiating their contracts for the upcoming season. Before that, Dodgers management had played one off against the other, the same strategy employed with great success by hockey owners. This time, though, rather than be divided and conquered, Koufax and Drysdale demanded that the Dodgers come up with $1 million, to be split equally between them over the following three seasons, representing an annual salary of $167,000, $47,000 more than what Willie Mays, the highest-paid player in the game, was earning.

The pitchers were represented not by a sports agent per se but by a lawyer named J. William Hayes, who took care of contract negotiations for actors, among them the then-popular television star Vince Edwards. Hayes' area of expertise came in particularly handy in creating a perhaps not-so-serious alternative for the pitchers, should the Dodgers fail to accede to their demands. Both players signed contracts to appear in a Hollywood movie called *Warning Shot,* starring David Janssen. If they weren't playing baseball, Drysdale would make his acting debut playing a TV commentator, while Koufax was assigned the role of a detective.

In the end, the strategy was only marginally successful. The pitchers gave up their nascent movie careers and settled for far less than they'd hoped – Koufax got $125,000 for what turned out to be the final season of his career, Drysdale $110,000. But the publicity the holdout received, and especially the way it inspired other players to consider their rights as employees, paid one enormous dividend. It made the work of a labour lawyer named Marvin Miller, then in the final stages of organizing the Major League Baseball Players Association, that much easier.

Al Eagleson, new to the sports world, a babe in the woods, whose business would be built on a single client, a teenage small-town hockey player hoping to make a decent living in a tiny, in many ways backwards, professional league, began to pay attention to the larger forces being unleashed. Maybe he quietly got a few extra bucks out of the Oshawa Generals for Orr, as he claimed, or maybe he didn't, as Blair always maintained. If they didn't cough up, it was because they knew they didn't have to, because they knew they owned Orr, because he'd already signed away his playing life, because he had only one route to the National Hockey League, because they were the only game in town. When the time came to negotiate that first professional contract, the Bruins promised to be equally inflexible, and there was no way in hell they were going to be dealing with any lawyers. But Eagleson wasn't thinking like a traditional hockey guy now. He was looking at baseball and football and a world that was quickly changing, at the NHL on the brink of expansion, at American television, at star making, at the real value of the brightest young talent in hockey, a kid not just the hard-core fans but also the younger crowd, and especially the girls, seemed to go for. There was potential here.

What Al saw in Bobby was the future. What he also saw was a

naive small-town kid, part of what he considered an unsophisticated, undereducated family, perhaps something a little too close for comfort to his own humble roots. Whatever affection he came to feel for the boy, and there's no question it was considerable, that underlying edge of contempt would remain throughout their relationship and come to the forefront the moment it ended. Eagleson had made something of himself. Through smarts and hard work he'd jumped class barriers, fine-tuned his brain, gained power and influence and had begun to make himself wealthy. This lot, who knew no better, who knew not much at all, were all too happy with their hardscrabbble life in Parry Sound. Not quite hillbillies, maybe, but in Al's mind not so far off.

What Bobby must have seen in Al was something else again. He was infatuated, though neither of them would ever dream of describing it like that. But any suggestion that it was all just business, that it was all professional, that their relationship could be summed up as lawyer and client belied a bond that would run far, far deeper. Bobby Orr was confident in his hockey-playing abilities. He understood what he could achieve on the ice. He could play against older, bigger, more experienced opposition and know that his own magnificent skills, coupled with his focus, his determination, his work ethic, would allow him to succeed and to star. He was a genius in that one narrow context. Outside of hockey, though, he was a blank slate. He hadn't really been anywhere, he hadn't really done anything or met anyone, he didn't know much about the outside world at all. He wasn't a scholar, wasn't a reader (aside from *The Hockey News*, the sports pages and comic books), wasn't particularly curious. His ambitions, from the earliest days, had been focused on the game and nothing but the game. (In that, among his hockey-playing peers of the time, he was hardly unique.)

And Al was everything else. Al was experience. Al was the big city, business and bright lights and pretty girls and the universe beyond Parry Sound, beyond Oshawa, beyond the Ontario junior hockey league. Al could show him things and tell him things and take him places his old man never could. Al was his ticket, and Bobby was smitten.

When they first met, Al did all the talking and Bobby did all the listening, while Doug handled the business from the family's end. But soon enough, it wasn't a three-way relationship anymore. Doug was shuffled off to the side (knowing that once the money started to flow, he could quit the job at the dynamite factory and spend the rest of his days full-time as Bobby Orr's dad). It was Al and Bobby now, Bobby and Al, two very different halves of an unbeatable whole. The greatest hockey-playing talent of his generation, perhaps of all time, coupled with a no-fear negotiator, an innovator, a brash, brilliant thinker. They'd own hockey eventually, the two of them, the way Elvis Presley and Colonel Tom Parker once owned rock-and-roll. They'd turn the NHL establishment on its head. They'd get rich. Together. To all that, Bobby Orr gave himself over. He put himself, his destiny, in Al Eagleson's hands.

Orr's last season in junior hockey, 1965–66, was different from the others. He was fully established now as the Generals' superstar, the team's captain, its quiet leader, the best player in the league, the best junior defenceman anyone had ever seen. He was one of only four holdovers remaining from that first ragged season in the Metro League (the others were Billy White, a slick, talented and rebellious forward named Billy Little and the team's trainer, Stan Waylett). Blair had once again changed coaches, replacing Jim Cherry with Bep Guidolin, whose claim to fame was that he had been the youngest player ever to suit up in the National Hockey League. Guidolin had played just one season with the old Oshawa Generals before joining the Boston Bruins as a sixteen-year-old. He was just thirty-nine years old, not far removed from his own playing days, and he was also, in every way that mattered, a Bruins company man and Wren Blair's guy. The players understood that from day one.

Still, they found Bep to be an unexpected ally. Even before the season began, a quiet revolution was brewing in the dressing room. The older players, the ones who had been around for two or three years, had grown tired of Blair's intimidation tactics. They didn't like being sworn at and screamed at when they lost. They didn't like having oranges thrown at them in the dressing room or being fined for every petty breach of his rules of conduct – precious dollars, considering the tiny amount of money they had to live on. (Billy Little, who was known for pushing Blair's buttons and pushing the team boundaries, had many weeks when his take-home pay was reduced to zero.) That was Wren's style, to make them play harder by scaring them, by making them angry, but surely there was another way to do things, one that wouldn't create such a negative atmosphere.

A few of the more senior players went to Guidolin in the fall, before the season began, and asked for a couple of changes. Could he do his best to keep Blair out of the dressing room after games, because the tirades were killing the team's morale? And was there any way he could loosen up the off-ice restrictions just a little bit? They weren't all kids now. A bunch of them were seventeen and eighteen and nineteen years old. They could look out for themselves. Allow them a bit of freedom, and there wouldn't be any real trouble, Guidolin was promised. And just maybe, if the guys could spend a little more time together socializing away from the rink, it might help to bring them together as a team.

Guidolin agreed to try to back off on the reins a little bit. There wouldn't be any more screaming after games. He'd do his best to keep Blair at bay. And on Saturday nights, after the Generals played at home, they'd be free to go out and enjoy themselves, without worrying about any kind of curfew. Thereafter, almost every weekend during the season, someone would hold a house party. The players gathered after the game, along with girlfriends and with parents (at least at the start). It wasn't a wild scene. A few of the guys might have a beer or two – Wayne Cashman, probably, or Danny O'Shea – but most of them drank only soda pop. They'd sit around and talk and listen to music, often until three or four in the morning. (Orr was almost always a part of the mix, as were Doug and Arva. He would sit quietly and talk and sip a soft drink, and then at some point the others would notice that he'd quietly slipped away home.) The next day would be a bit of a struggle, since there was usually a Sunday afternoon game and they'd all be a bit short of sleep. But the payoff was a team much closer than it had been in previous seasons – one that, for the first time, would find a way to succeed beyond the apparent limits of its talent.

No one picked the Generals to win that year. The Peterborough Petes, with their scoring star André Lacroix, and the Montreal Junior Canadiens, a team stacked with NHL-bound players, were more obvious choices. But whatever the expectations for the team, Orr's can't-miss star status was established beyond all dispute. He would finish the season with thirty-eight goals and fifty-six assists in forty-seven games, breaking his own records for a junior defence-man, finishing third overall in league scoring, fifth in goals scored, second in assists. (The other top scorers in the league that year were Lacroix, Danny Grant, Jacques Lemaire and Mickey Redmond, all of them the property of the Montreal Canadiens.) For the third consecutive season, he was selected a first-team all-star. And his status as a local pop star and wholesome sex symbol grew as well. At one point during the season, a false rumour spread in Oshawa that Orr was about to be traded away from the Generals. Calls flooded the switchboard at the Civic Centre, teenage girls crying and hysterical, desperate to be told that it wasn't so.

Though he left the inspirational speeches to others, Orr's quiet leadership skills were significant. He showed the way on the ice, and by how he handled adversity, how he played through injury, how he refused to be intimidated no matter which goons other teams sent his way. And on those occasions when his emotions did come to the surface, when the Orr temper flashed, everyone understood that it must have been serious. One night during a game against St. Catharines, he was hammered hard into the boards by Ken Hodge (who would become a member of the Stanley Cup – winning teams in Boston). He got up slowly, obvi-ously hurt, but managed to make his way back to the bench and didn't miss a shift during the rest of the game. Afterwards, as he was stripping down in the dressing room, Blair went to him and asked if he was okay.

"What do you mean?" Orr said.

"I saw you get hit. I want to know if you're all right."

Bobby said nothing. Then he reached down, picked one of his

skates up off the floor and threw it the length of the dressing room as hard as he could, just missing a couple of his startled teammates.

He stared up at Blair with a particularly hard, cold look in his eyes.

"Don't you ever ask me that again," he said. "If I'm hurt, I'll come and tell you. You don't come and ask me."

Blair didn't make the same mistake again.

On December 14, 1965, Orr and several other stars of the Ontario league joined the Toronto Marlboros for an exhibition game at Maple Leaf Gardens against the national team of the Soviet Union. This was the real thing, the Big Red Machine, coached by the great Anatoly Tarasov, featuring most of the players who had won that year's world championship, including an eighteen-year-old up-and-comer named Alexander Yakushev. Canadians, though, were still secure in the belief that all those world championships and Olympic gold medals meant nothing much at all, that if the Russians were ever faced with the best players from the NHL, it wouldn't even be close. The Soviets had begun their eight-game tour with an easy 4–0 win over Canada's national team in London, Ontario, then moved on to Maple Leaf Gardens, where a capacity crowd of 14,886 was drawn by the novelty of it all, by a rare in-person glimpse of the great unknown. What they must have expected was an exhibition of the Russians' skills overwhelming a bunch of Canadian teenagers, men beating boys. What they saw, at least in the first period of the game, was something else entirely. "The juniors, with only one workout together as a team, were most impressive in the opening period," Al Nickelson wrote in *The Globe and Mail.* "They took over to such an extent they forced the Russians into mistakes. In the face of persistent checking, the red-shirted tourists didn't have their usual puck control and it was the kids who played better positional hockey." The juniors led 3–1 after the first period, with Orr recording an assist on their first goal, scored by Ted Snell of the Niagara Falls Flyers. In the second period, though, fatigue seemed to set in among the Canadian juniors, many of whom had played league games the night before. The Russians got one goal back in the second, then two more in the third for a 4–3 victory. The winning goal was scored by thirty-two-year-old Konstantin Loktev, a veteran of world championships and Olympics past.

"Orr, a defenceman owned by Boston Bruins, probably was the outstanding junior," Nickelson wrote. "He was effective both ways." The Soviets' assistant coach Arkady Tchernishev agreed, singling out Orr and fellow defencemen Jim McKenny and Serge Savard for praise.

"They have a very good team," Orr said in a television interview after the game. "They pass that puck pretty well. Some people say that they would beat an NHL team. I don't think they would come close to beating an NHL team. They might do all right in the American League against some of the lower teams, but the NHL is out, I think."

The Generals finished the regular season in fourth place, comfortably qualified for the playoffs, but apparently no real threat to the first-place Peterborough Petes or the second-place Junior Canadiens, who had lost only two games during the entire second half of the season. (That said, the top six teams in the OHA that year were separated in the standings by only eight points.) In the opening round, Oshawa beat the St. Catharines Black Hawks, though it took eight games. (In those years, ties weren't broken by overtime or a shootout, even in the playoffs.) The Generals came into their own in the deciding game, winning it 8–1. Next up were the Junior Canadiens, with Lemaire, Carol Vadnais and Serge Savard in their lineup, and Scotty Bowman behind the bench, and playing in a home rink that was intimidating all by itself, the fabled Montreal Forum. The Generals walked in as though they owned the place, won the first two games in Montreal and took the series in five. That put them into the OHL championship, against the Kitchener Rangers, another team that would send a host of players on to the NHL, including Walt Tkachuk, Don Luce and Sheldon Kannegiesser. Oshawa beat them four games to one and now faced only two more hurdles before qualifying to represent Eastern Canada for the Memorial Cup. The first wasn't a test at all, a series against the

Northern Ontario champions the North Bay Trappers. The Generals won the four games 11–4, 11–2, 10–1 and 11–2, outshooting the Trappers 232–96 over the course of the series. During one game, with his team already ahead by ten goals, Orr ragged the puck for one long shift, holding it for two, two and half minutes, as his teammates recall, killing time during a blowout, sparing the Trappers further humiliation. The Shawinigan Falls Bruins of the Quebec league, whose best player was a young goaltender named Phil Myre, didn't go down quite so easily, but Oshawa still took that series and now would play for the junior hockey championship of Canada, the first Generals team to get that far in twenty-two years.

Their opponents, the Edmonton Oil Kings, were just a little more used to the drill. This would be their seventh straight trip to the final representing Western Canada, and they had won the trophy in 1963, upsetting the Niagara Falls Flyers. The Oil Kings could claim a small advantage in the fact that, though they were the ones travelling across the country, the games themselves would be played on what amounted to neutral ice. Apparently failing to anticipate the home team's success, those in charge of the Oshawa Civic Centre had rented the building out for a home show. So the games were shifted to Maple Leaf Gardens – and Generals players remember the letdown of leaving their building, filled to the rafters with devoted Oshawa fans, for a place that was too big for the event, that felt empty and hollow and cold.

But the Generals also had a much bigger problem. Bobby Orr was hurt. In one of the games against Shawinigan Falls, he had been slammed into the boards, suffering a groin injury that was later aggravated during a practice. Only the team and its inner circle knew the truth: their captain, their leader, wasn't going to be anything like himself. That didn't stop Blair from beating the promotional drums. "See Boston's $1,000,000 Prospect," one of the ads for the tournament blared. "Probably Your Last Chance to See BOBBY ORR Play Junior Hockey." Blair went a step further, cooking up a fictional subplot for the newspapers based around his star defenceman. Before the series began, he got in touch with his counterpart in Edmonton, a fellow by the name of "Wild" Bill

Hunter who had just taken over as the Oil Kings general manager. He would go on to become one of the great hucksters in hockey history, a founding father of the World Hockey Association and the guy who very nearly pulled off the impossible feat of landing an NHL franchise for Saskatoon, Saskatchewan. Just for publicity's sake, just to sell a few tickets, Blair suggested to Hunter, why don't we cook up a little phony rivalry? It would be like the wrestlers on TV, each one of us boasting about how good our team is, and how the other guys aren't all they were cracked up to be. Blair fancied himself a big talker, but he had no idea what he was getting into. At a pre-series press conference, Hunter won the battle of the blowhards with ease, touting one of his own defencemen, Al Hamilton, as the best junior in Canada, and putting down the Generals' superstar with ever-increasing degrees of bombast. "Who is this kid Orr?" Hunter asked the gathering of reporters. "He's nothing. We've got better players than Orr. Heck, we've got four or five players better than Orr."

The scribes, doing their bit, ate the sideshow up and wrote it as if it was real. But as the Memorial Cup final was about to begin, it didn't seem that they'd be able to take the story much further. The Bruins ownership had learned of Orr's injury and, unwilling to subject their most valuable property to any undue risk, whatever it meant to the Oshawa Generals, they sent an unequivocal message to Blair and to Guidolin: if he's hurt, the kid doesn't play.

Blair didn't deliver that news to Orr, at least not right away. The Generals were already comfortably ensconced in their Memorial Cup home, a Holiday Inn in the west end of Toronto, when Doug Orr came knocking on Blair's door. "I've heard a rumour," Doug said, "that Weston Adams doesn't want Bobby to play in this series because he's hurt." Blair confirmed that was true. And then Doug laid into him. Bobby wasn't under contract to the Bruins. If they didn't let him play, Bobby would never sign a contract with the Bruins. This was his chance to play for a historic championship, and it was never coming around again. Tell that to Mr. Adams, Doug said. Blair protested that he'd be fired if he put Bobby on the ice, but that possibility didn't seem to move Doug very much at all.

And then Blair decided to take a bold stand. To hell with Weston Adams. Bobby Orr was going to play. "You just have to have guts to stand up for some things," Blair says now. "And many times, you just have to have people respect your word." He might get fired for it. Bep Guidolin might get fired. But it was the right thing to do.

Orr played, much to the displeasure of Adams and Hap Emms, who by then had been elevated to the job of the Bruins general manager, but he didn't play very much or play very well. The series was close and exciting, a tribute in large part to the other, often overlooked, members of the Generals, who played their hearts out, knowing that Orr wasn't going to be there to bail them out this time. Edmonton won the first game 7–2. Oshawa came back and won the second 7–6, with Orr limited to fewer than five minutes on the ice because of his injury. They won again, 6–2, then dropped the next game 5–3, to leave the series tied at two. With Orr very obviously struggling in game five, Edmonton came within one win of the Memorial Cup, beating the Generals 7–4.

Before game six, the Bruins insisted that Orr be examined by a doctor, to assure them that their greatest asset wasn't risking his hockey-playing future. The doctor said that playing couldn't make it any worse, so he was cleared and took the ice for what would be the best, and the deciding, game of the series, not to mention Bobby Orr's last appearance in junior hockey – but not before his father repeated his earlier exchange with Blair, this time with Emms making the Bruins' case that Bobby shouldn't play and Doug reminding him that there was no deal, no contract yet. Oshawa took an early lead on a goal by Billy Heindl, who would become a tragic hockey footnote. (After a professional career spent in the minors, the World Hockey Association and briefly in the NHL, Heindl – who had been plagued by depression – jumped off a bridge in Winnipeg in an attempt to commit suicide. He survived as a paraplegic. In 1980, the only time they would share the same ice, Orr and Wayne Gretzky played together in a game to benefit Heindl. He died in 1992 at age forty-five, having reportedly succeeded in taking his own life.) Jim Harrison tied the game for the Oil Kings. Then, after Orr tripped over a stick on the ice and took himself out of the play, Ted Hodgson scored the winning goal for Edmonton. The Generals kept fighting to tie the game but couldn't beat the Oil Kings' superb goaltender Don McLeod. "I guess I played a little," Orr remembered years later. "I dressed for all the games. But our guys were great. I was really proud the way they played. We almost beat them. We lost the last game 2–1, and they won the series four games to two."[21]

The Bruins fired Guidolin from the Oshawa job after the Memorial Cup, in large part because he had allowed Orr to play. "If I'd had my way," he protested, "Orr wouldn't even have dressed. That wasn't my decision. He was so anxious to play that he went over the boards without my permission. . . . I almost had to put a strap on him to hold him down. If I'd just turn my head, he was on the ice. . . . He had a severe groin injury and it just wouldn't mend. If this hadn't happened, Bobby would have been a Memorial Cup champion and so would I."[22] (Bep eventually worked his way back into the franchise's good graces and wound up coaching the Bruins for a season and a bit, leading them to the Stanley Cup final in 1973–74, though they lost.) Adams and Emms didn't have to fire Blair. The fact was, he knew he had a soft place to land; he knew he had already choreographed his own exit before making the great moral decision to let Orr play. Soon after the season was completed, it was announced that Wren Blair would be put in charge of building the new NHL expansion franchise in Minneapolis – St. Paul, a team that would be called the North Stars. For the Bird, everything had fallen into place – seeing Orr, signing him, starting the Oshawa franchise, getting as far as the Memorial Cup final and now finally getting his big break.

As for Bobby Orr himself, he had turned eighteen but didn't officially belong to the Boston Bruins yet. He hadn't signed a professional contract. And maybe they needed him to help sell tickets for their godawful franchise just about as much as Bobby needed a job in the NHL. Maybe there was some leverage there after all. Weston Adams, Hap Emms, meet the best player who has ever lived. And meet his representative, R. Alan Eagleson. Your sport, your little fiefdom, will never be quite the same again.

Chapter Seven

NUMBER FOUR, BOBBY ORR

TWO BOATS OF CONTRASTING GRANDEUR converged by chance by a lock. The more modest was an eighteen-foot runabout, a visible sign that the Eagleson clan of Toronto was starting to climb the ladder. They had the cottage and they had the boat and the law practice and the political career. Things were looking fine all around. Heading out for a late-summer-afternoon cruise, Al was at the helm, playing skipper for Nancy and their young children, Trevor and Jill. They'd sailed over to watch the other boats coming and going from Lake Couchiching to Lake Simcoe in Ontario's near north. The youngsters got a kick out of that, seeing the water rise and fall, the gates swing open, one of those small mechanical miracles. Their parents were content just to soak up the sun.

The much more significant craft that pulled up alongside might as well have been Jonah's whale eyeing a meal, not quite a yacht but at forty-two feet long plenty big enough, with the name *Barbara Lynn* scrawled across the stern. Leighton "Hap" Emms had also done rather well for himself, a life in hockey paying more than modest dividends. He was the general manager of the Boston

Bruins, as well as the owner of the junior Niagara Falls Flyers. He had played the game way back when at its highest level, for the long-defunct Montreal Maroons and New York Americans and Detroit Falcons, along with the Red Wings and the Bruins, before really making his mark in nearby Barrie, Ontario, his hometown, where he started a junior franchise and prospered.

It wasn't by design that Emms and Eagleson crossed nautical paths that day, but when he looked way, way down at the young family, Hap certainly recognized the man at the wheel. Many times over the past few months, dating back to the Memorial Cup, in public and in private, Emms had been moved to declare that he'd never, ever deal with "that lawyer" under any circumstances. Nothing personal, mind you. (Well, maybe a little personal, but what would you expect from two strong, abrasive personalities.) It was just that the Bruins had spent the past four years promising their long-suffering fans that Bobby Orr would be their salvation. They had talked him up and fed the stories to the local sports press and even brought Orr's junior team into the Boston Garden to play an exhibition game to showcase the young star. (The Generals faced the Niagara Falls Flyers that afternoon, with a brash kid named Derek Sanderson in the Flyers lineup. Orr and Sanderson actually fought briefly during the game. Asked afterwards by a Boston broadcaster why he had dared to take on the saviour of the Bruins, Sanderson answered, "Would you have talked to me if I hadn't?") The Bruins had made Orr's ascension and his deliverance of the franchise into an article of faith. And now this big-talking brassy know-it-all, the same guy who had caused all that grief for the Leafs when he whispered in Carl Brewer's ear, had stepped in front of the kid and his old man and was telling everyone that Bobby wouldn't sign unless outrageous amounts of money were on the table, that the boy would play for nothing for the Canadian National Team rather than take his rightful place in the National Hockey League. As if that was really going to happen.

Well, Eagleson thought it might, at least temporarily, or at least he believed that enough to play the same card that Brewer had played. Al was a pal of Father David Bauer, who for years had run the national team, now rendered all but hopeless in its efforts to remain competitive with the quasi-pros of the Soviet Union. The hockey priest had stayed as a guest in the Eagleson family home, and he'd met young Orr there several times. With no other professional hockey alternatives, the national team had provided Brewer with a plausible alternative after his final falling-out with Toronto's coach and general manager, Punch Imlach. It gave him some small leverage against the Leafs owners, who controlled his professional rights (and being Brewer, the great iconoclast, he actually followed through on the threat, walking away from the money and the glamour, first enrolling in university and later playing for Canada's national team and in Finland before finally coming back to the NHL). Maybe that would have to be Bobby Orr's strategy as well, because there was no way they were going to lie down and beg for a contract as every other great young hockey prospect had done before. No way Orr was going to sign on the dotted line for whatever pittance Emms was offering – a five-grand signing bonus, and then $7,000 and $8,000 for the first two seasons in the NHL – and say thank you very much, Mr. Emms, for allowing me to play for your glorious team in this wondrous league. Generations of simple hockey-loving Canadian boys had been played for suckers just like that, while Conn Smythe and Weston Adams and the Norris family and the rest of them got fat on their sweat and toil. If this kid really was going to save the Bruins, if they were going to sell all those tickets on his back, if he was going to be the face of the coming NHL expansion into the untested hockey wilderness of the United States, he was worth a hell of a lot more than seven thousand bucks a year. How about $100,000 for two years as a starting point? That number made Emms laugh because it was so far above and beyond what anyone, including the biggest names in the game, was being paid in the NHL's existing salary structure, and then it made him furious. So there ended the negotiations, with summer almost done, with training camp and the new NHL season looming just beyond the horizon.

Interesting, then, that Emms' first response at catching sight of the good ship Eagleson was to open his arms in hospitality. "Why don't you folks tie up and come aboard?" The kids were thrilled to death to explore such a grand ship, and Hap eagerly played the proud captain, leading them on a tour of his magnificent vessel. His wife, Mabel, offered Al a beer, Nancy a glass of wine. Al asked her about the boat's name, and she explained that it was in honour of her granddaughter, her son Paul's daughter, who had been born intellectually challenged. Al told her that his sister's son was similarly affected, and the conversation evolved from there. When Hap returned with the kids, he sat down and joined in the small talk, then soon enough cut right to the point. "Well, Alan, we had better get together right away and get Bobby Orr signed. We both know he isn't going to be happy playing for Father Bauer." Maybe in their hearts they both knew that, but they knew a couple of other things as well. Emms knew that if he didn't deliver Orr to Boston one way or another, his new career as an NHL general manager was finished. And Eagleson knew that if he was going to turn this brand new, unprecedented hockey-lawyer act into something lasting, this was his moment, that Bobby Orrs came along all too infrequently, that if he managed to bluff his way into a big contract, his reputation would be made.

Nothing in the form of real bargaining transpired on the boat that day, though legend would later have it that the landmark deal was made on the spot. (The nature of the chance meeting did eventually prove useful to Emms when he was explaining to the press how the Orr contract got done. It wasn't as though he'd made the first move by calling Eagleson and breaking the stalemate. It wasn't as though he had given in to the lawyer's demands. Instead, it had all been happenstance.) Rather, Eagleson and Emms met on several occasions over the next couple of weeks, the talks long and arduous. There was a huge gap between the Bruins' opening offer and Eagleson's six-figure demand, and time was ticking away. Bobby didn't say much in those days, but he assured Al that he'd go along with the national team strategy if absolutely necessary. He also told him to do his best to get something on paper with the Bruins because he desperately wanted to play in the NHL.

Finally, Emms and Eagleson came to terms, terms that Eagleson promised for face-saving reasons he would never publicly

divulge – and despite the passing of three decades, despite the bitter dissolution of the Orr-Eagleson partnership, despite all that
has passed under the bridge, he has kept his word. For the record,
all he would say then, all he will say now, is that the original contract for two years was for less than $100,000 in salary, plus a
$25,000 signing bonus. That way, Hap could argue that he hadn't
fully acceded to Orr and Eagleson's blackmail. But whether the
real number was $50,000 or $70,000 or $80,000 (though specula-
tion included all three numbers, the accepted wisdom would be
that Orr earned $40,000 for each of his first two seasons), the fact
was that Orr stood to take home more from that contract than any
other player had made in the history of the National Hockey
League. Back in 1953, Jean Béliveau had been paid $100,000 by the
Montreal Canadiens when he first entered the league, but that was
for five seasons, and Béliveau was already an established star in
senior hockey, not a raw kid coming out of the juniors. In 1966,
Béliveau was making $30,000 a season, with an extra $15,000
thrown in for his role as a public relations spokesman for Molson
Breweries, owned by the same family who controlled the
Canadiens. Hull and Howe were each earning in the neighbourhood of $35,000 a season. Those were the reigning superstars of
the game, and just as soon as they heard about Orr's contract, all
of them marched into their owners' offices, demanding a raise,
demanding at least parity with the kid. So even if they didn't fold
completely, the Bruins had surrendered to a degree that would
make the other five teams in the NHL swallow very hard indeed.

When the time came for the official contract signing, they
decided to hold the ceremony back on the *Barbara Lynn*. Both
Eagleson and Emms liked the symbolism, since that was where
their relationship had blossomed, where the great accord had its
beginnings. (You could have read it as a surrender scene as well,
like the end of the war in the Pacific, but since it was all important that Emms and the Bruins retain their dignity, that certainly
wasn't the public posture.) Hap knew a guy from the Barrie Flyers
days, a former player named Red Favero who had become a professional photographer (Al knew him too – he had dated a friend

of his sister's). They invited him on board, and he set up a stagy contract-signing shot typical of the times, with Bobby and Doug and Hap, who was clutching a great big victory cigar in one hand, and making a tight, tense fist with the other. Eagleson didn't apear in that famous picture, but there was another shot taken that day. It showed the smiling lawyer and his famous client, both in white shirts and skinny dark ties, beaming for the camera, with Bobby holding a pen over the contract. After all that was done, Hap suggested they toast the moment. He poured everyone a glass of Teem – a cloying lemon-lime soft drink that has faded from existence – and everyone saluted Bobby Orr, Boston Bruin. What was he going to do with the bonus money, Bobby was asked. Buy his mom a refrigerator, and a washer and a dryer, he said. And he told Doug to start looking for a new house in Parry Sound.

The Orr contract would become, without an iota of overstatement, the most important in the history of professional hockey, and with all factors considered, it could be argued that no other single event had so dramatically altered the course of the game, or at least the business of the game. Consider the nexus, the factors that came together in that moment, and the consequences going forward. There was the emergence of a once-in-a-generation talent. There was a historically terrible, desperate franchise, willing to give in, to over-pay (if not in terms of true value, in terms of the existing market-place), to rewrite the league's salary structure in order to secure the services of a single player. Orr, and his family, who like most Canadians had been conditioned to worship everything about the National Hockey League, were still willing to challenge the sport's status quo, to hire a lawyer to handle the negotiations even though they knew the Bruins would hate the very idea. They were prepared to follow Eagleson's advice, to wait, to delay Bobby's NHL career if necessary, to forgo the fame and fortune at least temporarily in order to guarantee more money than any hockey player had ever received before. And if Eagleson hadn't been around and hadn't already gained some experience "unofficially" advising NHL players, if it hadn't been the beginning of the sports agent era, the family would have had no one to turn to, even if they felt sufficiently militant and emboldened.

The instant the deal was consummated, everything about the hockey business changed, though some of the new realities would take years to become apparent. For the players, even the ones who quietly seethed at a raw kid who hadn't played a minute of pro hockey getting all of that money, it was emancipation day. When Orr became the highest-paid athlete in the game, one of the highest-paid in any game – even if no one knew by exactly how much – every other player, every other star took notice and upped their asking price accordingly. (It would be many years before NHL players understood how it could be to their advantage to disclose salaries to each other and to the public. Eagleson pushed for it for years, arguing that it would give all of them added leverage, but the players resisted, maintaining that it was nobody's business but their own. It wasn't until 1990 that the first full list of NHL salaries was handed to the Montreal *Gazette* columnist Red Fisher at the All-Star Game. Since then, player salaries have been made public on an annual basis.) If Orr was worth that much as a rookie, what was Hull worth at the height of his powers? It would be several more seasons before the players would have real options, before the birth of the World Hockey Association gave them the chance to peddle their services outside the NHL. But from the day of Orr's signing on, the bar had been reset, and the thinking changed. Maybe it wasn't such a bad idea to bring someone else in to help with contract negotiations. Maybe you couldn't really trust your owner or your general manager to give you the straight goods. Maybe it was worth placing a call to this Eagleson guy, since he seemed to have found the key to the vault.

And on that rock, on that foundation, on that contract and the publicity it generated, R. Alan Eagleson would build his empire. First as an agent, with his sports business soon providing enough income to allow him to leave the rest of his law practice – and eventually politics – behind. In 1965, Eagleson had represented the players of the Springfield Indians of the American Hockey League when they fought back against the dictatorial rule of their coach and general manager, Eddie Shore (the same Eddie Shore who had been cited as Orr's only true stylistic precursor as an NHL defenceman). That victory won him a reputation as the most public, vocal and successful advocate for players' rights, which segued naturally into the founding of the National Hockey League Players' Association, of which Eagleson would be named executive director. (His myriad conflicts of interest in that role would evolve over time.) And finally, Eagleson would consolidate his power by becoming one of the driving forces behind Canada's re-entry into the world of international hockey, beginning with the mythic 1972 Summit Series against the Soviet Union and continuing with its exceptionally profitable offshoots, including the Canada Cup. Al Eagleson became the most powerful man in hockey – bigger than any individual star, any owner, than presidents and commissioners – while standing on the shoulders of Bobby Orr. None of that would have happened, at least not when it did, if Emms and the Bruins had held the old company line.

The Boston Bruins would begin the new season, the new Bobby Orr era, with a clean slate. This would be the last go-round for the old six-team league and of course the occasion of the saviour's debut. Milt Schmidt, who had done just about everything for the Boston franchise at one time or another since he was long ago part of the fabled "Kraut Line" in the 1930s, had managed to coach Boston out of the basement and into fifth place in the 1965–66 season, which was viewed as a qualified triumph. But now was the appropriate time to hire a new coach who might lead the Bruins into a very different, very optimistic future, somebody young and clever and of the moment. The team chose thirty-four-year-old Harry Sinden, whose career had intersected with Bobby Orr's several times before, when both were in the Wren Blair orbit. Sinden was, in his new profession, just as much a kid as Orr was in his, positively boyish by comparison to Punch Imlach of the Leafs and Toe Blake, the long-time bench boss of the Montreal Canadiens, and the other established coaches who dominated the big-league game. The season before, Sinden had still been playing defence every night, while also coaching the Oklahoma City Blazers of the Central Hockey League, a Bruins affiliate, to a championship. Now he'd have to finally take the uniform off, but in exchange for a remarkable opportunity, to coach at hockey's highest level without having served a long apprenticeship, to coach the sport's next great player and to take over a franchise that seemed to have nowhere to go but up.

Orr arrived at the Bruins training camp in London, Ontario, much as he had that first junior camp in Niagara Falls: quiet, deferential, full of "yes, sirs" and "no, sirs," unsure, it seemed, whether he could compete against these men, and unsure as well just how he might find a comfortable role in the dressing room. He walked into the motel room he had been assigned and saw lying on the bed, clad only in his underwear, his not insubstantial off-season belly rising from the mattress (one of his nicknames among the players was "Buddha"), the long-time captain of the Bruins, Johnny Bucyk.

"Hello, Mr. Bucyk," Orr said, a little startled at the sight.

"It's Johnny or Chief," Bucyk said, without getting up. "It's never Mr. Bucyk."

With Oshawa, Orr had grown into a leader, though in most ways a leader only by quiet example, and after four years he was the junior equivalent of a grizzled veteran. Here, he would have to become comfortable among players hard enough to survive in a very tough business, guys who smoked and drank openly, who spent the off-season working in blue-collar jobs like the one his father held in order to supplement their meagre hockey salaries and support their families. And here was Orr, eighteen years old but still much younger in appearance, a kid who was making five times, ten times, their salary, and he hadn't done a thing yet in the NHL. The reporters on the hockey beat surrounded him every chance they got and even surrounded his big-talking hockey dad, Doug, who seemed to always be around. That the vets viewed Bobby with something other than unqualified affection at the start was only natural. Sure, he might be their ticket to the playoffs, to better times, and maybe to bigger salaries in the end. But the resentment was there just below the surface, in the jokes about money, in the way they went at him during practice. He'd have to earn his place and prove his worth. In the meantime, they'd give him the full rookie treatment, including the Bruins' own preferred method of hazing. Orr was pinned down, naked, and shaved from head to toe with a rather dull straight razor, leaving little red cuts in the most uncomfortable places.

Despite the improvement the season before, when the Bruins finally escaped the NHL's cellar, the team was still weak in many areas. The goaltending was already in place that would win a Stanley Cup — several Stanley Cups, in fact, since the great Bruins duo of Eddie Johnston and Gerry Cheevers was augmented by a kid named Bernie Parent, who would go on to find fame and glory in Philadelphia. There was strength on defence as well, with Gary Doak and Ted Green joining Orr. But up front, Boston lacked scoring punch — only Pit Martin would reach twenty goals that season. Johnny Bucyk, the team's quiet captain, would be a bridge from the Bruins' years in the desert to the championship teams, and Johnny "Pie" McKenzie and Ed Westfall were also part of the mix. But in a season that featured a dominant Chicago Black Hawks team, a superior group of Montreal Canadiens and a bunch of geezers in Toronto who somehow won the Stanley Cup, Boston, but for a few brief moments of optimism, wasn't competitive with the rest. And when things did seem to be taking a turn for the better, when the team hovered around .500 and sat in third place in November, Emms managed to kill any growing confidence among the players. If anything united the team that year, it was their dislike for the general manager, who had built most of his hockey career in a position where he could bully and intimidate teenage boys but didn't understand leadership when it came to men. After a game at Madison Square Garden, at a point when the Bruins were playing relatively well, Emms made one of his frequent visits to the dressing room to inspire the troops. The line of Wayne Connelly, Ron Schock and Ron Murphy, the third in the Boston rotation, was then the most productive on the team. Emms took that as an excuse to unload. "If our third line is our best line," he told the players, "then we're in trouble." That vote of non-confidence upset a group of players who had no history of winning, who were a bit fragile to begin with. If their general manager didn't believe in them, it sure wasn't going to make it any easier for them to believe in themselves. (It was also Emms' bright idea to try playing Orr at centre – a notion coaches had flirted with throughout his career in minor and junior hockey and then abandoned. But there was precedent in the NHL, most notably Red Kelly's late-career shift from defence to forward, with great success. Sinden didn't buy it, though, and Orr didn't feel comfortable out of position. The experiment was shelved after a few shifts in a few games, and for the remainder of his NHL career, Orr played only defence, though of course he functioned at times very much like a fourth forward.)

Orr was under the microscope from the first minute of the first game, though to be accurate it wasn't the same as it would be years later for Wayne Gretzky or Mario Lemieux or Sidney Crosby. There wasn't twenty-four-hour sports television and radio; there was in fact precious little television coverage. There were only the newspaper beat guys and columnists, and for the most part they were just as interested as the team and the league in spinning Orr's heroic tale. And it was a very small world to begin with. It's tough for anyone born and raised since the end of the six-team era to really understand just how tiny and insular the NHL was then. Consider that, when the 1966–67 season began, there were only ten rookies entering the league, including Orr. Two of those, his Boston teammates and roommates Ross Lonsberry and Ted Hodgson, would be sent down early in the season, leaving an eight-player race for the Calder Trophy – an award that was all but conceded to Orr before the season began. His competition included his other roommate, Joe Watson, Ed Van Impe of the Chicago Black Hawks, Peter Mahovlich, Bob Wall and Bart Crashley of the Detroit Red Wings and Brian Conacher and Wayne Carleton of the Toronto Maple Leafs. The Canadiens and the Rangers featured not a single rookie between them. Only three other Bruins had ever been named the league's rookie of the year before: Larry Regan, Frank Brimsek and Jack Gelineau.

In training camp, Orr had been assigned jersey number 27 (the Bruins were notorious for recycling old uniforms to save money, eventually sending the big club's hand-me-downs on to their minor and junior affiliates). He wore it through the first eight games of the pre-season, and then the team's management offered him the honour of switching to number 5, the jersey worn by one of the franchise's great stars of the past, Aubrey "Dit" Clapper. Orr decided that wouldn't seem right and politely declined. He instead chose 4, a number worn for the Bruins the year before by a hockey journeyman named Albert Langlois, playing his only season with the team. Four. Orr. Even in the broadest Boston accent, it had a ring to it.

In his first regular-season NHL game, on October 19, 1966, Orr recorded one assist in a 6–2 Boston win over the Red Wings. (At 1–0, it was the only time all season that the Bruins would boast a winning record.) *Hockey Night in Canada* took the unprecedented step of sending a film crew to the game so that Orr's first NHL shift could be recorded and shown during a broadcast. More notable than the scoreline that night was the first professional encounter between the new star and the greatest player in hockey history to that point, Gordie Howe. On a shift early in the game, defending in his own end, Orr made the same mistake hundreds of others had made before him – he took liberties with Howe, whacking him behind the head with a bit of a cross-check, hoping to move him from the side of the net. Howe, who had a famous mean streak, took quiet note of the perpetrator. Then, when the opportunity presented itself, when Orr spent a second too long admiring one of his passes, he was subtly levelled by a Howe elbow. His new Boston teammates rallied to his defence, but as Howe remembers it, Orr told them to back off. "I deserved that," he said. Howe thought that showed something about the young man's character, though he certainly didn't pledge to ease up.

The Bruins lost their second game, at the Montreal Forum, on October 22. The next night, the back end of what were then traditional home-and-home sets between teams, a feature of the six-team league, Orr scored his first NHL goal against the Canadiens.

Early in the third period, he fired a slapshot from the right point past Gump Worsley, tying the game 2–2. (The Habs went on to win it 3–2.) No assists were awarded on the play. Gilles Marotte, playing the other point, skated to Orr after the puck went in and leaped into his arms in celebration, while the crowd at the Garden rose in what was said to be a five-minute standing ovation. "Never heard anything like it," Toe Blake said, and you had to figure he'd heard a whole lot during his many years in the game.

Time to come back to earth. Seven days after that shining moment, the Bruins were hammered 8–1 by the Red Wings, and Orr played what may well have been his worst game as a pro. He was on the ice for five of the Wings goals, and his mistakes led directly to three of them. But his coach, and his fans, were exceptionally forgiving. "He could have been on the ice for fifteen goals," Sinden said. "He could have scored five goals in his own net and the crowd wouldn't get on him. He's just too good most of the time. He gets caught sometimes, but it's only because when we're losing a game, which is often, he takes it on his own shoulders to tie it or win it for us. If we're down two goals in the second period, he wants to take the puck and score a goal. That way, he isn't always in good command of his position. We're always playing catch-up hockey, so it places that much more pressure on him."[23]

There was another kind of pressure as well, the same as he had faced in junior hockey. Almost immediately, Orr found that teams were trying to physically intimidate him, to negate his skills by force. Eventually, just as Bucko McDonald and Wren Blair had predicted, he knew he'd have to fight, to live by the hockey code. But after making his point against a couple of the league's reigning heavyweights, he at least wouldn't have to fight very often. Orr held his own against Orland Kurtenbach of the New York Rangers, and then won a clear decision over Montreal's Ted Harris, knocking him to the ice twice with clean punches to the head. And he seemed to enjoy it, to relish the battle, to unleash an anger, a fury, to let the Orr temper temporarily overrule the disciplined hockey brain. After that, the league's brawlers mostly kept their distance. In later years, when Orr did fight, he clearly meant it. He didn't dance. He didn't drop his gloves for show, or to make a point, or to stir some emotion among his teammates. It was never choreographed. He punched hard, sometimes throwing shots over a linesman's shoulder. And when the zebras moved in to break it up, he was never the first to surrender, never the first to let go.

On December 4, 1966, the Bruins (with a record of 6–10–4, clinging to fifth place) were struggling through a very tough night against the Toronto Maple Leafs at the Boston Garden. The visitors would wind up winning 8–3, including three shorthanded goals, and manhandled the Boston team all night long. But the truly crushing blow came early in the second period. Orr had banged up his left knee back on November 24 during an 8–3 win over the Detroit Red Wings and had missed the following game. Aside from the groin pull that ruined his Memorial Cup with the Oshawa Generals, it was his first real injury of any kind.

Against the Leafs, he found himself with the puck in his own end of the rink, and then started flying up ice at full speed. But he still hadn't completely adapted to the NHL or to the skills and strength and skating ability of NHL players. Maybe in junior hockey, Orr could have gotten away with having his head down for an instant. Here, as he was sailing along the boards, he glanced down at the ice just as he was being lined up by Marcel Pronovost, one of the game's elite defenceman, and one of its great pure bodycheckers. "I caught him with his head down and hit him low with my hip," Pronovost explained in the dressing room afterwards. There was nothing dirty about the check. Pronovost pinned Orr to the boards and pushed him up so high that one of his teammates, Joe Watson, remembers it looked as if he was heading right over the screen and into the seats. The worst of the collision, though, came when Orr's trailing left leg was crushed awkwardly into the boards. He crumpled to the ice, then hobbled to the bench and finally to the dressing room. The Bruins team physician, Dr. Ronald Adams, diagnosed the injury as a "strained internal ligament." "If he keeps his weight off the knee and we're lucky, we may have him back in three weeks," he said.

Sinden said afterwards that, if his club was going to succeed down the road, it would have to toughen up considerably. "It is obvious I have to shake up the team," he said. "We will bring in forwards with more muscle. I don't know from where, but they'll be here before we fall too far out of the playoff fight." That transformation of the Bruins into a team of physical intimidators would in fact take several seasons, but Sinden would eventually get his wish. What he couldn't have foreseen, what he couldn't have known, was that his meal ticket would be just fine, that he would learn and mature and excel to a degree that no other rookie defenceman ever had. What he also couldn't have known was that he had witnessed the first chapter of a small classical tragedy, the revelation of the hero's fatal flaw.

Orr returned to the lineup against the Leafs in Boston on December 25, 1966 – he looked rusty, and the Bruins were booed by their home fans as they lost 4–2. During the eight games he missed, the team went 1–6–1, scored only eleven goals and had thirty-one scored against them. By the time Orr returned, the season was definitively lost. Boston threw in the towel down the stretch, losing their final six games of the season, returning to the familiar confines of the NHL basement with a record of 17–43–10, fourteen points behind fifth-place Detroit, twenty-eight behind the New York Rangers, who grabbed the last playoff berth, and a full fifty points behind first-place Chicago. By any measure, even with Orr's promise, it had been a step backward for the franchise. Still, attendance at the Boston Garden (which had remained remarkably good even during the Bruins' worst years) jumped by forty-one thousand fans, and the team's revenues increased accordingly, making the investment in Orr's salary look absolutely prudent. Though the consensus around the league was that Orr had more than proven he belonged (he made the second all-star team, and some figured he would have been on the first team if he hadn't suffered the knee injury), questions remained – both about his possible fragility and about his risky, unconventional style of play – that would persist for several seasons.

But others harboured no doubts. Elmer Ferguson, the dean of Montreal's sportswriters, had seen Eddie Shore at his best and said that Orr was better. "This is because Shore was expected to play defence, while Orr plays both defence and attack and does fine at each." Gordie Howe – who even then seemed like the NHL's senior citizen, but was in fact only at mid-career – marvelled at what Orr could do. "When the other players start watching a kid like Bobby, he must have something. They used to watch me because I could use my stick with either hand, but Orr can do this and I hardly can see when he changes hands." (Joe Watson noticed something about Orr's hands as well – he held them high on the stick, and could pass or stickhandle or shoot without sliding them down the shaft. You knew Bobby Hull's slapshot was coming because he dropped his hands low, but with Orr, you could never tell what he was going to do next.) Emile Francis, who ran the New York Rangers, was another unabashed Orr fan. "I always said he'd be a better pro than a junior. I saw a lot of him as a junior. The kids would give him the puck, and then they'd stand around and watch him. In the pros, I figured they'd throw the puck to him and then set themselves up for a return pass. That's what happened. I've looked at my scoring sheet after each Boston game, and there's Orr with six, seven, eight shots. Hell, he's a defenceman. He's not supposed to get that many shots. I figure that since he's a defenceman maybe he should spend more time defending. But I try to think how many times we've caught him (out of position) for a goal and I can't find it happening too often. Kids that age aren't supposed to have that poise. I see veterans panic in a tough spot, and most of the time you can't blame them. Orr? He's standing there as if he owns the place. He's some kind of meal ticket, isn't he?"[24]

For Canadians, the most significant endorsement of all may well have come from Foster Hewitt. During Orr's rookie season, Hewitt appeared between periods of a game in which the Bruins faced his beloved Maple Leafs on *Hockey Night in Canada* and went way out on a limb. "I believe that Bobby Orr from the Oshawa Generals has done more in his first year than Bobby Hull ever thought of doing," Hewitt said. "If he keeps this up, he's going to be perhaps the greatest of them all. He's got everything. He's got a shift that seems to have the opposition really mixed up at all times. And he's got the physique. That's the only thing that I thought perhaps that he didn't have for this tough competition. But he's been right there all the time. Outside of an injury to his legs in the early part of the season, that was it."[25]

It was by statistical measure one of the best rookie seasons in the history of the National Hockey League, and unprecedented for a defenceman. Orr scored thirteen goals and twenty-eight assists, for forty-one points. Jean Béliveau debuted in the NHL as a mature twenty-two-year-old and recorded thirteen goals and twenty-one assists. Bobby Hull, a pure goal scorer, had thirteen goals and thirty-four assists in the 1957–58 season. The player Orr was most often compared to, Doug Harvey, broke in as a twenty-three-year-old rookie in 1947–48 and was sent back to the minors halfway through the year. It was absolutely no surprise, then, when Orr received eighty-eight of a possible ninety points in the voting for the Calder Trophy, awarded to the league's best first-year player.

Orr went back to Parry Sound at the end of the season to relax, to get away from all the attention and especially to go fishing. Later, he'd take up golf as a hobby, before his aching knees made it impossible, but angling would be Orr's lifelong passion, whether it was on the salt water in Florida, or pursuing Atlantic salmon at exclusive lodges on the Gaspé Peninsula, or catching humble pickerel back home. Fishing is both a social and a solitary pursuit, one that rewards patience and diligence and precision, but also one that runs counter to the kind of burning competitive drive that Orr had in spades. On the water, he could be a different guy. He didn't have to make the best cast or catch the biggest fish. He didn't have to win. (For myth spinners, Orr's annual summer return to his hometown, and to the great Canadian wilderness, took on a romantic cast. "He's a lad who's been brought up properly and it is inconceivable that he'll ever develop some of the irritating mannerisms adopted by less talented athletes," Toronto sportswriter Jim Proudfoot wrote. "He's the same kid who left Parry Sound to play hockey and he betrays the fact by rushing home every chance he gets – to fish, to hunt, to visit his folks, to simply loaf. He's been around, but, for him, Parry Sound is still the place to be.")[26]

One of his teammates from the kid hockey days, Bob Cardy, was back from the air force that summer, and the two of them went off on a boat, night fishing, sleeping on board, catching a few, catching up on each other's news. The second night on the water, long past midnight, they were fishing and talking, and Cardy was struck by how downcast and depressed his old friend seemed. It hadn't really been much of a season, Bobby explained. He'd struggled and he'd made mistakes and the Bruins hadn't made the playoffs. He wasn't sure, really, whether he could cut it at that level. Maybe he wasn't quite good enough.

As they were turning in for the night, one of them clicked on the radio. That's when Orr heard for the first time that he had been runner-up to Harry Howell of the New York Rangers for the Norris Trophy, awarded to the NHL's best defenceman. What they didn't know was what Howell had said on being informed of the honour: "I've been around for fifteen years, and thank God I finally won the trophy. I've got a feeling that for the next twenty years it will be known as the Bobby Orr trophy."[27]

Chapter Eight

SPIN THE BOBBY

I T'S TIME TO PLAY SPIN THE BOBBY. That's always good for a laugh. Daisy Buchanan's was packed most nights, especially in the fall, especially when the Bruins and Red Sox were both in town. By then, the cursed Sox tended to be long out of the pennant race, and the B's were in the early days of training camp. A nice, relaxed time for both teams for different reasons, though the truth was that this gang of hockey wild men weren't much restricted in their revelry in any season. A colourful, boozy gang they were, Espo and Cash and EJ and Cheesie Cheevers and the craziest of them all, Derek "Turk" Sanderson, the man with the circular bed. (That's him, hanging out in the back of the room, talking to Bill "Spaceman" Lee, the eccentric Red Sox pitcher. Now there's a conversation you'd pay to hear.) There were other bars they could try, other places for other situations, like Lucifer's, where you went after the legal last call. But Daisy's, tucked down below street level, as were so many of the old taverns in Boston – think of the fictional Cheers – was perfect most nights. Players and fans and reporters all enjoying themselves together, all understanding that nothing left the room. Jim Bouton had already blown the cover in baseball with his tell-all memoir, *Ball Four*, but the daily newspaper guys still weren't interested in poking around in anyone's personal life. Hell, they had too many of their own skeletons to worry about. Glass houses and all. And don't forget that times have changed. The repressed 1950s are a distant memory. There's nothing wrong with being free, nothing wrong with doing your own thing. Nothing wrong with loving the one you're with.

No shortage of famous faces here, but really, there's only one star of stars, bigger in this town than anyone is, than anyone has been since Ted Williams took his miserable self into retirement. Bobby Orr, golden Bobby Orr, who still looked like a kid, but when he felt like it could drink and . . . er . . . date like a man. (That's the great newspaper and fan mag euphemism: "date." "Who are you dating now, Bobby?" It always sounded as though the cute kids were going out for a soda, like in an Archie comic.) When Bobby walked into the place, you could hear the buzz, you could sense the heads turning around. That's real celebrity for you. As long as he stayed happy, as long as the drink didn't turn him dark and angry, there was nobody with a more charismatic presence. And who was going to be the lucky lady to date him at the end of the night? After everyone has been sufficiently lubricated, line the chicks up on the far wall, all giggles and miniskirts and open minds. Stand Bobby up in front of them, with his right arm extended, his index finger pointed straight ahead, with a great big goofy grin on his face. Then spin him around and around like a crazy top and, finally, let him wobble to a stop. Whichever way the finger was pointing, that was Bobby's girl. The other guys could fight over the rest.

Forget about January 1, 1960. Nothing started that day except a new page of the calendar. The sixties, or at least the massive societal shifts forever linked with that decade, began in different places at different times, unrelated to whatever the year might have been, anno domini. In the bohemian Beat world of Greenwich Village, in the jazz clubs where bebop was born, it started sometime right after the boys came home from the war. In many a conservative small town, the actual decade was all but over before the first signs of change crept in. There were places, probably, where they skipped it altogether, where the comfortable, confident post-war fifties melted into the cynical, post-Watergate seventies with hardly a bump in between.

The Parry Sound that Bobby Orr left in 1962 was rooted in every meaningful way in the 1940s and had remained largely unaltered since the end of the Second World War. Many of the dads were vets, like Doug Orr. There had been no real post-war economic boom. The local industries, the local hierarchy, remained pretty much unchanged from a generation before. Daily life was as it had been for some time, in terms of custom and mores and beliefs. Orr picked up a full decade when he moved to Oshawa as a fifteen-year old. By then, by the early 1960s, the town had at least fully entered the 1950s. These were salad days for the auto industry that dominated the small city's existence, and everywhere there was the comforting hum of progress and growth, with precious little threat to the old order. Rebellion for the kids meant sneaking a smoke or a beer and hoping like hell not to get caught. Nothing profoundly unsettling in any of that.

But the day Bobby Orr arrived in Boston to begin his life as a professional athlete, he was fast-forwarded into a brand new world – a different country, obviously, but also a different point in time, not because he was becoming part of big-league hockey but because he was becoming part of a wide-open, diverse, big-league city where new questions were being asked.

Professional sport itself, because it was so obvious, so visible, had always been looked to for signs of changing times, but anyone seeking the true societal cutting edge was bound to be disappointed. For the most part, this one aspect of popular culture lagged behind the rest. Consider the groundbreaking racial integration of major-league baseball. The miracle of Jackie Robinson's arrival wasn't that it happened when it did, pushing back deeply ingrained prejudices, but that it took so damn long, thirty years after Fritz Pollard, an African American, was playing in the nascent National Football League, half a century after Jack Johnson was crowned the heavyweight champion of the world. (The Boston Red Sox didn't get around to employing their first African American player until 1959.) Like baseball, most sports – or more precisely, the people who controlled them – were reactionary, not revolutionary. They tended to be dragged into the present kicking and screaming. Some teams prohibited players from sporting a whisker on their faces even as *Hair* was playing on Broadway. Recreational drugs seeped in more slowly than they did in the average high school. Professional sport was a booze-and-broads world for a long, long time after fashions changed, more Rat Pack than hippie. Gay athletes were deeply closeted then, and forty years later, with gay marriage blessed in some jurisdictions and gay characters a staple even on staid network television, not a single active male team athlete has felt he could openly acknowledge his homosexuality.

And if baseball was the stiff establishment game, if football was evolving into a slick corporate machine and basketball was the closest to thing to a counterculture because of the growing influence of great African-American players, then hockey was some sort of country cousin, all white, mostly Canadian, a little backward. So when the Big Bad Boston Bruins let their hair grow long, it was like a call to arms. The sideburns, the moustaches, the tresses creeping just over the collar at the back. (And, of course, in those days, no helmets to get in the way.) It had been a crewcut game until then, with the owners, the general managers, the coaches as absolutely empowered as military officers to enforce a behavioural code. The boys would still go out and pound a few, but there was no question just who was in charge. There was a question now, though. The league doubled in size in 1967. Players moved beyond the claustrophobia of the six-team world. They had agents, pushing for more money. They had endorsement deals. They were stars starting to act like stars. The "yes, sir," "no, sir" days were over. And if they wanted to let their hair grow, and to let their hair down, just who was going to stop them?

That new spirit of individualism came in lockstep with another change, a growing public interest in athletes' private lives and a growing willingness by athletes and their agents to exploit their colourful personalities for profit. (Joe Namath was the pioneer there, as he was in so many of aspects of what would define the modern athlete/celebrity.) There was not yet the quasi-investigative, scandal-sheet, celebrity-for-the-sake-of-celebrity sports journalism, but merely a need and desire to cast athletes in something closer to three dimensions, to spin a larger story involving flesh-and-blood characters. A new generation of sports writers and television producers now wanted to answer the question, What's so-and-so really like?

Over the entire history of professional hockey to that point, a player understood absolutely how his public image might be crafted in the sports pages or *The Hockey News,* in the fan magazines or on *Hockey Night in Canada.* It was all in subtle shades of square-jawed, bubble-gum-card heroism. A hockey player might be stoic or tough or funny or classy or fiery (the French guys tended to be hung with that adjective, especially the Rocket), but it was all expressed on the ice, or at least within the confines of the rink. What they did in the game, what they said afterwards in the dressing room, and that was that. If anyone followed them home, it was to paint a reassuring picture of domestic bliss, of the loyal wife and cute kids, team-sanctioned propaganda. No one followed them anywhere else, at least not while on the job. The private stuff stayed private. References to liquor and sex were absolutely off limits. Hockey players were not movie stars, whose marriages and divorces and moral peccadilloes had long been considered fair game. They were not pop stars, whose lifestyle excesses were a necessary part of the rebel packaging. They were virtuous and square and hard-working and God-fearing and just a little bit better than the rest of us. The fans may have enjoyed reading about how the glamorous folks on the big screen and on television had their failings and heartbreaks. It was reassuring to know that, for all of their wealth and beauty, they still had human flaws, that perhaps they were our moral inferiors. But no one wanted to read about sports stars with feet of clay. Their public purity was too deeply ingrained in the root-for-the-home-team mythology that drove the business and filled the seats.

What developed, then, was a funny hybrid, one that's still in many ways the norm today. Professional athletes were deemed to be public figures, to have sacrificed some of their privacy in return for the enormous rewards of their profession. They were – and still are – widely regarded as "role models," which meant that, in addition to their great physical gifts, they were required to behave in a way that would inspire their young fans to walk the straight and narrow. The possible contradiction in that – that young men, who in many instances were more narrow in their experience, more limited in their education, more isolated from the character-shaping aspects of ordinary life than the people watching them, would be held up as moral beacons simply because they possessed a particular genetic makeup, a particular set of motor skills – was glossed over by those charged with spinning the stories. It would become particularly uncomfortable in the late days of the twentieth century, as athlete salaries became out of sight, as press and fan resentment grew, as bad behaviour by spoiled sports stars seemed endemic.

When Bobby Orr was emerging as a public figure, though, even as the libertine realities of the times presented obvious opportunities for a healthy, handsome single young man, the mythmaking machinery of the sports business was still rooted in the more con-servative past. By virtue of his skills, and his good looks, and his prominent place in a big American city, he had a kind of pop-star potential. But because he didn't or couldn't flaunt it, because his aw-shucks Canadian persona was the polar opposite of Namath's big-man-on-campus swinger, his public image was also a remnant of that earlier innocent era. When Gordie Howe arrived in the National Hockey League in 1946, you can bet there wasn't a line written about whom he might have been dating. That was nobody's business but his own, but more important, that wasn't the story. By the time Orr came along, they could at least ask the question, but they didn't really want the answer. And the tales were written in euphemisms. No sports scribe was going to tell his readers about Spin the Bobby. For hints of what his life might really be like, of how the world might unfold for someone who was young, famous, wealthy, living in a big, vibrant city during ever-wilder, freer times, you had to read between the lines. You had to crack the code. You had to think about whether dating really meant dinner and a movie and a chaste kiss goodnight on the doorstep, or something else entirely.

When he first arrived in Boston to play for the Bruins, Orr moved into a beach house in Little Nahant that he shared with Joe Watson, another small-town Canadian boy, from Smithers, British Columbia. The two other roommates with whom they began the season, Ross Lonsberry and Ted Hodgson, were sent down to the minors, leaving Orr and Watson alone in the big, rambling five-bedroom place. Arva Orr wasn't so sure about the arrangement. She was leery about her boy going off to live in some wild bachelor pad and maybe not getting enough to eat. "But my dad and some relatives started coming down from Parry Sound, and I guess she was told that I was not starving myself to death or living it up and she was much happier," Bobby said. "In fact, we did very well in the eating department. Some of the married players living in the neighbourhood occasionally had Joe and me over for dinner."[28] Many of those players, married and otherwise, adopted the Little Nahant house as their preferred party locale. How wild could it have been, with Orr and Watson both under the legal age, with teams still exerting tremendous control over their players' lives, with the burden of celebrity shaping their behaviour? Well, perhaps not a twenty-four-hour bacchanal, but there was that time when the skaters from the Ice Capades came over for a visit – they were into hockey, and Orr and Watson . . . well, maybe they weren't into figure skating, but they were certainly into girls. (Joe looks back now and says he sometimes wishes he could relive those days, but will have to settle for the movie in his head, waiting for it to be replayed someday when he's an old man sitting in his rocking chair.)

The next season, Watson was shipped out in the expansion draft to the Philadelphia Flyers, so Orr needed a new roommate or three. He wound up in a different set of digs, a rented, relatively posh two-garage house in suburban Lynnfield, Massachusetts, twenty minutes' drive from the Garden. His companions there were the goalie EJ Johnston, who became Orr's closest running buddy on the team, fellow defenceman Gary Doak and the Bruins trainer John "Frosty" Forristall, so nicknamed because his build resembled that of a snowman. Being a team trainer in professional sport is now a quasi-medical job requiring specialized training and knowledge. Trainers are involved in conditioning the athletes, in keeping them fine-tuned throughout the season, in providing emergency care when an injury occurs – all that is crucial to keeping a franchise's most valuable assets, its playing talent, fit and in running order. Forty years ago, though, the job was considerably less formal. Trainers were one step up from the equipment boys, more gofers than paramedics. They could stitch a guy up when necessary, and they could provide whatever was available from the team's medicine chest. (Consider that, during most of his time as owner of the Toronto Maple Leafs, Harold Ballard employed as the team's trainer his cottage boat mechanic, the post a perk for previous favours rendered. Any Toronto player injured during a game knew that he wasn't in the most competent of hands – and knew that nearly every complaint, up to a broken leg, would be treated with a particular lemon-flavoured over-the-counter cold medicine.) Forristall was typical of the breed. He got into the business because his mother worked in concessions at the Boston Garden. Harry Sinden would bring him along with Team Canada in 1972, and later he had brief stops with the Toronto Blue Jays and the Tampa Bay Lightning before dying of a brain hemorrhage at age fifty-two.

During the Bruins years, Forristall was the players' pal and confidant and co-conspirator. He was divorced and enjoyed being in the company of some of the city's biggest stars and the female entourage that followed them around. He was especially happy to be Orr's right-hand man, to the point that he signed autographs for him when the volume of mail at the house became overwhelming. "I've got it down pat. You can't tell our signatures apart." Frosty would do anything for Bobby, and Bobby thought that was just fine. Over the years, there would be a long line of other admirers who came after him, eager to fill that same role and to bask in the glow. Orr loved having them around, loved the security and protection they afforded. He was never one to easily mix with strangers.

Every once in a while, during Orr's bachelor years, a reporter would be assigned to produce a story on the private life of the great young hockey star, and they would be granted carefully controlled access behind closed doors. Orr was never comfortable in the spotlight away from the hockey rink. He fiercely defended his privacy. But in the early days in Boston, writers were occasionally allowed to breach the walls, and as the rules of engagement changed with the times, they gradually felt emboldened to move from old-school iconic portraiture to something more closely resembling flesh and blood.

In 1968, it still read like a teen fantasy: Bobby didn't drink, didn't smoke, had only been dating for two years. "He is constantly being called by young girls, but always turns down their advances." That's because, as Bobby pointed out, "The type of girls who call you aren't the type I would like to take out anyway." When he did go out, it was with "airline stewardesses and secretaries, but [he] has no single best girl." One of those dates, unnamed, described him as the perfect gentleman. "Bobby said that being in the limelight sort of forces a person to behave yourself at all times. Signing autographs and making appearances are just part of the job of being a hockey player. He is very polite at all times and is a wonderful escort."[29]

His older sister, Pat, called on to fill out the story, marvelled at how much her little brother had matured. "I am three years older than him and he used to come to me and talk about things a lot. Now, I feel almost younger than Bobby."[30] He was certainly nothing like that dangerous, sexy, hirsute bad boy Derek Sanderson. (There again, a reference to Turk's circular bed.) Bobby, presumably, slept on something both square and rectangular.

Two years later, the story had changed slightly. Bobby acknowledged that he had a "special girl" named Julia but added that he wasn't ready to settle down quite yet. "Playing hockey and travelling around like I do is not exactly fair to any girl who might marry me. Anyway, I am pretty young yet, and want to enjoy myself now."[31] Later that year, in the next round of stories, Julia was history, apparently. "No, I don't have a special girl at the moment. I don't go steady or anything like that. Why? Well, I'm away so much. Travelling all the time. It would be nice to settle down and have a family. My parents still are young and my father's more like a friend than a father.

"But it wouldn't be fair for me to marry now. What kind of home life could I give anybody? Wouldn't be fair to the girl. Some day after I call it quits. But not now."[32]

Then back to Frosty. He was always willing to talk to the writers and, as the roommate of the great man, had a unique, up-close vantage point. Doak and Johnston were out of the house by then, both of them married off. It was just the two swinging singles, living on their own, and the tone had become quite a bit more forthright. "I always answer the telephone at home," Frosty said. "We've had to change the number twice already this season. I usually know the people Bobby wants to talk to. . . . It's unbelievable. Women keep phoning. And people keep driving past the house and pointing to it."[33]

Those lucky girls who got past the front door were in for a treat. "When the broads come to the house, they're speechless," Frosty said. "The place is spotless. Even the guys on the team are surprised when they come over for a party. They think we had a cleaning lady in because it was a special occasion. But it's always like that. If Bobby passes an ashtray and it's dirty, he cleans it. I do the same. I cook – roast beef, chicken, things like that. And he does the dishes." Bobby entered the narrative only briefly, playing the voice of reason. "People think athletes lead a pretty fast life. They think they drink a lot and spend all their time at parties or in bars. I don't come into town much to go to the clubs. There's always some drunk who wants to prove he's tough by fighting with you or something."[34]

Then, in the spring of 1971, Bobby sat down at home for an interview with a writer named Keitha McLean, who was producing a regular feature for the now-defunct *Montreal Star* called "Beauty Spot."[35] She was young and very pretty, and maybe that in part explains why Orr opened up to her in a way that he never did to any other reporter, before or since. (McLean went on to become a pioneering figure in Canadian women's magazine publishing, and died, too young, of cancer.) The language was finally, fully of its time. "Beauty Spot Raps with Bobby Orr," the headline read. The subject, almost exclusively, was women, or at least being young and famous and meeting women and trying to have a private life in public. "That's the trouble with too many of the guys," Bobby said. "They talk too much about their women. Keep your mouth shut, you can have a very groovy time, and nobody bothers you." (Yes, Bobby Orr said "groovy.")

All those groupies, he explained, could get on your nerves, "especially with the ones who are always trying to get into the Garden. But then sometimes a groupie can turn into a girlfriend, so . . ." Sometimes, Bobby explained, being famous had its drawbacks, was a double-edged sword. "I can ask a girl to dance and she'll turn me down so she can tell her friends. On the other hand, if a chick comes after me, and I tell her to leave me alone, she will say that I think I'm too good for her."

And sometimes the guys could be nearly as pushy, but there was at least a remedy for that. One night, Bobby explained, he was sitting in a bar. (There's a big change right there, a professional athlete acknowledging that he might go to such a place, and that he might drink something stronger than soda pop, though apparently some folks still felt comfortable passing judgment. "Sometimes I can't stand it. I'm in a bar minding my own business and a complete stranger will tell me that I shouldn't be there, that I'm a bad example to his son . . . and then he'll brag to the kid about seeing me.") This night, a fellow he didn't know from Adam came up to Orr and asked if he'd help him impress a girl he was trying to pick up. Maybe if she thought he was Bobby Orr's pal, she'd be bowled over, and that would help close the deal. Would Bobby mind just walking by and saying hi, as though they were best buddies? "I thought that every man should help another with that kind of thing." And maybe teach him a little lesson, as well.

Bobby went further than requested. He sat down with the couple. He put his arm around the girl. He acted as if he was trying to pick her up himself.

"The guy, forced into playing the role, finally said, 'Hey, that's enough now, Bob, find your own girl.' He had really blown his chances and he didn't realize it. . . . He should have kept his mouth shut in the first place, but no, he had to be the big shot."

McLean drew her own conclusions about Bobby. She compared him to Namath, but minus the flamboyance. She found him humble and found him sexy, and probably didn't entirely buy his protests that his single life wasn't quite as wild as it appeared. The other players joked about his being a casanova. But it wasn't really like that at all, he claimed.

"I have a few girls and a lot of dates. But I'm no Rock Hudson and they're not falling all over me, no matter what these guys say. Marriage? I'm not ready for it. I'm too young and have a lot to learn. First I have to learn you can't take a game home with you. When we lose, I'm ugly, hard to live with. I have to get over that before I marry. It wouldn't be fair to a girl now, especially during the season. I'm away a lot. It would be hard on her. What kind of a life would it be for her?

"Of course there are plusses. Your children would be growing up when you're still young. You could have fun with them. I know I have had a lot of fun with my dad. He's only 48 and we get along great. But there are a lot of things to do before I get married."

On the afternoon of Saturday, September 8, 1973, Bobby Orr was married in what was widely described as a "secret ceremony" back in Parry Sound. The bride was the former Margaret Louise Wood – known to all as Peggy – a former speech therapist who had grown up in Detroit and was now a resident of Fort Lauderdale, Florida. Bobby had met her in a bar in Boston. She was twenty-six. He was twenty-five. The wedding took place just before the beginning of the Bruins training camp.

Details were sparse because Bobby wanted it that way. The reporters and photographers who were staking it out, having heard small-town rumours – not mobs, obviously, not paparazzi, but enough – were largely frustrated in their efforts to get the story. Doug told them that morning that Bobby had gone fishing, and it turned out he wasn't just trying to throw them off the scent. Bobby had indeed escaped to the water for an hour or three. He returned in plenty of time for the ceremony, which took place at the home of the Presbyterian minister Rev. Robert A. Crooks. The bride wore a pale blue pantsuit, the groom a light-coloured business suit. Bobby's sister Pat was the maid of honour, and her husband, Gerald Murphy, was the best man. There were no other guests. "Peggy and I just decided on the date a few days ago. I would have liked to have had a big wedding for Peggy, but we decided to just do it . . . get in the church and get it over with," Bobby explained later. None of his Bruins teammates knew it was coming, though he'd let Harry Sinden in on the secret. Bobby's parents didn't attend because they didn't think it would have been fair, since Peggy's mother and father couldn't make it.

The happy couple's first stop as man and wife was for a short visit to the Orr family home. A reception followed at the Parry Sound curling club. Bobby and Peggy dropped in on Al and Nancy Eagleson the next day at their home in Toronto, on their way south, and then left for a short, pre-training camp honeymoon on Cape Cod. (Eagleson distributed a wedding photo to the press. It remains one of the very few pictures of Peggy Orr in public circulation.) Their first home as a married couple was a two-bedroom apartment in downtown Boston that Bobby had been sharing with Frosty Forristall. "Frosty tells me he's not moving out," Bobby said. "He says he was there first and he ain't moving."

Three months later, several newspapers published a photo of Bobby and Peggy at a Christmas skating party. The cutline below the picture said that the new Mrs. Orr was expecting the couple's first child. Darren Orr was born the following August. No pictures of the baby were provided to the press. That's the way Bobby wanted it. Damned if his life was going to be an open book. "He's a good, big kid. He's a good sleeper and a lot of fun," the proud father said.

But he wouldn't tell them much more about his first son, or his second, Brent, or about anything else that went on away from hockey. And he certainly never went out of his way to tell anyone that Bobby Orr's boys never played the game that made their father famous. Never. Two of Gordie Howe's sons would play professional hockey by his side. One of Bobby Hull's sons would become one of the greatest NHL goal scorers of all time. Bobby Orr's sons didn't even learn to skate.

Sports celebrities' private lives might be becoming part of the story, part of the wider marketing pitch, but Bobby Orr was never going to play that game. A couple of decades later, when the next great hockey superstar got married, it was nearly as public an event as a royal wedding. Fans knew the name of Wayne Gretzky's actress bride, Janet Jones, just as they'd known about his past girlfriends, about his family back in Brantford, about his growing up in public, just as they would eventually know about Gretzky's own children, their likes and dislikes and talents. Not with Bobby Orr. Not with his wife, who would remain all but anonymous even as he scaled the heights. Not with his sons, who were taught to never casually mention who their father was. Watch him on the ice. Talk to him in the dressing room (if it was one of those nights when he felt like talking). But stay away from his family, stay away from his home life. That would remain forever off limits.

Chapter Nine

HOCKEY ACHILLES

THE BOYS FROM THE LOCAL DAILY scrambled down to the dressing room during the first intermission, only to find the door barred. That didn't seem right. It was a big night for Winnipeg, after all, a rare summer hockey game at the old Arena, featuring at least a few familiar faces from the far-off National Hockey League. And now the brightest star on the ice was suddenly off limits to the same scribes who had done their civic duty by pumping up the event, helping the organizers sell four thousand tickets for a good cause. The game matched the Pro All-Stars, as they were called for the night, against Canada's national team, a benefit in aid of the Manitoba Hockey Players Benevolent Association, which helped old players who had fallen on hard times. Most of the big leaguers who turned out for the occasion were Manitoba boys, back home for the summer: Ted Green from St. Boniface; Pete Stemkowski and a Boston prospect named Bob Leiter from Winnipeg (though Green and Stemkowski were nursing off-season injuries and in the end wouldn't step on the ice); and Joe Daley, a goalie from East Kildonan who was going to get a shot with the expansion Pittsburgh Penguins. It was big news that Carl

Brewer, late of the Toronto Maple Leafs, would be part of the show, even though he wasn't technically a pro at all. Just about the time that Bobby Orr was signing his rookie contract with Boston, Brewer, with the help of Al Eagleson, had forced the Toronto Maple Leafs to allow him to "turn amateur" and join Father Bauer's national team. It seemed a lot of effort just to get out from under the angry stare of Punch Imlach, but Brewer was that kind of guy. He eventually made his escape and played for Canada in the 1967 World Amateur Championship, though he was barred from the 1968 Olympics (which operated under a stricter set of rules) because he still carried the taint of having once played for pay. Now there were rumbles that he was on his way back to the big league. Not that Brewer was prepared to let anyone in on exactly what he was thinking. When asked about his plans before the game, he'd offered only an enigmatic smile and said politely, "No comment." That was Brewer, playing by his own rules as always. On the other side, the national team lined up with some of its veteran stalwarts, including Fran Huck and Morris Mott, along with a group of raw youngsters auditioning to play for their country. Among the latter were a couple of talented kids named Brian Glennie and Butch Goring, for whom bigger things were in store.

But the real marquee name had left the ice early in the first period and quickly disappeared from the Pro All-Stars' bench, not to return. The reporters naturally wondered where Bobby Orr had gone. What had happened to the reigning NHL rookie of the year must not have been obvious from the press box. Maybe he had only planned on making a cameo appearance. Maybe a few minutes was all a big-time hockey star could spare for a backwater like Winnipeg. Downstairs between periods, while Orr remained behind closed doors, the local press corps was offered a couple of possible explanations for his sudden absence. "One official said Orr broke the blade of his skate and no one could find another set," Jack Bennett told his readers in the *Winnipeg Free Press* the next day, "while another claimed Orr wasn't in shape to go a full game as he hadn't skated in months."

Orr was hustled out of the arena and soon enough out of town, without saying a word, without anyone being the wiser, which certainly didn't sit well with the fourth estate. "The organizers of this game received all the publicity they asked for, yet when their turn came to fulfill a request, they turned their back on us," Bennett grumbled in print.

The truth was that Orr had to get his story straight for the Boston Bruins before telling the press anything at all. Bobby had come to Winnipeg of his own volition, without the blessing of his team, without the blessing of Al Eagleson. He liked the cause and he liked the chance to get back on the ice; and Green had treated him especially well during his rookie season in Boston. Though the Bruins might have owned him as far as the NHL was concerned, as far as Orr was concerned they didn't own him in August.

He had been injured before, when a groin pull ruined his Memorial Cup with the Oshawa Generals, and later when Marcel Pronovost's hip check almost lifted him into the rinkside seats and twisted his left knee during his rookie season in the NHL. It was his right knee this time, and the timing couldn't have been worse. Expectations were high for the Bruins in the coming 1967–68 season, the first for the new, expanded league. There were many who believed that, by the end of his rookie season, Orr had already become the best defenceman in hockey, on the verge of leading the franchise at least into the playoffs. To that end, the Bruins had been considerably strengthened during the off-season, through a trade with the Chicago Black Hawks that had brought three talented veteran forwards into the fold.

Now Orr was on a plane headed back to Toronto, his knee swollen and painful, the kind of grim journey he would be forced to make many times, in many variations, over the course of his NHL career. He was wondering how badly he was hurt, and he was wondering just how he was going to explain it to Al, to Milt Schmidt (who had taken over as general manager when the Bruins finally tired of Hap Emms' act the previous spring) and to Mr. Adams, all of whom would surely be furious.

There had been a three-way collision, he told them sheepishly. Leiter got some of the blame for it, but Bobby tried to assure everyone that it wasn't really his fault. Just one of those things that happens in the course of a hockey game, an unhappy fluke, an accident. "A guy steered me into the boards, and another guy, who was on my side, hit me," Orr said. Of course, that wasn't really the point. What the hell was he doing playing hockey in Winnipeg in August in the first place? Who told him it would be okay? Orr mumbled something about how "permission was given somewhere for me to play," and suggested that it was Tom Johnson, assistant to Weston Adams, who had extended the organization's blessing.

That was news to Eagleson, and Schmidt, who was livid, certainly didn't seem inclined to buy it. "I'd rather not elaborate until I know all the facts," he said. Afterwards, the Bruins would make their new team policy regarding off-season activities explicit. No exhibitions, no lacrosse, no rodeos – yes, rodeos (Johnny McKenzie, for one, was known to take part) – during the summer for any player with a Boston contract. "You know, we didn't even give the boy permission to play in that game. He could have ruined his career in a meaningless game," Schmidt said.

The Bruins sent Orr to the best knee man they could find, Dr. John Palmer at Toronto General Hospital. "The knee was investigated under anaesthetic this afternoon, but we did not find any damage to require surgery," Dr. Palmer reported. "The knee was placed in a cast, where it will stay for two to three weeks. He should be ready to play three weeks later – just about the time the schedule opens.

"There's no reason to believe the recovery will be other than complete."

He was telling the truth there. The right knee, the one Orr hurt in Winnipeg, would never trouble him again during his hockey career. They'd never have to open it up. "A minor strain of a minor ligament," the doctor explained. But those kinds of doctor's statements, assurances that this time all was well, that this time, this surgery, was the miracle cure, that nothing was going to prevent Bobby Orr from returning to the ice and playing like his old brilliant self began to ring hollow over time. He was the perfect hockey-playing machine, born with the power, the grace, the instinct, the genius's shinny IQ. God couldn't have built a better hockey player. And then He decided to play one of His little cosmic jokes, as He is wont to do. Yep, the kid has everything. He's the total package. He could dominate the sport for fifteen years, maybe more. His team could win a string of championships. Except that . . . well, you'll figure it out soon enough.

Achilles' mother, Thetis, the sea goddess, hoped to make him immortal by bathing him in the magical waters of the River Styx. But when she immersed him, she held him by his heel, which remained dry. Achilles grew up to become the greatest warrior anyone had ever seen. The Trojans' arrows and swords couldn't harm him. But then Paris, the son of the Trojan king, with a little assist from the god Apollo, shot an arrow into the mortal heel, and from that wound Achilles died.

Orr's injuries in his second professional season certainly didn't end with the twisted knee in Winnipeg. He would spend five weeks with the leg immobilized in a cast and only start skating with the Bruins on the first of October, in a rush to get ready for the beginning of the 1967–68 NHL schedule. Still, Orr showed few ill effects on his return and seemed his brilliant, blossoming self until December 9, when, in a game against the Toronto Maple Leafs, he was flattened by Frank Mahovlich, breaking his collar bone and separating his shoulder. People were starting to wonder if he was a little bit brittle, if what still looked something like a boy's physique couldn't stand the rigours of playing against men. That injury kept Orr out of the lineup until January, when he returned just in time to suit up for his first NHL All-Star Game. Played on January 14 at Maple Leaf Gardens, it marked the last time the exhibition matched the defending Stanley Cup champions, Toronto, against the rest of the league's best. The all-stars were led by Toe Blake, the coach of the Montreal Canadiens, the other Stanley Cup finalist. In future years, the All-Star Game would be transformed into a battle of division against division and lose any vestige of serious competition. Then, it still seemed like a real contest, with pride on the line. (The 1968 game is also remembered because it took place just two days after Bill Masterton of the Minnesota North Stars suffered fatal head injuries in a game against the Oakland Seals, the only on-ice death in the league's history, an event that naturally overshadowed the festivities.)*

Watching the action, Sinden and Schmidt could see that Orr was labouring, that he seemed to be battling through pain in his left knee. But he was still playing well, and Blake, who wanted to win the game, wouldn't take him off the ice, even though Sinden and Schmidt found themselves hollering at him to protect their

---

* Bill Masterton is remembered today as the only player to die from injuries suffered during an NHL game, and because his name is now attached to the trophy awarded annually to the player who "best exemplifies the qualities of perseverance, sportsmanship, and dedication to hockey." He grew up in Winnipeg, and played junior hockey there before making the then-unusual decision to defer taking a crack at the pros and continue his education at Denver University, where he earned a Bachelor of Science degree. In 1961, he led the school to the NCAA championship and was named the most valuable player of the NCAA Tournament and an All-American. Masterton signed with the Montreal Canadiens organization after graduation, but following two years in the minors, realized he had little chance to crack the team's powerful NHL lineup, and so opted to go back to school, earning his Masters in finance. He married and settled into a job with Honeywell. That seemed to be the end of Masterton's hockey career. But after four years out of the game, he was contacted by Wren Blair, who knew Masterton from the minor leagues and was trying to fill out the roster of the expansion Minnesota North Stars. Blair persuaded Masterton to give hockey one more shot, and bought his rights from the Canadiens. To his surprise, Masterton made the North Stars, and he scored the first goal in franchise history on October 11, 1967, in St. Louis. "I realize it's going to be tough," Masterton told the *St. Paul Dispatch*, discussing his chances of sticking in the NHL, "but if I get the opportunity to play, I'm confident that I can make it." (*St. Paul Dispatch*, January 15, 1968.) In his last game, he had carried the puck into the Oakland Seals' zone, and then dropped a pass for teammate Wayne Connelly. Masterton then either fell or was knocked down while in a crowd of players. The back of his head hit the ice, and he was knocked out, bleeding profusely. He died twenty-seven hours later from massive brain injuries, without ever having regained consciousness. Masterton was twenty-seven years old and had two young children.

investment. Orr's sore knee forced him to sit out the first five games following the all-star break. Then, on February 10, during a game at the Olympia in Detroit, the joint simply locked up, and it was all he could do to skate off the ice and limp to the Bruins dressing room. There was another sad, anxious, painful flight home, another set of probing questions from the reporters, and now there would be no holding back the knife. Bobby Orr's first knee operation was conducted at Newton-Wellesley Hospital in Boston, with Dr. Ronald Adams doing the honours, repairing some torn cartilage and pronouncing afterwards that all was well. "The operation was completely successful and badly needed," he said. A bit of ligament damage repaired, a bit of cartilage removed. Nothing out of the ordinary.

It would be like that every time. The knee would be pronounced better every time. Orr and the doctors would wax optimistic about the future every time. And every time the truth was that it was getting worse. Every time the scalpel was involved, Orr's career was shortened by days and months and whole seasons. Maybe the doctors didn't do him any favours; maybe they were too eager to operate rather than employ rest and therapy and patience; or maybe they just didn't know any better, since that was the style of the times, the limit of medical knowledge and technology when it came to knee injuries. Maybe Orr didn't do himself any favours, either. He was always restless, always impatient, had little time or interest in the boring business of rehabilitation. He was indifferent about doing the work and rushed himself back on the ice. A lot of hockey people would blame the Bruins for that, endangering their most valuable asset for their own selfish purposes, but the truth was that they couldn't have kept Orr away even if they had wanted to – just as they couldn't keep him off the ice during the Memorial Cup. He was bullheaded and ultra-competitive, and he was going to do it his way.

Still, the Bruins can't be entirely let off the hook. Scotty Bowman remembers a game when he was coaching in St. Louis, during the early days of the Blues expansion franchise. The Bruins arrived in town in the midst of a winning streak, but with Orr hobbling and favouring one leg. Harry Sinden summoned the Blues team doctor into the dressing room to give his star defenceman the once-over. The doc was new to hockey, new to sports in general. After doing the exam, he wandered into the Blues dressing room and told Bowman, "There's a guy on their team who I advised them not to play tonight."

"Who's that?" Bowman wondered.

"I don't know the players," the doctor acknowledged, "but it was a blond guy with a brush cut. I looked at his knee. He was very polite. I said that I wouldn't take a chance tonight. I wouldn't dress him. Get it X-rayed and looked at. Then, my God, the coach nearly took my head off."

That was Sinden, shooting the messenger.

Orr played, but only on the power play, perhaps a half-dozen shifts, and it was obvious that he could barely skate. After the game, he asked to see the St. Louis doctor and apologized to him for Sinden's behaviour.

A fan can dream of how it might have been had Bobby Orr come along ten or twenty years later, how they would have cleared up so many of his problems with a scope and a local anaesthetic rather than full-blown surgery, how they know so much more now about knees and the damage done through sports. There would have been more years, and more good years, and he would have been able to play against the Russians in '72, and won further Stanley Cups and retired gracefully when the time was right, happy and wealthy and satisfied. But instead, he was the hockey Achilles, and because of that his fate was sealed.

At the beginning of that second season in the NHL, Orr had hardly heard a discouraging word. He was a boy-god back in Parry Sound, who at worst might have inspired a little jealous grumbling when somebody else's parents felt their kid didn't see enough of the puck. The fans loved him unconditionally in Oshawa, where he was celebrated in the hometown paper and in those from every town the Generals visited. In Boston, the beat reporters and columnists of the sports press – pretty tame back then, almost retainers of the team – marvelled at Orr's magnificent hockey skills and buffed and polished his squeaky-clean image. They were in the hero-making business, real or otherwise, and Orr, who was everything they had been promised he would be, certainly fit the bill. What had he ever done to disappoint anyone? How had he ever failed? It had been like a fairy tale so far.

But there was another Bobby, a different Bobby, who only showed himself on occasion, when challenged to a fight on the ice, or when he'd had a little too much to drink. He could be angry and mean and dark. When his temper flashed, those who knew him best knew enough to steer clear. On the ice, there were only glimpses, and most of those came in fights, fair and square, in which Orr stood up against the league's toughest brawlers and didn't give an inch. That, of course, only added to his allure. It was what hockey players were supposed to do when challenged. What happened on Sunday, November 5, at Boston Garden was different, though. It made even Orr's many admirers squirm just a little bit.

The Toronto Maple Leafs were the visitors that night. In the second period, the Bruins were on the power play when the puck came loose and the Leafs' Brian Conacher skated to the boards to pick it up. Conacher was certainly no goon. A tall, lean forward, he carried both the privilege and the burden of one of the most famous names in hockey history. His father, Lionel, had been honoured as Canada's best athlete of the first half of the twentieth century. His uncles Charlie and Roy would join Lionel in the Hockey Hall of Fame, making the Conachers a kind of Toronto sports royalty. Unlike Orr, Conacher was a big-city boy, and unlike Orr, he would grow up in privilege, beginning his hockey-playing life at Upper Canada College, the private school of the local establishment. He graduated from there to the Toronto Marlboros, played for the national team, and then had two seasons with the Maple Leafs. He was there through the 1966–67 season, which means his name, like those of his father and uncles, is engraved on the Stanley Cup. But he didn't have their talent, and he didn't have their burning desire to play the game. What happened in Boston would force him to question how much he really wanted to be part of the National Hockey League at all.

Just as he picked up the puck, Conacher saw Orr bearing down on him. Orr dropped low so that he could better block Conacher's shot. Conacher responded by chipping the puck left along the boards.

Then he moved to his right, hoping to skate around Orr and retrieve the puck on the other side. As he made his move, with Orr still coming forward, his stick struck Orr square in the face. Conacher said afterwards that he had no idea what had happened, and no idea of the consequences. He continued on with the play, picking up the puck, skating over the Toronto blue line, convinced that he had a chance to score a short-handed goal. But before he could shoot, he was flattened from behind. It was Johnny McKenzie who had blind-sided him, then pounded away with his fists while Conacher crouched, face down, covering up, absorbing the beating. Seeing Conacher helpless, the Toronto captain, George Armstrong, led the Leafs off the bench.

Back up the ice, Orr lay bleeding heavily from a cut on the bridge of his nose, staining the ice red around him. The Bruins trainers jumped over the boards as soon as the play stopped and ran to his aid. In the stands, the Boston fans reacted with shock and outrage. Orr's teammates, understanding his value to the Bruins, understanding the unwritten hockey rules that required standing up for your own, immediately joined McKenzie and went after Conacher. It's still a part of the hockey code to which officials often turn a blind eye, allowing players to enact their own brand of justice. (That's why Todd Bertuzzi thought he was doing nothing wrong, nothing out of the ordinary, when he attacked Steve Moore from behind in Vancouver in the spring of 2004.) The referee and two linesmen seemed confused as to where to turn, whether to go to the aid of the injured Orr or to protect Conacher from the attacking Bruins. When Orr finally rose, battered and still bleeding, he pushed away the Boston trainers, ignoring whatever feeble protest they might have offered, and skated hard toward Conacher. No one was going to get in his way.

Afterwards, Orr explained that it was the stick that bothered him, that if Conacher had hit him with a shoulder or a fist or an elbow, it would have been different. But stickwork in hockey was, and is, regarded as cowardly, both dangerous and unfair. When Orr reached Conacher, he pulled McKenzie off him and then let fly with a terrible, irrational fury, flailing away as Conacher cowered, his hands shielding his face (he was worried, among other things, about what might happen if he was struck in the eye – Conacher wore contact lenses). "All I know is that I wasn't mad at Orr before or after the play," Conacher explained the next day. "I can understand Orr being mad. But I'm not going to fight a crazy man, bop a guy in the nose who is already hurt and bleeding." (Asked later whether he planned on fining his players, the Leafs coach, Punch Imlach, said, "They'd be fined by me if they had not left the bench.") The officials desperately and unsuccessfully tried to restore order. Linesmen Neil Armstrong and Walt Atanas pulled Orr off Conacher's back. Orr had to be held, pushing back at the officials, pointing his finger at Conacher, screaming at him. Conacher's jersey had been stripped off, and his face and underwear were spattered with Orr's blood. He escaped briefly, only to be sucker-punched in the back of the head by Ken Hodge, dropping to the ice again. Still, Conacher refused to fight back. At one point he broke free and skated behind the net, hoping that the physical barrier might keep the Bruins at bay. Finally, belatedly, a few of the Leafs came to Conacher's rescue, surrounding him and escorting him off the ice. He had to pass the Boston bench on the way to the exit, and then through a public area under the stands before reaching the visitors dressing room. The Bruins spat at him and threatened him and promised that there was more to come. Boston police helped him get to the dressing room, while fans cursed and threw whatever they could get their hands on and played the angry mob. As he was being patched up, Conacher knew that he'd have to go back on the ice or forever be branded a coward. He returned to the bench after fifteen minutes and played one shift that for him must have seemed interminable. Eddie Shack skated all the way across the ice to hit him with an elbow, and didn't receive a penalty. One Bruin after another ran at him and bullied him and continued with the threats. It was, most neutral observers agreed, a dark, savage moment for hockey. In Toronto, where they would soon take to booing Bobby Orr every time he touched the puck at Maple Leaf Gardens, it was also viewed as an outrage.

Afterwards, Orr didn't seem particularly bothered by the incident. He joined some of the other Bruins for drinks that night, with three stitches closing the wound in his nose, and was still a little angry to start, but it passed soon enough. His right thumb was aching from some of the punches he landed, but the injury wasn't anything serious. While his fellow Bruins promised they'd deal with Conacher again the next time the two teams met, really, that was that. (It was years before Conacher and Orr spoke again. "He thought I had done it intentionally," Conacher remembers. "Number one, that wasn't in my nature. Number two, I definitely didn't do it intentionally." After he left the NHL as a player, Conacher was for a time the assistant general manager of a team in the low minors, the Mohawk Valley Comets. Ronnie Orr, Bobby's brother, was then working for one of the other teams in the league. "Bobby thinks you did that on purpose," he told Conacher. Still, the two of them eventually became friendly, and Bobby Orr and Conacher finally made contact when Conacher was the operations manager of Maple Leaf Gardens and Orr was the annual star of an Easter Seals skate in the building. No apologies were offered, and the topic wasn't raised directly. "I think it was water under the bridge," Conacher says. "You realized that it was a thing of the past, and you never really talked about it.")

In truth, there would be some lingering after-effects. You could argue that this was the night the Big Bad Bruins were born. The team came to dominate the NHL in succeeding seasons through a mixture of supreme skill and a kind of upfront physical intimidation unseen before in big-league hockey. They'd beat you with a beautiful play, and then they'd beat you with their fists. And they stuck together, always – challenge one and be prepared to face the rest. (The Bruins would eventually be pushed aside by the team that took that style to its unfortunate extreme, the "Broad Street Bully" Philadelphia Flyers of the mid-1970s.) Orr's own public image also shifted ever so slightly. He was still the golden boy, the nonpareil, the greatest young player in the game. But for the first time, the press box gang decided that he might have a few warts, after all. Naturally, the Toronto reporters doled out criticism with the most enthusiasm, since an innocent Maple Leaf had been the victim of a mass assault. Even in Boston, where Orr could do no wrong, not everyone was cheering him on this time. It's worth noting, though, that the disapproval had nothing to do with the violence itself but with the sense that Orr, by losing control of his temper, might have hurt the beloved home team. That sentiment was expressed most directly in an "open letter" to Orr written by the reporter Kevin Walsh and published in *The Boston Globe:*

Bobby, what did you prove Sunday night? That you are tough? That you have a low boiling point? That you're not going to be pushed around on the ice?

It was a mistake – chasing after Brian Conacher and getting into a fight with him after he hit you in the face with his stick. It hurt your team. It led to a series of events that marred an excellent hockey game.

Instead of Conacher going to the penalty box with a five minute major, you got involved in a fight and erased the Bruins' advantage.

At that point in the game the Bruins might have scored a goal or two and broken the game wide open.

You lost your temper and it may have cost the Bruins a victory.

I'm sure you are aware of it now. The Bruins are paying you to play hockey.

Hockey is an emotional game. At times it's rough and players get injured. A player's boiling point can be low when his nose is broken and blood is rushing from a cut. But the superstars have self-control.

They don't lose their temper. It's rare when Gordie Howe or Bobby Hull is put off the ice for fighting. They are too valuable to be off the ice. The stamp of a great player is self-control.

When you arrived in the league the only "unknown" concerning your chances of making the jump from junior hockey to the pros was how tough you were.

You don't have to prove you're tough now. Everyone in the league knows you won't step away from anyone.

That is why it was a mistake to go after Conacher. He was gone for five minutes.

The littlest Oshawa General.
Fourteen-year-old Orr in
the uniform of the junior team
he helped to revive.
(Getty Images)

Alan Eagleson (left) with his two most important early clients, Orr (far right)
and Carl Brewer (second from right), both of whom would eventually help to
bring him down. Also pictured is future NHLer Danny O'Shea.
(CP photo/*Globe and Mail*)

In Niagara Falls, Ontario, at his first training camp as a member of the Boston Bruins, Orr confers with the team's rookie head coach, Harry Sinden. Note that Orr is wearing his original Boston number: 27. (Frank Prazak/Hockey Hall of Fame)

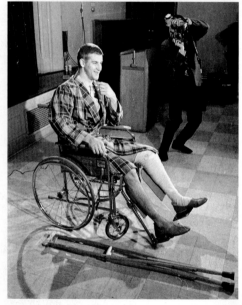

In what would become a familiar image, Orr–fresh from knee surgery–explains to the press that he has "no idea yet" how long he will be out of action. February 16, 1968, Newton-Wellesley Hospital, Boston. (Bettmann/Corbis)

Orr playing for the NHL All-Stars against the Stanley Cup champion Toronto Maple Leafs in the 1968 All-Star Game at Maple Leaf Gardens. (Graphic Artists/Hockey Hall of Fame)

The Goal. The Boston Bruins win the Stanley Cup on May 10, 1970, and
Bobby Orr takes flight. One of the most famous images in the history of sport.
(Ray Lussier/*Boston Herald American*)

The conquering heroes.
Orr, flanked by teammates
Don Marcotte and Bill
Speer, riding in the Stanley
Cup victory parade
through the streets of
Boston on May 11, 1970.
(Bettmann/Corbis)

A real Beau Brummel. Orr in September 1972, when he skated with Team Canada but was unable to play in the Summit Series against the Soviet Union because of his bad knee. (Getty Images)

Wren Blair, the hockey bird dog, seen here during his days as general manager of the Minnesota North Stars. (Hockey Hall of Fame)

The wrong uniform. One of the few times Orr was able to suit up and play for the Chicago Black Hawks in October 1976. (London Life-Portnoy/Hockey Hall of Fame)

The last hurrah. Orr practicing with Team Canada in 1976, preparing for the inaugural Canada Cup. (Bettmann/Corbis)

The last great game he'd ever play. In the first game of the Canada Cup final, Orr was masterful in a 6–0 win for Canada over Czechoslovakia. In the second game of the best-of-three final, his bad knee slowed him down considerably, but Canada still came out on top. Orr was named the tournament's most valuable player.
(CP photo/*Toronto Star*/Jeff Goode)

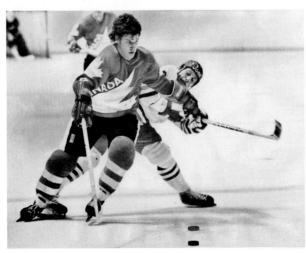

Saying goodbye. Orr announces his retirement on November 8, 1978. He had attempted a come-back after missing the previous twenty months while recuperating from knee surgery, but had lasted only six games. He was just 30 years old. (Bettmann/Corbis)

A rare photo of Orr suited up in the uniform of the Minnesota North Stars for an old-timers game shortly after his retirement. Later, his knee problems–which would eventually lead to replacement surgery–restricted his on-ice activities to charity skates with kids. (Larry Sexton/Hockey Hall of Fame)

The agent. Some controversy arose when Orr, who had become a player-agent, also served as coach during an annual junior all-star game. There was no small irony in the fact that he finally found his post-playing career in the business pioneered by Al Eagleson. (Kevin Frayer/CP photo)

If you lose your temper and go after everyone it's going to hurt the Bruins. Every team in the league is going to send its hatchet man after you. They are going to attempt to draw you into the penalty box. The opposition will lose a fixture from the end of the bench. The Bruins lose an All-Star defenceman.

It isn't a fair trade in any market.

You don't belong in the penalty box or in the trainer's room having your injured thumb treated, Bobby. You belong on the ice playing hockey, the way only you can play.

Conacher isn't being absolved for his high stick that hit you in the face. It's a long season, seventy-four games, and Conacher will have to skate up and down his wing all season. Brian probably won't be too anxious to carry the puck along the boards or go into the corners against Boston.

You're lucky the X-ray proved negative and your thumb isn't broken. You were able to practice with the team Monday. You could have been out of action six or seven games.

At nineteen, you are on the threshold of being a superstar. Don't let a low boiling point overshadow your ability.[36]

Orr read the letter. He read all of the Boston sports sections, every day. And when a writer penned something that displeased him, he would instruct Eagleson to call the offender and let him know he wasn't happy. Then he would simply cut the scribe off. Over the years, Orr's relationship would grow testy with some members of the Boston press corps – at times, a full half of the hockey contingent wasn't in his good graces, and so wasn't allowed access to his post-game thoughts. Some national writers were excluded for a time as well. It wasn't necessarily permanent. One day, out of the blue, all would be well again. But any reporter who needed to speak to the biggest star in hockey, to the biggest sports figure in Boston, understood that he or she took a considerable risk criticizing Bobby Orr in print.

Despite the injuries and the fallout from the Conacher incident, the 1967–68 season, the first for the new, expanded NHL, would represent a personal triumph for Orr, as well as a team triumph for the Bruins. Though he played in only forty-six games and his production fell to thirty-one points, he would be named the NHL's top defenceman, winning the Norris Trophy for the first time. And after having missed the playoffs every season since 1958–59, the Boston team finally made it to the post-season. Orr was back on skates just a month after the February knee operation and pushed himself hard to return to the team for the final days of the schedule. But that turned out to be a mistake in every way. The Bruins shouldn't have let him do it, and Orr shouldn't have forced himself onto the ice before he was ready. Boston had actually played rather well in his absence and held its place in the standings. On Orr's return, he clearly wasn't himself. In the first game back against the Red Wings, he lashed out angrily, taking two ten-minute misconducts, one for making a gesture toward his throat, a comment on the work of referee Bill Friday, and another for slamming the door to the Bruins bench a little too hard for the zebra's liking. Boston lost that game, and lost three of the final four down the stretch. Finishing third, they were drawn against the first-place Canadiens in the opening round of the playoffs, and played as though they were just happy to be there. The Habs, who would go on to win the Stanley Cup, swept Boston in four games. Orr finished the series with just two assists and dazzled no one with his defensive play.

Despite the ignominious finish, the season as a whole represented a step forward for the Boston franchise, for which Orr would receive much of the credit. But he was only part of the story. Another huge factor in the Bruins' renaissance was a trade made during the previous off-season that would be celebrated as one of the most savvy, and lopsided, in the history of the sport. It remade the Bruins, remade the character of the team and marked the arrival of the only player and personality who would rival Orr as the Bruins leader and number-one star. Theirs would be an uneasy, but fruitful, relationship.

After finishing on top of the NHL standings during the 1966–67 season, the Chicago Black Hawks seemed poised to win the Stanley

Cup, as they had back in 1962, led by the great Bobby Hull. In the first round of the playoffs, the Hawks drew the third-place Toronto Maple Leafs, an old team, apparently on its last legs. But those Leafs, backstopped brilliantly by the ancient goaltending duo of Johnny Bower and Terry Sawchuk, upset the Hawks and then went on to beat Montreal for the Cup. Change for the sake of change became the mantra in Chicago. The team's management had run out of patience with a big, strong, gifted scorer from Sault Ste. Marie, Ontario, who had done a fine job as the centre on Hull's line but who had flopped against Toronto in the playoffs. And Phil Esposito had a habit of speaking his mind, for better or for worse. Before heading home to take up his off-season job in a steel mill, while several sheets to the wind, he had told Billy Reay and Tommy Ivan, the Hawks coach and general manager, exactly what he thought of their team-building talents. What better way to get even than by sending the big mouth to the worst franchise in hockey, the Boston Bruins. Ivan got on the phone to Milt Schmidt, and soon enough they had an agreement, just hours before the league's trade deadline. Like so many deals made out of emotion, it turned out to be a terrible one for the Black Hawks. Schmidt, the happy beneficiary, found himself wondering where the catch was, wondering if there was something wrong with Esposito that he'd missed. In return for Orr's regular defence partner, Gilles Marotte, forward Pit Martin and a goaltender named Jack Norris, Boston received Esposito, plus wingers Ken Hodge and Fred Stanfield. The latter two would be key contributors to the Bruins' glory years, and Esposito would evolve into the greatest goal scorer the sport had yet known.

He was also a large personality, a talker, an egotist, a joker, a drinker, a carouser, a womanizer, a guy who would dominate the dressing room, who was in so many ways Orr's opposite number. Espo ran hot where Orr ran cold. Over the years, there would be plenty of stories alluding to an uncomfortable Esposito-Orr rivalry, and just as many public assurances from the two players that they were actually the best of pals and teammates. The truth, of course, lay somewhere in between. Orr and Esposito co-existed as friendly, and at times not so friendly, rivals. There was no question who was the larger, louder presence in the Bruins dressing room – that was Espo's schtick, just as it would be when he led Team Canada against the Russians in 1972. Orr wasn't a speech maker, wasn't much of a talker of any kind. If a Boston player did something on the ice that he disapproved of, he'd send a message not with words but with an icy, angry stare. The rest of the team divided between them. There were a few Orr guys, like Eddie Johnston, his closest pal on the team, and there were a larger number of Espo guys, like Don Awrey, but it wasn't as though the two factions didn't mix. Esposito liked to be the centre of attention, the life of the party. Orr was often the first guy to slip out of the bar, to retreat to the sanctuary of his home.

On the ice, anyone outside of the team itself would have been hard-pressed to see any evidence of their differences, though there were times, especially when the two were duelling for the NHL scoring championship, when Orr confided to those closest to him that he thought the "Chicago guys" were quietly conspiring against him, whether they were feeding Espo an extra pass or denying Orr one, just to make sure their long-time buddy came out on top.

But there's a truth that applies to all teams in all professional sports: harmony is way overrated. Many a championship had been won with players who didn't socialize away from the park or the rink, who didn't say a lot to each other in any circumstance, whose personalities naturally clashed, who came from backgrounds that were irreconcilable, who rubbed each other the wrong way, who hated each other's guts. Talent goes a long way toward patching over those kinds of differences. Success goes a long way toward achieving workplace calm. And as for the other side of the coin, a team spiralling downward will invariably begin to pick at itself, to magnify its rifts and tensions and jealousies. There is a long, long list of jerks who won many a championship, and of nice guys who finished last.

Every one of the Boston Bruins understood an essential truth: that both Orr and Esposito helped make them and their team a whole lot better. The two principals understood as well that they were complementary parts of a greater whole, that when Orr floated a perfect pass, or sent a slapshot in from the point, when Espo stood in front of the net absorbing all manner of punishment in order to gobble up a rebound, they needed each other and became greater than the sum of their parts. In the end, that's all that mattered.

In June 1968, Bobby Orr was back in Parry Sound, fishing as usual, when he decided he just couldn't take the pain any longer. He had won the Norris Trophy by then, and had been named a first-team all-star. It had been nearly two months since he was last on skates, and he'd been taking it easy, but still the left knee, the one that had been operated on back in February, wasn't getting any better on its own. Orr went to the family doctor first, who took one look and said that he'd better get himself to a specialist right away. A few days later, he'd find himself under the knife again, with Dr. John Palmer at Toronto General, who had taken care of his right knee the summer before, in charge of the proceedings.

No big deal, Dr. Palmer explained afterwards. The operation in February had removed a piece of torn cartilage. But there had been a chip inadvertently left behind, which had aggravated the joint. He had removed it and then poked around a bit, and everything seemed just fine.

"Bobby won't have any problem with the knee in the future," Dr. Palmer said, and you have to assume he really believed it.

Chapter Ten

THE ARTIST AT WORK

T HERE WAS NO OTHER PLACE LIKE the Boston Garden. The great arenas constructed during the professional sports boom of the early twentieth century weren't the product of cookie-cutter architecture. They all looked different and felt different and even smelled different, and those idiosyncrasies could be a tremendous advantage for the home team. In Montreal at the Forum, the spirits of the ancient greats always seemed to hang heavily in the air – maybe it came from knowing that they'd laid out Howie Morenz on a bier at centre ice after he died from the catastrophic after-effects of a broken leg. Chicago's Stadium was magnificently claustrophobic. The upper deck hung out over the lower like a balcony, and the great pipe organ, the sound of which could make the place shake to the foundations, was literally built into the walls. Detroit's Olympia was a bit of a graceless barn, and Maple Leaf Gardens at times seemed as much a church where one dutifully worshipped the blue and white as it did a hockey rink, though don't tell a Toronto fan that. Even in that context, the Garden in Boston was by far the most eccentric of an eccentric lot. Built over a train station, it had the smallest number of seats, the smallest ice surface and strange corners from which the puck might bounce at angles only a veteran Bruin could readily predict. Fans sat crowded together, uncomfortable but remarkably close to the action – close enough that a visiting player could hear and see and touch them, which most often wasn't a very good thing. The funk of circuses past seemed to have permeated the bricks and mortar, never to completely depart. And the rats, they said, were the size of alley cats, with plenty of dark, dank corners where they might be fruitful and multiply.

In the two Canadian cities of the original six, hockey fans, at least in the expensive seats, tended to turn out in suits and ties well into the 1970s. It was the establishment game, the biggest show in town. Tickets were dear and tickets were scarce, and acquiring them normally involved connections. In many American cities, though, Boston certainly among them, hockey was and is a working man's game. Those who filled the Garden were a little rough around the edges, and without the segregation and class distinction that came later with the invention of private boxes, they filled even the best seats in the house. Especially in the glory years, the years of the Bruins' ascendance in the 1960s and early 1970s, the fans could intimidate as well as the team's band of brawlers. It was no wonder, then, that of all the teams in the NHL, Boston was most different at home and away. In 1968–69, which would be the real beginning of the franchise's golden era, the Bruins lost more games on the road than they won. But in the Garden, in thirty-eight regular-season games, they were beaten only three times, by teams that must have managed to remain oblivious to their surroundings.

The Garden may have been of more ancient origin, but in those days it seemed like the house that Bobby Orr built. No athlete was ever so beloved there, not Cousy or Russell or Bird, not Milt Schmidt or Eddie Shore, not even Marvelous Marvin Hagler, who would make it his de facto home base. They loved Orr unconditionally, would defend his well-being irrationally, found in his combination of skill and toughness and boyish charm the object of their hearts' desire. (The Irish in him didn't hurt, either.) Entering his third season in the National Hockey

League, he was now acknowledged as the best defenceman in the game. More than that, a passionate but notoriously fickle, sometimes bitter sports town had given itself over to him without reservation. The Boston fans saw in Orr something of themselves, or of themselves as they wanted to be seen: humble, working class, honest, diligent, brilliant. In their eyes he was as infallible as the pope. Still, in the days before the beginning of the 1968–69 season, as he struggled to return from two rounds of knee surgery and carried the public burden of his lucrative, precedent-setting new contract, Orr found himself racked by doubt, about his leg, about his popularity, about the money he was making, even about his new modish haircut, now finally starting to creep down around his ears. "Maybe I don't show it," he told the New York – based hockey writer Stan Fischler, "but I worry. About my health, the legs. I was worried at the start of the year that I might not be able to play. I mean, you get a little doubt and you worry. Lately I've been throwing up. The doctor says it's just nerves – I've been getting worked up too much. . . . There are people who say I'm not worth that much money. You get it in a lot of ways. . . . I used to have a brush cut, but I let my hair grow. Now some people bug me about getting a haircut. At the games you get a few wolves here and there. But you got to take the good with the bad."[37] (For Orr it was a remarkably unguarded moment in the presence of a journalist, but that warm, trusting relationship with Fischler wouldn't last long. When the writer published his book *Bobby Orr and the Big, Bad Bruins* in 1969, Orr was on the phone to Eagleson, wondering if he could sue over the use of his name in the title.)

Orr didn't feel healthy enough to play during the exhibition season, but he was in uniform, ready to test the knee, when the Bruins opened the regular season against the Detroit Red Wings on October 11. By the early days of 1969, he was playing exceptionally well, but there were subtle signs that the knee was again bothering him. Sinden and the other players could tell that Orr, though always some degree of superb, wasn't quite the same player night in and night out. The knee was swelling after every game, and by now the ice pack in the dressing room was part of his regular routine. But the pain, and Bobby's confidence in the leg's ability to carry him, would waver. The other Bruins learned to pick up on that and to cut their own play to suit. Some games, it was obvious from the opening seconds of the first period that Orr was feeling just fine, and so they'd step back, let him play his game, let him freewheel and improvise and then try to do their best to keep up, knowing that he'd make them look good. On other nights, though, which would become far more frequent as the years passed, they'd sense during warm-up that Bobby wasn't quite right. He'd never say a thing, and certainly would never pull himself out of the lineup or limit his own ice time. But his teammates would see him struggling to get up to speed, see the occasional grimace as the pain kicked in. In those games, without saying so, the other players entered into a silent pact to try to pick up a bit of the slack, to take more responsibility on their own shoulders, to not sit back and expect number 4 to play Superman.

On January 30, 1969, during a game against the Los Angeles Kings at Jack Kent Cooke's Fabulous Forum, Orr was skating backwards on a routine play when his left skate caught in a crack that had formed in what was no doubt lousy California ice. His knee twisted, and Orr felt the twinge instantly, but he stayed in the game to the end. The next nine games, though, he was forced to sit out, waiting for the discomfort to subside, hoping that another operation wouldn't be necessary. After the surgery the previous spring, the doctors had told him to expect pain and swelling for at least six months. That time was up now, and it wasn't going away, especially after being aggravated. Still, Orr resigned himself to gritting his teeth and playing on, and was back in the Boston lineup.

Whatever he was feeling, whatever the circumstances, whatever the state of his health, most nights of the season he was the best player in hockey. On December 14, in a game against Chicago, Orr recorded his first NHL hat trick, and added two assists. Sinden called it "the greatest offensive game ever played by a defence-man." Historically, and by any aesthetic measure, he was no doubt correct. The fans at the Boston Garden stood and cheered after his third goal and littered the ice with hats, as per the tradition. Orr, of course, was embarrassed at the display and seemed eager for it to end. By year's end, he would score his twenty-first goal of the season on his twenty-first birthday, breaking the record for a defenceman set in 1944–45, one of the statistically suspect wartime seasons, by William "Flash" Hollett of the Detroit Red Wings. He would win his second Norris Trophy, again be named to the league's first all-star team and finish the year with sixty-four points in sixty-seven games, also a new single-season record for a defencemen, breaking the mark held by Pierre Pilote. (Orr also piled up a career-high 133 penalty minutes that season, an accurate reflection of the more aggressive, edgier play that was his response to the injury woes and the suggestions of his own fragility the year before.) But the season belonged equally to Phil Esposito. With forty-nine goals and seventy-seven assists, he led the NHL in scoring, setting a record for points in a season, and then added eighteen points in ten play-off games, making a lie out of Chicago's rationale for trading him after a bad post-season with the Black Hawks. In addition to the Art Ross Trophy as the league's top scorer, Esposito won the Hart Trophy as its most valuable player. Orr was still the God of the Garden, but they needed to make room for another name on the marquee now. One fan's homemade sign became a fixture inside the arena: "Jesus Saves . . . And Esposito Puts in the Rebound."

There was one darker moment during what was otherwise a happy coming-of-age season for the team. It was in some sense the book-end to the brawl with Brian Conacher the year before, when Orr had been clipped – accidentally or otherwise – on the bridge of the nose by the Toronto Maple Leafs forward's stick, and then attacked him, with the other Bruins providing enthusiastic bench-clearing support. In Boston, the brawl had only reinforced the belief that these Bruins were a tough team who stuck together. In Toronto, though, the management of the Maple Leafs noted what had taken place, saw how their players were a little slow to come to the aid of one of their own and decided that something essential was lacking in their dressing room: the bravery and toughness and tribal cohesiveness that was the mark of the best, most successful hockey teams. Following their surprise Stanley Cup win in 1967, the Leafs were struggling, and the new realities of the NHL, brought about by expansion, had robbed them of what traditionally had been their biggest advantage, having first crack at the best players in and around English Canada's largest city. The team's owners, along with coach and general manager Punch Imlach, were eager to right the ship, but not entirely sure how.

Heading into the 1968–69 season, they decided that the Leafs' apparent lack of heart might in some part be corrected by offering a job to a big, mean, slow-footed defenceman named Pat Quinn, who otherwise seemed destined to spend his career kicking around in the minor leagues. Quinn had grown up in Hamilton, Ontario, and because of that, before the days of the amateur draft, was deemed the property of the Detroit Red Wings, who operated a junior team there. But when he came of age, he almost immediately ran afoul of Hamilton's mercurial coach, Eddie Bush. Quinn tried to escape by accepting a university scholarship to play in the United States, only to be told he was ineligible because he had already signed away his rights to a professional team. (Years later, he would complete his university degree and eventually finish law school.)*
Stymied, he moved on to the Edmonton Oil Kings and was part of

---

* Though he made his reputation as a big, tough defenceman from the streets of working-class east-end Hamilton, Ontario, Quinn was in many ways an atypical hockey player. He continued his education during the off-season, eventually earning a law degree – though he never practised. After his playing career ended in 1977 with the Atlanta Flames, Quinn moved into coaching and management with Philadelphia, Los Angeles, Vancouver and Toronto. He took both the Flyers and the Canucks to the Stanley Cup Finals before being fired by both teams. In 2002, Quinn guided Canada to the men's hockey gold medal at the Winter Olympics in Salt Lake City, the first for the country in fifty years. He was back at the Games in 2006 in Turin, but Canada failed to qualify for the medal round. That spring, Quinn was fired as coach of the Maple Leafs after Toronto failed to make the playoffs for the first time during his tenure there.

their Memorial Cup – winning team in 1963, breaking the leg of the Niagara Falls Flyers' Gary Dornhoefer during the final series. Quinn shuffled around in the low minors after graduating from junior hockey, a journeyman defenceman who wasn't going to crack the six-team league and wasn't a top-of-mind prospect for anyone even when the NHL doubled in size. Then the Maple Leafs unexpectedly came calling, acquiring his rights from the St. Louis Blues in a trade for the rights to veteran Dickie Moore. As Quinn remembered it years later, "They thought, Well, here's a young guy who could handle himself – and you know, tough guys help some other guys that in a lot of cases aren't that tough but gain some courage from having some protection around."[38]

Quinn's famous feud with Bobby Orr began during a late-season game between the Leafs and the Bruins. Orr followed a shot from the point that had been stopped by the Leafs goaltender, Bruce Gamble, and tried to knock the puck loose, piling into the crease and whacking Gamble on the back of his hand with his stick. Quinn saw that, and immediately reacted by doing what hockey players have been trained to do since the murky origins of the sport, coming instantly to his goalie's defence. He cross-checked Orr, flattened him and then stood over him, as if to let him know who had done the deed. Orr's temper flashed. He kicked at Quinn's stomach with his skate, and Quinn answered back in kind, kicking him in the butt. When Orr finally scrambled to his feet, he found Quinn more than ready to rumble, excited and pleased at this opportunity to showcase his pugilistic skills. If Bobby Orr wanted a fight, well, Quinn would be happy to accommodate him. May the better man win. Alas, the bout never got off the ground. By the time the two of them faced off, other players had piled in, and the linesmen intervened before they could start swinging. But Quinn took note – and no doubt Orr did too – understanding that the league was small enough that they would meet again.

The opportunity would present itself in the playoffs later in the spring of 1969. After finishing fourth, the Leafs were matched against the second-place Bruins, who ended the year just three points behind first-place Montreal. Imlach's team seemed determined from the outset of the series to employ what seemed a suicidal strategy, attempting to intimidate the nastiest team in the NHL right in their own building. (As a measure of the Bruins' chippiness, their 1,927 minutes in penalties during the 1968–69 season were nearly a thousand more than the total racked up by the next most penalized team, the Philadelphia Flyers. "We're not exactly the best team to play that kind of game against," coach Sinden dryly observed.) Needless to say, it didn't work out very well. The Bruins were in ascendance, the Leafs in decline, and in addition to beating Toronto in the alleys, Boston could outskill them at nearly every position. Late in the second period of the first game at the Boston Garden, the home team was already ahead 6–0 when Orr picked up the puck in his own zone and wound up for one of his now familiar end-to-end rushes. Quinn was lurking just outside the Boston blue line and saw what was coming. The Garden crowd had been on him from the opening faceoff, remembering the hit on Orr back in Toronto, hollering, "Get Quinn" every time he touched the puck. The opportunity now unfolding so perfectly in front of him, the chance to shut them up and settle an old score, was just too sweet. "I could see he wasn't watching. . . . He could skate, the greatest skater maybe in the game at that time, and he was really flying. He didn't have his head up. So I thought, Well, I have a chance to throw a check on him here, and stepped right into him, and he didn't see it coming. I caught him with my shoulder." It was a perfect collision, the unstoppable force meeting the immovable object right in front of the penalty box, with the object scoring a clear knockout. In Boston, they maintain to this day that it was a cheap shot, an intentional elbow to the head, though the video record is inconclusive. Orr dropped to the ice as if he'd been mortally wounded and lay motionless, unconscious. It took a second for that frightening scene to sink in at the Bruins bench and in the crowd: the franchise player down and out. The building was for a moment eerily silent. And then, all hell broke loose.

The referee, John Ashley, moved decisively, handing Quinn a five-minute major for elbowing, which Quinn naturally disputed. He took his place in the penalty box with Orr still lying dead-still on the ice. Eventually, they loaded him onto a stretcher. "But when they started to take him off, then the place got all restless and loud," Quinn remembered. "In those days, they only had one penalty box. You sat in there, and there was a big cop, a Boston cop, that would be sitting in there in case there was anything that happened. And so I end up sitting there, and suddenly I got whacked from behind by someone. I ducked to get out of the way, and I turn around and there is some guy trying to get at me over the glass, and now he's joined by a few others. So I stood on the bench, and I swung my stick a couple of times and the cop gets up and he has a hold of me. . . . We're standing on the bench, and on one of the swings I hit the glass and the glass popped and exploded. That cut the cop, so now I have a cop bleeding and the crowd surging back down again to get after me. I just dove out to the middle of the ice, and the place erupts. They just flooded garbage down. Some guy even threw a coin changer . . . and of course I checked it later on, and there were no coins in it."[39]

They brought down extra police to protect Quinn on the ice, and another contingent to get him safely to the dressing room between periods, with the crowd spitting and throwing whatever they could get their hands on and cursing and hollering for his blood. ("The fans here don't like anybody to touch Orr," an anonymous Boston cop told *The Globe and Mail*'s Lou Cauz. "He's their Frank Merriwell and Jack Armstrong rolled into one. To my thinking, it looked like a clean check.") Meanwhile, Orr was coming to in the Boston room and said that he wanted to play the third period, but the team's doctors held him back. As far as the folks inside the arena knew, their hero was still on death's doorstep, and so they continued to howl for vengeance. In the third period, Forbes Kennedy, a hard case from the Maritimes who was also hired to give the Leafs some grit, took it upon himself to defend his team's honour. He challenged the Bruins and the crowd and the officials and anyone else within earshot, he fought goalie Gerry Cheevers twice, fought Johnny McKenzie and landed a punch on a linesman, which finally got him thrown out of the game. Kennedy ran the disciplinary table during that brawl, drawing a historic combination of four minor penalties, two majors, a ten-minute misconduct, a game misconduct and a match penalty all at once. It turned out to be his swan song in the NHL.

It seemed almost beside the point that the Bruins won the game 10–0. Esposito scored four times and added a couple of assists, though that personal accomplishment was pretty much lost in the chaos. The Leafs dressing room was closed to the press afterwards. Imlach fled the arena without sharing his thoughts with reporters. The following night, the second game of the series, again in Boston, was a much tamer affair, though the Leafs villain still merited a police escort and the fans chanted "Kill Quinn" in unison even before play began. The Bruins won that one 7–0, humiliating the Leafs, then completed the sweep at Maple Leaf Gardens, winning two much closer games 4–3 and 3–2. Orr, back in the lineup once the series shifted to Toronto despite a persistent, pounding headache as the result of a concussion, had two assists in game three, helping the Bruins win on the Leafs' home ice for the first time since 1965. In game four, Orr was dominant, dictating the play with his rushes, at one point stepping in when Cheevers was caught out of position and blocking a George Armstrong shot that was destined for the back of the net.

He also heard a sound he had never heard before. Away from Boston, fans had been almost universally admiring of his skills. As Orr toured the other five original NHL cities and then branched out to the new hockey hinterlands following expansion, the best young player in the game was naturally a ticket-selling draw. They rooted for the home team, but they also appreciated his brilliance, just as a later generation would turn out to marvel at Wayne Gretzky wherever he came to play. That had been at least equally the case in Toronto, where Orr's Parry Sound and Oshawa roots made him nearly a hometown boy. Now, though, and forever after, until his final visit as an NHL player, boos cascaded down in Maple Leaf Gardens every time he touched the puck. It was a bit perplexing – hadn't he been the one who was cold-cocked by Quinn? – and perhaps in the beginning it was more of a reaction to the bloodlust of the Boston fans than to Orr personally. But long after the Quinn hit had faded in memory, never mind Orr's earlier attack on Brian Conacher, they were still doing it, and the boos had taken on a tint of bitterness, of envy. The Leafs' glory days were long gone, while the Bruins were the class of the league. And Orr, who grew up cheering for Toronto as a boy, who might have played there had the Maple Leafs scouting department been on the ball, was made to pay for all of that, pay for his brilliance and his team's success, pay for the Leafs' own failings.

Quinn and Orr shook hands as part of the traditional hockey ritual at the conclusion of a playoff series, though not with much conviction. They would never really be bosom buddies after that. Imlach, too, took time to congratulate the victorious Boston players, greeting them as they walked off the ice, wishing them the best in the Eastern Finals, where they'd play the Montreal Canadiens. Moments later, while reporters were still working the dressing rooms, Imlach was fired by Stafford Smythe, an impulsive, emotional act that signalled the end of an era.

So often in professional sports, teams with no history of winning can make an enormous leap forward in the course of a season but then suddenly realize where they are, suddenly become conscious of their surroundings and stumble, especially when faced with more seasoned opposition. Sometimes that's it, a flash in the pan, a one-year wonder. They come apart before ever reaching those heights again. And sometimes it's an essential learning experience that hardens and builds character and imparts a critical lesson. Heading into their series against the Canadiens (which, in the early, post-expansion years, was the de facto Stanley Cup final), the young Bruins had a bit of a swagger. They were very good, they were very tough, and they had competed successfully all year long against the best of the NHL. They had destroyed the storied Maple Leafs in four games, beaten them every way imaginable, and so the Habs, though they were the defending champions, presented no great psychological obstacle. The Bruins arrived at the Forum confident enough and naive enough to believe they couldn't be beaten, and they were very nearly right. In the first two games at the Forum, they held a one-goal lead with less than two minutes to play in the third period, only to be edged out both nights in overtime, 3–2 and 4–3. When the series returned to Boston, they rallied to win games three and four, by 5–0 and 3–2 scores. They then lost the pivotal game five in Montreal. Facing elimination on the comfortable home ice of the Boston Garden, the Bruins fought tenaciously, extending the Habs into double overtime, before finally going down 2–1 on the only overtime goal of Jean Béliveau's magnificent career. It was a devastating way to lose, so close to glory – Montreal went on to easily sweep the St. Louis Blues for the second year in the row and claim the Stanley Cup.

The team reacted to that loss not by imploding but by becoming wiser, more seasoned and better. By the time the Bruins arrived in training camp in the fall of 1969, they were a more mature, experienced bunch with growing talent still to be tapped. For a change, Orr had been able to relax and enjoy the summer without having to endure the cycle of surgery and rehabilitation that had ruined the 1968 off-season. It had been more than a year since the last operation on his knee, and the optimism surrounding his health extended to a general optimism regarding the Bruins' chances. In hindsight, the steady development of the club since Orr had arrived on the scene is obvious. Though the franchise had taken a small step backwards in his rookie season, falling to last place again, each subsequent year it had shown improvement, first making the playoffs, then winning a playoff series and coming within a couple of goals of winning it all. The only disheartening news came during the pre-season, when Ted Green became involved in a savage stick-swinging brawl with Wayne Maki of the St. Louis Blues during a game played in Ottawa. Maki flattened Green from behind. Green slashed Maki. Maki speared Green. They slashed each other. Then Maki hit Green over the head with his stick, fracturing his skull. It is remembered as one of the ugliest moments in the history of the NHL. (Both players were charged with criminal assault but acquitted.) Green certainly paid the price for his involvement. It seemed for a short, frightening time that his life might be in danger, and in the end he would miss a full year of hockey. He was lost to the Bruins for the entire 1969–70 season, their second-best defenceman gone, but the truth is they would hardly seem to miss him.

Great teams, no matter what the sport, all have a look. The individual parts, the individual players fit together with the logic of a jigsaw puzzle. Really, though, it's always as much a matter of luck and chance as it is of grand design. The recipe for a sports championship involves not just the best talent but the best talent in the right combination, at the right stage of development, with the right coach and the right management. One devastating injury, one destructive, divisive move by ownership, and it could all come apart. But looking back at the 1969–70 Boston Bruins, we can see that every element was in perfect balance. And the chemistry of the team, now long past the period of adjustment that followed the arrival of Esposito, Hodge and Stanfield, was harmonious as well. The players didn't all love each other all of the time, but the important part was that everyone understood each other's value, knowing that the skills of the guy at the next locker made them all better. So maybe Espo wasn't exactly Orr's cup of tea – but who was a better finisher, who was more likely to anticipate one of his perfect passes and put it in the back of the net? And if Orr wasn't Esposito's soulmate, Espo understood well that so many of those goals he was scoring wouldn't have happened without the flawless playmaker behind him. Harry Sinden was secure enough in his own abilities and knowledge, and still close enough to his own playing days, that he was willing to let the boys be boys, to refrain from imposing his will just to prove who was boss. Gerry Cheevers and Eddie Johnston split the duties in goal, and both were reliable, occasionally spectacular, which was plenty for a team with so much offensive firepower. On defence, Dallas Smith and Rick Smith and Gary Doak and Don Awrey were steady, stay-at-home types, though Dallas Smith could carry the puck a bit when called upon. They made precious few mistakes and knew enough to compensate when Orr took flight. Up front, there was the veteran presence of

Johnny Bucyk, who had lived through some of the worst years of the franchise, and perhaps because of that seemed imperturbable. There was Wayne Cashman, who was a little bit mean, a little bit dirty, but could also play the game. Fred Stanfield just seemed so smooth, and Ken Hodge had the perfect combination of power and strength and a deft scoring touch. Johnny McKenzie was always in the middle of the action. He could skate, and his shot was as accurate as any on the team. Derek Sanderson provided plenty of excitement and, though he had considerable offensive skills, had transformed himself into a defensive master, winning faceoffs and working to neutralize the other team's top line. Esposito was like no one else in hockey. He was strong, willing to stand in the slot and take a beating. He had a fine, accurate shot. And his knack for scoring goals, for being in the right place at the right time, ready to scoop up a rebound or to place himself on the end of a teammate's pass, was impeccable. A lot of his goals weren't pretty, but they counted all the same.

Orr was the key to the enterprise, the maestro in full command of his powers, his game complete. In the defensive zone, he would occasionally be caught out of position, but only because he had taken the kind of chances any coach would encourage. Watching those games, we see how often he seems to be leading a Boston rush, circling around the opposition goal, and then, even if the action shifts suddenly, is back in his own zone in time to make the crucial defensive play. He dropped to block shots, he could poke or sweep check, he could take the body when necessary, he was all but impossible to beat one-on-one, and he could handle himself with his fists. If his goaltender wandered, Orr would sometimes find himself standing deep in the crease, fearlessly throwing himself in front of shots. For any opposing team on the attack, there was the ever-present knowledge that one mistake, one turnover, and Orr would instantly be in transition, headed the other way, anticipating a quick pass, in high gear, leading the rush. His slapshot is rarely mentioned as being in the same league as Bobby Hull's. But if not quite as hard, it was more accurate, and because of his remarkably quick release, goaltenders found it at least as difficult to stop.

But it is those great, graceful flights down the ice that mark Orr as different from any other defenceman, any other player, in the long history of hockey. Taking the puck behind his own net, he seems utterly relaxed, surveying the ice in front of him, assessing the obstacles in his path, in no particular hurry. The opposing players long ago learned that there was no point in pressuring him, no point in aggressively pursuing on the forecheck, because Orr would just skate by or around, leaving them out of the play and looking foolish. Passing his own blue line, he cuts back and forth across the ice, as graceful as a figure skater, accelerating, flying now, but it seems effortless. Orr sees resistance coming, he anticipates, he appears to be thinking three moves ahead of everyone else on the ice. The moment of decision comes as he crosses the opposition's blue line. He tests the defence like a great basketball point guard, probing, pushing, looking for a lane, a crease, or looking to lure the defenders into a trap. Sometimes, arriving at that crossroads, he'll give the puck up, finding a perfect angle, finding a teammate breaking free on the wing and leading him to the net. Sometimes he'll take it himself, straight to the net, to deke and shoot. Sometimes he'll pull up short and fire a slapshot. It comes off his stick nearly as quickly as a wrist shot, so there's little time for the goaltender to react. Sometimes, at his most beautiful, his most balletic, he'll swing wide on a graceful arc and carry the puck all the way behind the net, and from there dish it out, or sweep around to the far side and shoot.

Orr did his best to explain how the game looked to him when he spoke to the *Sports Illustrated* writer Mark Mulvoy, who taped his thoughts and transformed them into the authorized biography *Bobby Orr: My Game,* published in 1973:

Hockey simply is a game of instinct and mistakes. When I am on the ice, I look for openings. That is what the game is all about. I see an opening on the ice – maybe one of my teammates has skated into the clear or maybe I know I can beat a particular defensemen because he has turned the wrong way, things like that – and I instantly react to it. Maybe I react to openings quicker than other players, I don't know for sure. When I see something that looks open to me I go, See you later! Believe me, nothing I do on the ice is the result of any grand master plan. I never stand behind my net with the puck and decide that I'm going to skate down the right wing, cut through center at the red line, stop at the far blue line, and fire a slapshot two inches off the ice and one inch inside the near post. I simply stand behind my net and head wherever my instinct tells me to go. . . . I know that may sound pretty farfetched, but it's true. Many times after a game I sit in the dressing room and ask myself why I did certain things that night on the ice. As a rule, I cannot even answer my own questions.[40]

But that's how it always is for the great improvisers, for those who create in a moment of inspiration. Every one of Orr's rushes is a little bit different. Every one is a virtuoso performance. Every one is familiar but unique, like Charlie Parker running a standard chord progression and then turning expectations on their head, or Jimi Hendrix doing with an electric guitar what no one had imagined before, and no one could duplicate afterwards. It is Muhammad Ali's jab, Michael Jordan's takeoff, Willie Mays running down a fly ball. It is the place where sport and art converge.

Chapter Eleven

STAR POWER

MARCH 15, 1970. THE BOSTON GARDEN.
BOSTON BRUINS 2, DETROIT RED WINGS 2.
OPENING MOMENTS OF THE SECOND PERIOD.

H E CARRIES THE PUCK BEHIND HIS OWN NET, angling from right to left, digging in hard on his edges to make the turn. Eddie Johnston in the Boston goal glances back for just an instant, then turns his head to face forward again, his gaze scanning the ice in front of him like a radar beacon, one side, then the other. Johnston must be reassured. He has learned over the past few seasons that if Bobby Orr has the puck, he has precious little to fear. The Bruins are down a man, with Rick Smith still in the box serving out the final seconds of a penalty he picked up late in the first period. The Wings will naturally take their chances here, in a tie game on the road, late in the season, right in the thick of a tight five-way race for the four playoff spots in the National Hockey League's Eastern Division – only the suddenly downtrodden Toronto Maple Leafs are out of contention in what amounts to the old Original Six. Detroit will throw just about everything and everyone into the power play, while Boston tries to break the pressure and clear the zone.

As Orr cuts hard behind the goal line he is pursued by Frank Mahovlich. The Big M arrived in Detroit almost exactly two years before, as part of a memorable trade. The Wings sent a complete line to Toronto – Norm Ullman, Floyd Smith and Paul Henderson – for Mahovlich, ironman Garry Unger, Peter Stemkowski and the rights to Carl Brewer. Mahovlich had graduated from the St. Michael's College junior program in Toronto, where the Leafs hot-housed their best junior prospects under the watchful eyes of the Basilian fathers. He was hailed as the next big star for English Canada's favourite team and lived up to those expectations early by beating out Bobby Hull as the NHL's rookie of the year in 1957–58. During the 1960–61 season, Mahovlich scored forty-eight goals for the blue and white. But he stalled there, just two short of Rocket Richard's magic fifty, and some figured the pressure must have done him in, that he choked, which for an athlete is the greatest slight of all.

It was a glorious time to be around Maple Leaf Gardens. Mahovlich had his name engraved on the Stanley Cup four times with Toronto, but he was also one of those big men who on the ice seemed to be forever taking it easy, coasting along, lazy, when in fact it's just a trick of perspective. Big men always looked a little slow, a little lethargic, just as Mario Lemieux would, or Eric Lindros, just as, by contrast, all of those little guys with pinwheel legs seemed to be forever working their hearts out. The Toronto fans got on Mahovlich, booing because he looked uninterested, because he hadn't become quite the superstar they desired, because in those days they were spoiled by success. The story was that they even took time out of their celebration to boo him off the ice the night the Leafs won the Cup at home in 1963. Mahovlich was a sensitive soul, and Punch Imlach, the Leafs coach and general manager, had decided that picking on him, chipping away at his fragile confidence, was the key to his motivation. Punch was dead wrong about that, just as he was dead wrong about a lot of things. Mahovlich left the team in 1964 to be treated for depression, then again in 1967, when he suffered a nervous breakdown.

During Mahovlich's last season in Toronto, the Leafs held their annual open practice around Christmastime at Maple Leaf Gardens, a rare opportunity for those who couldn't afford the exorbitant price of admission to a real game to see their heroes up close for a token price. The climax of the event was always a penalty shot contest, and Mahovlich, whom the kids all loved, wound up scoring the winner after several of his teammates mysteriously shot wide or into the goalie's pads. Only later, after Imlach shipped Mahovlich off to the Wings, did the story come out that the other Leafs had conspired to let him win that afternoon, that they figured it would be good for him. How pathetic that seemed – at least it did until Mahovlich rediscovered his game in Detroit.

On this night in Boston, he has already scored his thirty-first goal of the season, and he'll have his thirty-second by the time the game is over, on his way to thirty-eight for the season – not a bad follow-up to the forty-nine he potted the year before. Nevertheless, halfway through the following season he'll be traded to Montreal, where Sam Pollock is in the process of transforming a team that missed the playoffs in 1970 into the Stanley Cup champions of 1971. Mahovlich will score twenty-seven points in twenty playoff games for the Habs that spring, and follow with twenty-three points in seventeen playoff games when they win the Cup again in 1973. He will play for Team Canada against the Russians in '72, alongside his brother, Pete. In 1981, in retirement, he'll be named an honoured member of the Hockey Hall of Fame, and after that he will be appointed to Canada's Senate. Old Punch was fired not long after the Mahovlich trade, and his Leafs haven't won a Stanley Cup since.

With Mahovlich nipping at his heels, forechecking, applying considerable heat, Orr falters for just an instant. The puck slips off his stick in front of him, far enough removed that it's no longer fully in his control. Out of the corner of his eye, he sees a second Detroit forward bearing down on him, a flash of red and white charging toward the corner. Gordie Howe looks like someone's dad, with his dark hair now receding in a widow's peak. He has been in the league since 1946, and the height of his powers, most agree, came back in the mid-1950s, when a series of powerful Detroit teams were duelling with the Canadiens every season for the Stanley Cup. In any discussion of the greatest hockey player of all time, Howe's name tops most everyone's list. He is now said to be in decline. So feeble that during the 1968–69 season he put up the best numbers of his career, finishing with 103 points, becoming only the third player in league history to reach the century mark. (Phil Esposito and Bobby Hull were the other two, and all three of them did it that same year, their stats obviously inflated by the diluted talent pool in the first post-expansion seasons.) So ancient that, though it will be only one more season before he enters his first, short-lived, "retirement," it will in fact be another decade before Howe plays his final NHL game.

Orr understands that he has to make a decision right away, that if Howe arrives while he's still within spitting distance of the puck, he'll be slammed into the end boards and taken out of the play, probably handing Detroit a scoring chance. (Given that it's Gordie, given that he still has that notorious mean streak, Orr might also wind up with one of those famous elbows planted in his chops, just for good measure.) Orr bends low, reaching forward, lets go of his stick with his left hand, and with his right chips the puck just out of Howe's reach. His teammate Derek Sanderson waits for it along the side boards.

In many ways, Sanderson's early career has been similar to Orr's. He excelled in junior hockey, leading all scorers during his final season with the Niagara Falls Flyers in the OHL, and then adapted to the NHL with hardly a pause. He was named the rookie of the year in 1968, one season after Orr captured the Calder Trophy. But the two players reacted very differently to the big-league spotlight. Where Orr was a bit hesitant, a bit unsure at first and maintained a self-effacing public image, Sanderson took to fame and fortune as though he'd always expected it, as though he absolutely belonged front and centre. He is extremely handsome, and like the great soccer player George Best (who once said that had Pele been born ugly, no one would have remembered him) he loves women, loves the nightlife, loves being thought of as Boston's most eligible bachelor — and it costs him. Sanderson dresses in a flamboyantly stylish way, on the cutting edge of the times, and during the 1970–71 season becomes the first NHL player to sport a moustache since Garth Boesch wore one while playing for the Leafs back in the 1940s. By the time the Bruins win their second Stanley Cup of modern times in 1972, Sanderson has played a bit part in a long-forgotten movie, had his own weekly television talk show in Boston and has invested in a couple of bars – not a great match, it turns out, for his addictive personality.

They started to call "Turk" the Joe Namath of hockey. He was a guest of Merv Griffin's, on *60 Minutes,* and hit the pinnacle with an appearance on Johnny Carson's *Tonight Show.* There were more movie roles, a couple of ghost-written books designed to exploit his swinging image. *Cosmopolitan* voted him one of the ten sexiest men in America. In 1973, when the birth of the rival World Hockey Association finally gave hockey players some leverage with their NHL teams, Sanderson was one of the first to jump at the opportunity, signing a $2.65 million contract with the Philadelphia Blazers – making him not just the world's highest-paid hockey player but the highest-paid athlete of any kind on the planet.

And that was the beginning of the end, really. Sanderson played just eight games for the Blazers before an injury ended his first and only WHA season. Eventually, the boozing that was always part of the hockey life combined with cocaine and Quaaludes. Sanderson would quit and then come back, go on the wagon and tumble off. He never became the player he might have been. The Pittsburgh Penguins were the last team to give up on him. Out of hockey, out of mind, he was broke and wound up living on the streets. Sanderson pulled himself out of that death spiral finally and, through willpower and a little help from his friends, managed to make a new life for himself. The same guy who had pissed away millions of his own dollars wound up managing the investments of others, including a number of professional athletes. Of those Sanderson credited with helping to haul him out of the abyss, with moral support, with money, with tough love, the first mentioned was Bobby Orr.

Orr deftly avoids the onrushing Howe with two graceful steps as precise as a dancer's. Howe lets him go, his focus shifts and he continues after the puck, turning his attention to Sanderson. In that instant, as a second ticks off, perhaps two, on the Garden's clock, Bobby Orr makes a choice that is absolutely emblematic of his genius, his daring, his originality. It goes against what generations of defencemen have been taught to do. It would be, for anyone else, reckless.

Knowing that his team is still killing a penalty, that they are at a disadvantage, that the Red Wings are throwing all of their manpower forward to score on the power play, he goes on the attack himself while his team is short-handed. In two strides, he shifts direction, turning his shoulders square, facing down the ice at the Detroit goal. He begins to accelerate, assuming that Sanderson will spot him, that he'll work the old give and go, that he has played with Orr long enough to expect the unexpected. (Two months later, they'll use the same kind of unspoken communication during the fourth game of the Stanley Cup finals against the St. Louis Blues. The play will finish with Orr flying through the air, parallel to the ice, his arms raised in celebration, the aftermath of that championship-winning goal one of the most famous images in the history of North American professional sport.) Sanderson controls the puck and, with Howe having turned to fix him in his sights, flips a pass to his teammate, who takes it in stride just inside the Boston blue line.

Then Orr turns it on, in five powerful strides reaching the centre-ice red line at full throttle. From the time he was a boy, playing hockey in Parry Sound, those who shared the ice with him all said the same thing. You couldn't really tell how fast he was moving. You couldn't see the extra exertion. There were no little chopping steps, no apparent increase in effort. You'd do the normal calculations and get ready to check him, figuring that the two of you would meet at one moment and one place on the ice, only to arrive at the appointed destination and find that time and space had played tricks on you, that Orr was already gone.

Most of the Red Wings are hopelessly stuck back in the Boston end, still in power-play mode. But Mahovlich gamely gives chase. He is skating as hard as he can, leaning forward to at least try to get a stick on Orr and slow him down. But he never gets closer than

Orr's wake and eventually falls out of the play. Bobby is already fixed on his next challenge, his next obstacle. Detroit's two defence-men have retreated quickly from their position on the point and are skating backwards now, Gary Bergman to Orr's left, Ron Harris to his right. Bergman sees a Boston winger hoping to join the rush, hoping to pick up one of Orr's perfectly timed passes, or to scoop up a rebound, or just to get a good seat for what's to come. It is Bergman's responsibility to make sure none of that happens, which leaves Harris alone, one-on-one. He is an NHL journeyman, a guy who will manage to last nearly nine full seasons in the league over several stops, but who plays the best hockey of his career for Detroit. Harris is trained to defend the centre of the ice, to prevent the shooter from finding open space in the slot, in front of the net. So he hopes to steer Orr wide, to use his momentum against him. Let Bobby try to beat him to the outside and then push him into the corner, pin him there, don't let him shoot or drop a pass. There's no way there should be enough room for him to get by and swing around in front of the net, and there's no way he's getting through Harris. Since those first days of kid hockey, since they first told you that you were going be a defenceman, since you first learned to skate backwards, this *mano-a-mano* challenge has been a fundamental, a play repeated again and again in practice, part of every game. Harris couldn't count the number of times he'd eased a rushing forward out of harm's way. It was a bonus if he got to punish him with a bodycheck, to achieve that satisfying thunk as he was stopped dead, pinned between shoulder and board.

Orr looks up, measuring the opposition, reassessing the situation. Again, there's no change in his stride, but it's obvious he's flying simply because there are no other Red Wings in the vicinity. He takes his left hand off his stick, keeping the puck to his right, out of Harris's reach, in case the defenceman tries to poke it free. Orr's tremendous, deceptive strength is an asset here. Back in Parry Sound, he used to lift weights at the house on Great North Road, but he never bulked up in any obvious way. Instead, he achieved long, natural muscle, powerful through the shoulders and forearms, the hips and thighs. A hockey body, the kind that guys used to build working out on the farm. Orr uses his free left hand to control Harris, to fend him off and create some leverage. When he dips his left shoulder low, his intentions become obvious. He is heading for the goal, though there still doesn't seem to be the time and space necessary for him to swoop wide, then cut left toward the crease. But then you realize he is indeed moving fast enough to find that angle, as though Harris were no more an obstacle than a pylon during a skating drill. Orr's blades are now running on nearly the same straight line. He looks like a figure skater, trying to cut a perfect "eight." Once his left shoulder is past Harris, and he begins to make the turn, there's a clear path to the goal, where Roy Edwards stands alone.

Edwards is enjoying his first steady NHL employment, splitting the Wings goaltending duties with Roger Crozier after spending nearly ten full seasons in the minors in seven different leagues — beginning with Wren Blair's Whitby Dunlops, where he played alongside Harry Sinden, with stops in Fort Wayne, Buffalo, Calgary, Sault Ste. Marie, Portland, Pittsburgh, Spokane, St. Louis and Fort Worth since then. Finally, expansion opened things up, opened doors for guys like him, when the twelve available big-league goaltending jobs on the planet doubled to twenty-four. The NHL's great gamble changed life for a whole host of players who otherwise might have spent their lives in the minors, never earning a big-league paycheque, never appearing on *Hockey Night in Canada,* never gaining the state of perpetual celebrity grace that goes with being an NHL player in the country that, in those days, produced just about all of them.

The moment Orr cuts past Harris with one stride and starts to slice across the front of the net, Edwards is doomed, and he knows it. He tries to go with Orr, to slide from his left to his right, following the motion, but he can't keep up, can't cover all of that empty net behind him. The goalie falls to his right, making a feeble swipe with the catcher on his right hand. But the puck is already by him then. Orr could have placed it there. He could have stick-handled it over the goal line. He doesn't really even have to shoot. Just slide it softly, gently into the far corner.

From beginning to end, the play takes perhaps ten seconds.

Orr raises his hands in celebration. The crowd stands and cheers for five full minutes following the announcement that the goal represents his hundredth point of the season. No other defenceman has ever come near that mark. Before Orr, it was unimaginable that any ever would. Orr indulges in his usual head-down non-celebration, the very picture of athletic modesty, then skates toward the Boston bench. Ken Hodge gives him a hug, pats him on the butt. Orr stands at the boards, waiting for the applause to subside and the game to resume. It won't, it doesn't. Even the referee seems determined to let the moment continue. And then Orr finally gives the Boston fans what Ted Williams had always denied them, no matter how much adoration they showered on the Splendid Splinter. He takes a couple of steps and waves with his left hand, a short curtain call acknowledging their affection. It's love now. It's full-blown crazy love.

For someone too young to remember, or who didn't grow up in this country, how to explain *Front Page Challenge,* the longest-running show in Canadian television history? It was a game show, but that doesn't really do it justice, since there were no prizes involved, since the contestants worked collectively and not against each other. There were several hosts over the thirty-eight seasons the show was on the air, but the best remembered, and the one this night, is Fred Davis, with his hair jet black and oiled in place, a guy who had begun his showbiz career as a big band trumpet player. Likewise, the panel of celebrity contestants changed over time, but all three of the best-remembered stalwarts are here. Betty Kennedy, a well known Toronto radio personality, is sort of like the perfectly coiffed Kitty Carlisle without the high society airs. Pierre Berton, a journalist and most notably a writer of wildly popular Canadian historical non-fiction, always wears a bow tie along with a collection of exceptionally loud sports jackets. Then there is Gordon Sinclair, long ago a foreign correspondent and adventurer, now a talk radio curmudgeon, famous for addressing the three subjects any good Canadian would be loath to raise in polite company: money, sex and religion. The mystery guest, a newsmaker of some sort, is seated out of sight of the panel but in plain view of the audience, which becomes sort of a co-conspirator. The panelists take turns asking questions, trying to guess the guest's identity (the more famous work to disguise their voices), either succeeding in their quest for the truth or finally running out of time. No one is really keeping score. The game itself is followed by a short chat segment. It's all very civilized, very restrained, very, very of the place and time, so unlike anything you would see on television today, and so beloved in its time. Perhaps you had to be there.

To be called upon to appear as a mystery guest was undeniably a kind of high national honour, since everybody – or at least everybody's parents – watched the show. That spot was reserved for true celebrity, and in the case of athletes only for those who had done something completely extraordinary in the Canadian context. Something like a defenceman scoring an outrageous hundred points over the course of a National Hockey League season.

The live band plays a little bit of insipid jazzy background music. The live audience buzzes, seeing Orr appear behind the panel. The set is bathed in sixties television colours, garish, slightly washed out reds and yellows and aqua blues, the way *The Ed Sullivan Show* looked once you finally had a colour television on which to watch it.

"Are you a player now?" Sinclair asks the mystery guest, homing in on the story.

"Yes." No need to disguise the voice. The accent is indistinct small-town Canadian.

"Are you on one of the Original Six teams?"

"Yes."

"Are you Bobby Hull of the Chicago Black Hawks?"

"No."

Betty Kennedy jumps in.

"Are you Bobby Orr?"

"Yes."

A bell sounds like the one at an old-fashioned hotel front desk. The mystery is solved. The audience applauds.

The startling part is to see the nervous boy from Parry Sound, the same kid who could hardly make eye contact with Ward Cornell during that first *Hockey Night in Canada* intermission, now transformed. He's still a little jittery as the interview portion of the show begins, blinking, licking his lips. He has let his hair grow longer, though it doesn't yet creep over his ears. It's neat and tidy and perfectly shaped, with the bangs sweeping across his forehead, like the photo on the Dry Look hairspray can, just slightly more rebellious than the old brush cut, but just about everybody is at least inching in that direction. Orr has by now learned how to deal with these slightly uncomfortable situations under the spotlight, how to play a character named Bobby Orr, who can disarm an interviewer with a shy smile, who can josh around and use his own magnetism, his own star power, to his advantage. They feel special being in his presence, not the other way around, and still he gives little of himself away, offers up almost nothing real. This is Aw-Shucks Bobby, and decades later he'll still be around, appearing in wordless television commercials, sending a message with a wink and a smile and a shrug. He can slap you on the back and tell you a little joke and make you feel like one of the boys in the dressing room – or at least like one of the boys if they were full of clean thoughts and pure motives and minus any rough, boozy, aggressive, angry edges. He can be a mother's favourite son or a dad's pal kibitzing over a few beers or a teen idol–style non-threatening boyfriend (maybe a little threatening, maybe behind closed doors, maybe . . . well, that's someone else's fantasy), a great guy, which in the Canadian small-town hockey parlance is the highest compliment there is. That Bobby Orr, he seems like a great guy, and if you told him that he'd look at his feet for a second and blush and smile and shake his head in an aw-shucks way and look a little embarrassed at the compliment, the same way he looks when he scores a goal. Orr learned to turn up those aspects of himself, and it protected him, it enriched him, it gave him a comfortable public face, and it meant that whatever he didn't want to reveal, whatever he didn't want to talk about, whatever fears or insecurities lingered within him, no one would ever know.

"Now, Bobby Orr, I'm told you're the highest-paid twenty-two-year-old Canadian in the history of this country. Is this true?" That's Sinclair, of course. Right to the point.

"Well, I'm very happy with what I make." Then the look down, the disarming smile. "Before I came on this show they told me you'd ask this question." Everybody chuckles. They probably did tell him – or at least Al told him – and he turns what then was the height of rudeness, what today seems like a very gentle inquisition, on its head.

"I sure will ask that question." Sinclair doesn't let it drop, though, as so many others would. He is old enough and curmudgeonly enough to be beyond embarrassment. "As a matter of fact, Eagleson and you are going to sit down with the Boston team pretty soon and talk money for next year. And the story around the sports fields is a hundred grand a year. Is that reasonable?" A hundred grand. A number to make the audience at home shake their heads in wonder, and perhaps in disgust, at how out of balance the world has become. A hockey player making $100,000 a year. But who's going to begrudge this great kid, this great player, even those unimaginable riches?

"Well, I still have one more year to go on my contract."

"And how much is it for?"

"The contract I'm under right now? Well, I, uh, I'm very happy with my contract."

The audience laughs and applauds. Orr's stonewalling, repeating the same line again – the line Eagleson must have fed him – is utterly charming because of the humble delivery. "I don't like to discuss money or anything like that."

Sinclair is finally defeated. A warm, grandfatherly smile flashes across his face. The old crank is melting.

"Oh no. Isn't that a great thing. The guy doesn't like to discuss it. Look, when I was twenty-two years old I got nineteen bucks a week and no more. Betty, you're on."

That's supposed to be the last word, of course, the "I walked five miles to school in my bare feet" lament of the oldster, and a good boy like Bobby Orr would never talk back to his elders. But before Betty Kennedy can weigh in, Orr leans into the mike and delivers his own punchline.

"And I made $10 a week the four years I played in Oshawa."

Touché. The whole room breaks up. Bobby smiles. Even Old Sinc has met his match.

That's the Bobby Orr who will linger in memory, who will never seem to age, who will never become more complicated or problematic, who will never break anyone's heart by being revealed as less than they imagined him to be.

Chapter Twelve

THE BOBBY BUSINESS

T HE MONEY STUFF, MAYBE IT WAS none of Gordon Sinclair's concern. But that didn't mean the rest of the world wouldn't be hearing plenty about the rosy financial health of Robert Gordon Orr, as managed, protected, directed and enhanced by his friend, attorney, agent and adviser, R. Alan Eagleson.

Until Orr's arrival as the highest-paid rookie in the history of hockey, the subject of personal finances had been all but off limits in the sport. There was the polite, reserved, inherently conservative Canadian explanation for the tendency toward discretion, since of course nearly the entire playing population of the National Hockey League had its origins there. The players were more often than not sheltered small-town or farm boys whose first experience of the larger planet would come through hockey road trips. They understood from their parents what to think of as their business, what might be considered the business of others and how those two would only rarely intersect. They wouldn't have dared to tell anyone what their fathers made, if indeed they knew, and their own salaries were equally a guarded secret, even from a roommate or the guy sitting at the next locker in the dressing room.

What a boon for the NHL owners, who understood exactly how they benefited from the "don't ask, don't tell" tendencies when it came to pay. It wasn't as if the players enjoyed real leverage, since before the institution of the amateur draft, they signed their rights away as young teenagers, and even after expansion, after the draft was established, there was no realistic alternative that would allow them to ply their trade outside the NHL universe. But just so that no player became too emboldened and decided to hold out when a new contract wasn't to his liking, just so they didn't pick up any more delusions of the kind they harboured during the 1950s, when Ted Lindsay and his pals thought they might try to start a union, it was best to keep salary a closely guarded secret between the player and his trusted employer, the general manager. That the players went along like sheep, that for decades they didn't understand either their true market value or even what their own teammates were making, was as much a factor in their exploitation (and in the entire labour history of hockey) as were the misdeeds of any greedy, evil owner.

With Orr, Eagleson had found not just his entree into the hockey business, not just his first real client, but also a way of spreading a larger message, one that would eventually help make him the most powerful man in the history of the sport. When the precedent-setting rookie deal with the Bruins was signed, Eagleson made sure that the information went public, though not the absolute, specific amount Orr would be paid, since he'd promised Hap Emms and Weston Adams that those numbers would never be divulged. No harm, though, in letting the boys in the press box (no girls in those days) speculate a bit, especially since they were just as likely to shoot high as to shoot low. How much was that original contract worth, Al? Well, he certainly couldn't say, because he and Hap and Mr. Adams had a gentlemen's agreement, but if you guessed that it was worth closer to $100,000 than $50,000 over two years, let's just say you wouldn't be too far wrong.

At the same time, the culture of the sports pages was changing. Writers who in the past would have shied away from financial matters, believing that their role was to cover the game and only the game, to remain within the bounds of the commercial fantasy of professional sports, were beginning to take a larger interest in what transpired in the boardrooms. For those determined to take a more independent journalistic approach to their job, someone like Eagleson was a godsend, providing plenty of fodder and inside information, and real numbers, even if some of them weren't quite as real as they at first seemed.

Orr was in the first weeks of his rookie season when Eagleson's attentions turned to the nascent National Hockey League Players' Association. His reputation as a player-friendly, no-nonsense renegade had been made with the Orr contract, and again in December 1966, when he represented the poor beleaguered inmates of the Springfield Indians of the American Hockey League against their dictatorial boss, Eddie Shore. (Among other things, Shore had his players making popcorn, blowing up balloons and sweeping out the arena when they weren't playing hockey, and even forced some of them to sharpen their skills through tap dancing.) Sympathetic press coverage was a big part of that story as well. Eagleson's heroics in Springfield were given blanket coverage: Bob Pennington of the Toronto *Telegram* spent a week in the town covering the story, and even *The New York Times* dispatched a reporter to see what was going on.

The movement to organize NHL players was driven by grassroots discontent with the system and mirrored stirrings of rebellion in other professional sports. But the hockey players desperately needed leadership from outside their own ranks. No individual player, no group of players, was going to front for a hockey union. They were undereducated, they didn't have the expertise, and many were loath to risk their careers. What they saw in Eagleson, why they trusted him with their collective interests, was obvious then and remains so in hindsight. He was smart, he was innovative, he was on the cutting edge, he was brazen, he was unafraid of the sport's powers, and he got results. The history of the attempts to organize hockey players up to that point reads like a sad cautionary tale. Way back in 1910, before there was a National Hockey League,

Art Ross (after whom the trophy for the league's top scorer is named) was the first to lobby for basic workers' rights. He failed miserably and was scorned by the hockey public for his efforts. The fans thought he was uppity. In 1925, the Hamilton Tigers went on strike in the hopes of being paid extra for the playoffs. They missed out on a chance to win the Stanley Cup as a result, and the team was moved to New York the next season. A group of NHL players tried to win pension benefits in 1947, only to wind up with a plan in which they, and not the owners, made all of the contributions. Most notoriously, there was the 1957 drive led by Lindsay and Doug Harvey, which the owners managed to undermine by stirring doubt and dissent within the players' ranks. (Then, for good measure, they did their best to ruin Lindsay's career.)*

By 1966, though, there were larger forces at work. The baseball players' association was taking shape under Marvin Miller, and the Teamsters, under the leadership of Jimmy Hoffa, were threatening to organize the National Football League. Eagleson, who by then had player clients on all six teams, was seen as someone

---

* "Terrible" Ted Lindsay made his debut with the Detroit Red Wings in the 1944–45 season. His father, Bert, had been a goaltender for the Renfrew Millionaires, one of the greatest teams from the early days of professional hockey. As a member of the Production Line, with Gordie Howe and Sid Abel, Ted Lindsay became one of the key members of the Detroit teams that won three Stanley Cups during the 1950s. Not a big man, he was both tough and skilled. Following what may have been his best season as a pro, 1956–57, in which he led the NHL in assists, Lindsay was traded to the Chicago Black Hawks, along with goaltender Glenn Hall. It wasn't really a hockey move. Detroit general manger Jack Adams, to whom Lindsay hadn't spoken for three years, was punishing the player for his efforts to organize a players' union by sending him to what was then the worst team in the league – the NHL equivalent of exile in Siberia. Lindsay played three seasons for Chicago before retiring. He was persuaded to come back and play for Detroit in 1964–65. The Wings finished on top of the league that year for the first time since Lindsay was traded away. He had twenty-eight points during his final season as a player and also led the team in penalty minutes, with 173.

who could break down the doors of the boardrooms, who would confront the owners on their own turf as the players' trusted advocate. He had made the cheapskate Bruins pay a raw rookie more than anybody in hockey, so his negotiating skills were beyond question. There was resistance in pockets to the association, especially in Toronto, where the owners, Harold Ballard and Stafford Smythe, and the coach and general manager, Punch Imlach, remained great intimidators in the dressing room. But by early 1967, support was nearly unanimous, and so the National Hockey League Players' Association (NHLPA) was formed, with Eagleson as its first executive director, and his old lacrosse pal, Bob Pulford, as its first president. The owners were finally forced to accept the reality that the players had organized, and preferred a known commodity like Eagleson to someone far scarier, like Hoffa. Marvin Miller would argue – and still argues, well into his eighties – that it was never a *real* union, that there were always too many links between the NHLPA and management. But in the moment of its formation, it represented a great leap forward. By becoming its face, its voice, its point man, Alan Eagleson, already a huge force in the sport through his work as an agent, instantly became the second most powerful man in hockey, behind only the league's president, Clarence Campbell. Two-thirds of what would become his unassailable power base, the agent business and the union, was already in place. The third – shepherding Canada's return to international hockey – was only a few years away.

Orr was still recovering from the second of two knee surgeries in the summer of 1967, when Eagleson began negotiating his next contract with the Bruins. There were suggestions already appearing that perhaps Orr was too fragile for the NHL, that he was damaged goods, that the chances of his enjoying a long and prosperous career had been severely diminished by his problematic left knee. That wasn't the story Eagleson was interested in telling, though, and by then he had fully mastered the art of sowing seeds in the sports pages on his client's behalf. This time, Orr would be shooting for a salary that seemed astounding, even for such a stellar talent:

$100,000 a season, a number no NHL player had ever approached. The Bruins now had a proven commodity on their hands, an all-star, a Norris Trophy winner, who was just beginning to come into his own. And so, Eagleson argued, they had better be prepared to offer the going rate, even if the number was one they had never even contemplated before.

Eagleson couldn't really negotiate through the press since he lacked real leverage. The fact was, Orr couldn't play anywhere other than Boston. (Though, having played the Canadian National Team card while negotiating Orr's first professional contract, Eagleson certainly wasn't above trying to create a phony alternative. Years later, while haggling over what turned out to be Orr's last Boston contract, he suggested that his client might cross the Atlantic to play if nothing was resolved. "We've been approached by some people from Europe. If the money was good enough, and if something happened with the Bruins, who knows?") But Eagleson would let slip a few details of what they were looking for, allowing the writers and, through them, the fans, to understand that the boy wanted only fair compensation for his magnificent talents. Then Eagleson might drop a few comparables into the conversation, because, after all, this was the new NHL, not the cozy old six-team loop but something approaching a true major league, equivalent to pro basketball, akin to the National Football League and in some places even to the great god baseball. Never mind what the next-highest-paid NHL defencemen was earning. How about Joe Namath or Wilt Chamberlain, the stars who defined their sports? Let's look at the biggest heroes in Boston – Ted Williams and Carl Yazstremski of the Red Sox and the Celtics stars John Havlicek and Bill Russell. Were any of them more important to Beantown than Orr? Even the great Celtics teams didn't always play to sellouts, but did you see any empty seats in the Boston Garden when the Bruins were in town? Why shouldn't Bobby Orr be paid at least as much as any or all of them, since he was the reigning star of his sport, the young, handsome face of the great American expansion, the only hockey player likely to get his picture on the cover of a big-time U.S. magazine, the greatest hockey player of all time?

Bobby would never, ever talk about money, and he certainly wouldn't say that last part, in public or even in private. But Al was saying it all the time now, as was Harry Sinden, the Bruins coach (who was by now calling Orr not just the greatest player in hockey but also the greatest athlete in any sport). Yes, Howe was great and Richard was great and no one could take anything away from Hull or from the ancients like Howie Morenz. But the best player to ever lace up skates was in his prime right now, folks, and those who employed him had better understand that and be prepared to ante up.

What Eagleson stumbled upon, or perhaps what he had understood to be lurking there latently all along, was a remarkable aspect of sports fan behaviour. The same people who in the old days would have immediately considered their heroes greedy if the news had broken that they had asked poor old Conn Smythe or Jim Norris for a raise – and would have viewed anyone earning a salary three or four times those of the average working stiff's for playing *a game* as entirely immoral – started to find themselves coming down on the player's (and by extension, his clever agent's) side. Just as long as he himself wasn't out front doing the asking, just as long as he appreciated his lot in life and knew his place, just as long as he remained a loyal, diligent, honest worker who cared as much for the home team as those buying the tickets to watch him in action.

The player's public posture was to make it clear that he really didn't think about the money all that much, that he preferred to concentrate on winning games, that he only wanted what was fair. The agent could do the dirty work for him. He could explain that there was plenty of money in the team coffers if the owners could only suppress their greed. The fans, the ticket buyers, would take their cue, applying pressure on ownership, lobbying on their hero's behalf. *Pay him, you cheap bastard. Give the kid what he's worth. Don't you want to win the Cup as much as we do?* Thus the owner of your favourite team, in the past a beneficent custodian of a great cultural institution (in the case of Smythe, something of a hero in his own right, having fought in both wars, and having built Maple Leaf Gardens partly with his own money in the depths of the

Great Depression), became the *other*, the fat-cat boss, the enemy. He was probably squeezing out extra profits rather than trying as hard as possible to win a championship. He didn't really share your die-hard passion, didn't bleed the team colours. He started to take on the look of a heartless cartoon capitalist, wearing a top hat and smoking a big cigar lit with a $100 bill, keen on exploiting the talents of the still-unsullied athletes in his employ for the sake of his own ever-expanding riches. Those early sports union leaders – not just Eagleson and Miller, but also Larry Fleisher of the National Basketball Players Association, Creighton Miller of the National Football League Players Association and Don Augustin of the American Football League Players Association – understood that that was the story they had to tell. All of them actually sat down in the same room to discuss their respective predicaments in the weeks before the NHLPA was formed. They knew they had to start by swaying public opinion. Every time Eagleson made a speech in those days, he referred to a thirty-page draft he'd written, titled "The Business of Sports," which laid out in no uncertain terms that it was the owners who were greedy, and that it was their system that forced players into the role of indentured servants. (It's fascinating, and perhaps inevitable, that the pendulum would eventually swing back, that by the time the NHL owners decided to effectively break the players' union four decades after Bobby Orr's debut in Boston, they did so with much of their fan base cheering them on. It was the players, then, who were labelled greedy and heartless, and the owners who managed to paint themselves as the true guardians of the game, unselfishly losing bags of money in the hopes of keeping hockey alive.)

Eagleson understood all of that, and so understood that it was in his client's interest to make sure that everyone had a pretty good idea what Bobby Orr was making, not to mention exactly how much he ought to be making. Orr himself, though, was allowed to remain pristine simply by deferring to Al, by flashing the boyish smile and looking shyly at his feet and saying that he really didn't pay too much attention to all of that money stuff. One minute, Orr could say something like "I don't think a player's salary is anybody's

business. That's strictly between the club and the player."
Meanwhile, on the other side of the room, Eagleson would be
telling the same sportswriters, "Bobby will be a millionaire by the
time he's twenty-five." Every one of Orr's contract negotiations
with the Bruins (and finally, most dramatically, with the Chicago
Black Hawks) was played out in the sports pages as though it was a
game itself, with the Eagle providing the expert commentary and
the owners reluctantly dragged into the open, asked to explain and
defend the way they operated their teams. It wasn't close to a fair
fight, and those were odds Eagleson liked a whole lot.

Orr's second contract with Boston, signed in August 1967, was
treated as a major news item in sports sections across North
America. Initial reports had his salary over three seasons at
$300,000. Then *The Toronto Daily Star* upped the grand total, citing
knowledgeable sources in reporting that Orr would in fact earn
$400,000. That number was outrageous enough to force the Bruins
owner, Weston Adams, to go public. He popped up to assure everyone – most especially his fellow NHL governors, who must certainly have been displeased at the inflationary pressures of such a
deal – that the total was nowhere near that high, that the reports
were erroneous and irresponsible. A press conference was held to
clear matters up, and just as Eagleson would have wanted, it did no
such thing. Orr himself dismissed reports of one of the clauses that
was supposed to have been part of his deal – the Bruins' pledge to
pay for him to further his education if he so desired. For Orr, fur-
thering his education would mean finishing high school, something he said he hoped to do someday, something his mother was
encouraging him to do, but that had nothing to do with his contract. "I was a little lazy in school," he admitted to Stan Fischler.[41]

In fact, the deal Eagleson negotiated was a step forward for
hockey players not so much because of the salary but because of
some innovative thinking regarding Orr's off-ice earning potential.
This time, because of its relative complexity, the contract was negotiated not with Weston Adams, or with Milt Schmidt, but with
Adams' own lawyer, Charles Mulcahy Jr. Orr's pay over three years
did indeed fall somewhere between $300,000 and $400,000, but

only about 60 per cent of that was directly tied to hockey – so Adams, technically, was telling the truth. The balance of the money came from what was actually a separate agreement, paying Orr to make public appearances on the club's behalf. But the real key, at least from Eagleson's point of view, was that the team granted Orr permission to use the Bruins logo and uniform in any endorsements he might arrange on the side, from which he had to pay the team only a minority share. Until then, every NHL club had carefully guarded its rights, to the point that players who appeared in ads had to have the crest on a jersey airbrushed out or even had to don a different set of colours. (Later, the NHLPA would negotiate the right to sell endorsements without the consent of the owners.) And there was indeed an education clause in Orr's Boston contract. The Bruins agreed to pay for Orr to complete high school by correspondence, or during the summer, and also agreed to pay his university tuition if he decided to carry on. Orr never took them up on the offer, passing even on the chance to finish high school

In the fall of 1970, at the height of his hockey powers, with the Bruins having just won the Stanley Cup, Eagleson began negotiating with them on what would turn out to be Orr's final contract with the franchise. This would be the motherlode. Athlete salaries in other professional sports had begun to skyrocket. Namath was making $400,000 a year. Lew Alcindor, who later changed his name to Kareem Abdul-Jabbar, was making $1 million over the duration of his NBA contract. "Pistol" Pete Maravich's rookie deal in the NBA paid him nearly $2 million over its term. And Eagleson was telling everyone who asked that, by the time he was finished with this next contract, Bobby Orr would be a millionaire as well, the first NHL player to reach those heights. When Orr finally signed, in August 1971, Eagleson announced that his five-year contract was the "highest in the history of hockey and one of the highest in the history of professional sports."

And perhaps, it was suggested, this would be Orr's final professional contract, that he'd hang up his skates at the end, at the ripe old age of twenty-eight. "Well, he'll have played ten years when he finishes it," Eagleson said, "but I think that's for him to decide at the time. As far as I know, he hasn't said he would quit hockey at the end of the contract."

But how much is he really making, Al? Give us the numbers. Of course, he couldn't do that because he'd guaranteed the Bruins confidentiality – and because, he'd quietly confide, off the record, of course, the Bruins had acceded to all of his demands.

"One thing you can be sure of. Bobby Orr is going to be the highest-paid player in history. In his first eight years he is going to make more money than any other player ever made in twenty years.

"Why? Just one reason. Bobby Orr will be the highest-paid hockey player in history because he is the greatest player in hockey history."[42]

The greatest player, the wealthiest player. And by extrapolation, represented by the first, the greatest, the most cunning, the most savvy agent in the history of the game. Any other player who wanted that kind of advocate, who wanted to get on the gravy train, knew exactly whom to call. This perfect partnership of Orr and Eagleson was the model for how the new NHL was going to work.

When it came to handling all of that money, Eagleson took care of everything for Bobby. *Everything.* Orr didn't waste much time fretting about where the cash was coming from or where the cash was going, other than how he might spend it, which he did with no small enthusiasm. He made no pretence of understanding either the business of the NHL or the business of Bobby Orr. Eagleson's job was to handle all of that for him. But it wasn't simply a financial relationship. Eagleson didn't just work for Orr. Their ties ran far deeper, as Bobby was more than happy to explain. "Alan Eagleson handles my finances. He's my attorney, as you know, but also a very good friend. I trust him and believe in him. I've done very well because of Al. He calls me, but if he can't get hold of me he can go ahead and do it and tell me later."[43] And it wasn't just the hockey salary. That wasn't even the half of it. Eagleson was one of the first to understand that you could take a player – or, more specifically, the *idea* of a player – and turn it into all kinds of income-generating opportunities, one piled on top of another, each spreading the brand name, each building equity.

To some degree, professional athletes had been trying to make money from their fame for decades. The first and most obvious angle they exploited was to open a restaurant or a bar with their famous name on it – Jack Dempsey's, Stan Musial's, Toe Blake's et al. – though such businesses were potential sinkholes, ripe for exploitation, especially if the star attraction wasn't really paying too much attention to the fine details, to the freebies, to how many pals were eating and drinking on his tab. And there were limited commercial endorsements, first in print, then on radio and television, with players putting their good name on the line to sell cars and cigarettes and sporting goods. Only the big stars made real money that way – in the lower ranks, it might pay off merely in a local dealer's offering a break on the price of a brand new ride. Almost invariably, the endorsements were piecemeal, since the athletes tended to handle their own businesses and didn't really know what they were doing, and since all they were looking for was a quick buck to supplement their playing income.

Those same pitches were made to Orr, but as Eagleson explained, he had a response at the ready. "People come to Bobby with all kinds of schemes. He'll just tell them to come and see me. Half of them will quit right there. They don't want to talk to a lawyer."[44] He wasn't much interested even when they did work up the nerve to talk to him, because he had his own marketing plans for Bobby Orr, far more extensive and sophisticated than anything seen in the NHL before. At the time of Orr's professional debut, hockey player incomes with very few exceptions remained exceedingly modest, even by real-world standards. (Consider that Orr's first roommate, Joe Watson, went home and worked on a road gang in Smithers, B.C., the summer after his rookie season with the Boston Bruins in order to make ends meet.) On the endorsement side, only a handful of players made a nickel off the ice. Eagleson was going to change that. Before meeting Orr, through his friendship with Bob Pulford, he had begun working with a small group of Toronto Maple Leafs, helping them to invest their money and to find opportunities off the ice. (It was called, informally, the Blue and White Group.) Pulford put money into mortgages and took an off-season job with a car dealer friend of Eagleson's. Billy Harris and Harry Neale set up a summer hockey school in Woodbridge, Ontario. Bobby Baun went into business with a contractor and spent summers building ponds in the country.

Orr, though, would provide an entirely new set of opportunities. The day he signed his first contract with the Bruins, Eagleson already had an endorsement deal lined up with Ostrander's Jewellers in Toronto, one of Al's clients. Then he put in a call to Old Mills Pontiac Buick: in return for a few appearances at the dealership, Bobby would get the use of a car. (The owner was a member of the Lambton Golf Club, where Eagleson also belonged.) Eventually, there would be a deal with General Motors – even Doug Orr got a new car out of that one; Yardley's (print ads featured a hip-looking Orr vouching for their aftershave. *Bobby Orr, star defenseman of the Boston Bruins says: It's a Man's World with Yardley Black Label. "Sure, I put a lot into the game," says Bobby Orr. "That's why I like the fresh feel you get with Yardley Black Label men's products – you will too.");* Labatt's (personal appearances only – professional athletes were forbidden to actually endorse alcohol); Bic pens; Munro games; Crestliner boats. For a time, there was a chain of Bobby Orr Pizza Places.

In the summer of 1970, the sports columnist Scott Young suggested to Eagleson that he'd tallied up Orr's off-ice earnings for the year and figured it was close to $250,000. "Well, you're pretty close," Eagleson said. "And if you're talking about the end of the fiscal year we're in, you're low."

(Late in his career, he'd make that kind of money from a single deal. Through an Eagleson connection with Standard Brands, later RJR Nabisco, Orr signed a five-year contract with the company that paid him between $250,000 and $300,000 a year.)

Orr's ability to generate income off the ice became almost as much a part of the story as the way he played the game. Over and over again, he and his adviser were celebrated as the models of modern sports marketing, always a half-step smarter, a half-step better, than anyone else. As a writer for *The Hockey News* put it during the summer of 1970, "Boston's brilliant Bobby Orr just can't seem to avoid making money. It literally falls into his lap."

The money was pouring in. There was absolutely no question about that. Where it went after that, according to Orr, was pretty much up to Eagleson. "I never see any money," he claimed. It was invested on his behalf. One of the few financial decisions Orr made on his own was when he insisted on helping out the proprietor of his favourite clothing store (a great tailor but a lousy businessman, Eagleson said). The investment was made, and Orr's youngest brother, Doug, ended up working there, which suggests that for all of Orr's public disclaimers when it came to his business interests, in at least this one instance a bit of the famous stubbornness carried over off the ice.

The most public venture of the Eagleson-Orr partnership would be a summer sports camp for boys that would carry Bobby's name and that of another of Eagleson's clients, Mike Walton, who began his NHL career with the Toronto Maple Leafs. Orr and Walton had met through Eagleson and become close friends. Eagleson got wind that the Owaissa Lodge property near his summer cottage in Orillia, Ontario, had been put on the market – a summer camp property that included a four-sheet curling rink. What he envisioned there was a boys' summer hockey camp, like the Haliburton Hockey Haven that Wren Blair had once operated and where Bobby Orr had once been an instructor. Eagleson put together a group of six share-holders to buy the place: four investors of his acquaintance – a doctor, an architect, an accountant and a builder – as well as Eagleson and Orr themselves, each in for one share. Five years after that initial investment, Orr bought the others out. What was to be known as the Bobby Orr – Mike Walton Sports Camp became an immediate success. Both Tom Watt, who later coached in the National Hockey League, and Bill Watters, a future agent, assistant general manager and Toronto broadcast personality, were involved as camp directors. At its peak, there were a total of seventeen hundred students over the course of the summer, with each boy paying $125 – a gross of $212,500 a season. The kids got hockey instruction from the pros – though Bobby wasn't all that enthusiastic about putting in the hours – and could also enjoy the more standard summer camp lineup of swimming and boating and the great outdoors. It was an attractive mix.

Orr drew against the money he generated on and off the ice to pay his living expenses, which not surprisingly grew increasingly lavish as his fame and wealth increased. He also looked after his family back in Parry Sound. Doug quit his day job first, but it was a little while after that before Arva finally agreed to stop working as a waitress. Ron ran a clothing and sporting goods store on the main drag in Parry Sound with Bobby's name on the sign and Bobby's money as its underpinning. His brother-in-law, Ron Blanchard, would eventually operate Bobby's autograph and memorabilia business. And like any good Canadian boy, Bobby insisted on building a new house for his folks, which cost in excess of $100,000, a significant sum at the time, especially in Parry Sound. "I owe a lot to them," Bobby explained. "They raised me right. I like to go fishing with Doug – and my mother is something else. She doesn't like a lot of fuss around her, and she can spot a phony from a mile away."[45]

The rest of the money Eagleson managed. That story, like the story of the contract negotiations, was spun over and over again by the sports press. The Bobby Orr business was what all other hockey players, all other professional athletes, aspired to: a hefty salary to begin with, and then all kinds of money just for being who they were, for showing up and smiling and lending their name or their image – that money creating more money, turning into the kind of long-term security they pined for, knowing that playing careers were short and unpredictable, that it could all end tomorrow. Eagleson would eventually claim that Orr earned three times as much outside of hockey as he did from the game itself, and there was absolutely no reason to doubt that assessment. Orr's name was everywhere, so the evidence was all around.

At one point, a reporter asked Orr about his taxes – was he paying in the United States or in Canada? "My taxes? Some here, some in Canada," he said, also making vague mention of the Bahamas.[46] Still, Orr made it clear that wasn't really his concern. "Everything is handled for me. That's what lawyers are for. I don't like to sit down and fight over anything. I stay out of it."[47]

Bobby vouched for Al. He encouraged his teammates and other players to sign up with him, to hand over their contractual negotiations, to let Eagleson help them with endorsements. If they wanted to be like him, if they wanted to earn money the way he did, Al was the ticket. And Bobby Orr was the best advertisement imaginable for the value of his services.

There were questions that weren't being asked, but then again, who would have had the imagination to ask them? What happens if the cash flow stops abruptly? What happens if the hockey career is suddenly cut short? What happens if a tax dodge doesn't pass muster? What happens if not every investment pans out? What happens if that beautiful, trusting friendship turns sour, if the inseparable partners stalk off in different directions? What happens if, after all those years as equals, one of you needs the other less and less? What happens if, as it does sometimes in life, love morphs into something closer to hate?

"The Eagle has handled me well," Bobby said. "After all, he puts his own dough into most of the ventures I'm in. I couldn't ask for a much better show of faith than that."[48]

Even after retirement, Orr continued to tell much the same story about the happy relationship, about the clever investments, about his success as a businessman, about the unqualified trust, about the two of them, Bobby and Al, being like halves of the same whole, body and brain, heart and head, partners, pals. One earned the money, one invested the money; both made out like bandits.

And then the story changed.

Chapter Thirteen

ASCENDANCE

B Y THE END OF THE 1969–70 SEASON, the Bruins could no longer be regarded as plucky underdogs, as a team temporarily achieving beyond the limits of its true talent. Boston was now established among the National Hockey League's elite, finishing tied in points on the final day of the schedule with the first-place Chicago Black Hawks (the Hawks were awarded the top spot on the basis of recording more wins). Just behind Boston, completing the new hockey world order, the New York Rangers were making their own push for respectability. Temporarily at least, the old hockey powers had fallen from the heights. Gone – though it would prove a blip rather than a trend – were the previous season's Stanley Cup champions, the Montreal Canadiens. They missed the playoffs entirely that spring, as did the Toronto Maple Leafs, marking the first time in NHL history that both Canadian franchises had been left as spectators during the post-season. Sadly for Toronto and its fans, that tumble from glory would prove more than temporary.

The young, confident Bruins certainly weren't untouchable. They still struggled away from their cozy home rink, and they surrendered more goals than they should have, turning many of their games into wild, high-scoring shootouts. But Boston had proven that it could thrive employing that wide-open style of play because it enjoyed such overwhelming offensive power, borne out by the fact that the Bruins scored twenty-seven more goals over the course of the season than anyone else in the league. By now, the lineup that had been all but carved in stone by Harry Sinden not long after the big trade that brought Phil Esposito, Ken Hodge and Fred Stanfield to town was balanced and without glaring weakness, the perfect mix of hockey skills, each player seemingly in harmony with those around him.

The core of that club would change very little through Boston's glory years (really, until the day in 1975 that Esposito was traded to New York, the true signal of the dynasty's end). On the top line, Espo was the centre between Ken Hodge and first Ron Murphy, then Wayne Cashman. The second line, with Fred Stanfield between Johnny McKenzie and John Bucyk, would remain all but permanently intact, a close-knit trio on and off the ice. The third line, the checking unit, which could neutralize an opponent's best players and a score a few goals on its own, had Derek Sanderson at centre, with Ed Westfall on one wing. The other spot was originally Eddie Shack's, then was passed on to Wayne Carleton, Don Marcotte and finally Orr's summer camp partner, Mike Walton, when he arrived by trade from Toronto in 1971. Ted Green had missed the 1969–70 season because of his head injury, so either Rick Smith or Gary Doak took his usual place alongside Don Awrey as part of one defensive pairing. (Later, Carol Vadnais would be part of the mix as well.) The other blue-line duo, Orr and Dallas Smith, changed only when one or the other was hurt, or when Orr was summoned for extra duty. The continuity of that alignment, enhancing players' familiarity with their roles and with each other, was both a part of Sinden's grand plan and something close to the NHL norm in the era before free agency made it more difficult to keep teams intact over the long haul.

Until the spring of 1970, those Bruins could be considered a work in progress, yet to fully prove themselves. The Stanley Cup playoffs represented a separate test, during which plenty of regular-season wonders had foundered in the past. The year before, the Bruins had learned a very tough lesson when they got a little bit too cocky against Montreal and paid the price. As it turned out, that gut-wrenching loss to the Canadiens had been a formative experience. They would learn from their mistakes, mature and evolve, as became obvious when they faced the now-formidable Rangers in the opening round.

New York's last Stanley Cup victory had come in 1940 – the year before Boston had last won the Cup – and the team hadn't won a playoff series in two decades. They had been fellow cellar-dwellers with the Bruins in the old six-team league, the two-part punchline of a long-running hockey joke, though like the Bruins they were still loyally supported by their fans through the lean years. But now, just as Boston was in the ascendance, the Rangers were building their own elite side, anchored by their own brilliant young offensive defenceman, Brad Park. Park would draw comparisons to Orr throughout his career, whether he appreciated it or not, including in later years, when he came over as part of the Esposito trade and donned a Boston uniform. In almost any other hockey era, Park would have won a string of Norris Trophies himself, but then the best he could hope for was to be considered Orr's closest competition, the next best thing.

The series kicked off at the Boston Garden on April 8, and the Bruins opened with a flourish. Esposito staked the team to a quick 2–0 lead, and then Orr added the next two to make it 4–1. The second of his goals was a short-handed masterpiece: Orr picked up a rebound just off the Boston crease following a Tim Horton slapshot, then swung around his own net and made a quick move, leaving the forechecking Ron Stewart literally tumbling in his wake. Orr continued up ice, then, on reaching the Rangers blue line, fed the puck to Johnny McKenzie. He awaited the seemingly inevitable return pass, an example of that familiarity, that team chemistry at work, and beat Ed Giacomin with a wrist shot. When Sanderson added a second short-handed goal during the same Boston penalty, the Rangers were beaten. The game finished 8–2, Boston.

The next night, in game two, New York broke an early 1–1 tie when Orr fell down in his own end, turning the puck over to the Rangers' Jack Eagers, who fed Rod Gilbert for the go-ahead score. Orr slammed his stick against the post, knowing that he'd given one away. But with the once-great Terry Sawchuk in the New York goal, and unable to stop much of anything, the Bruins tied the score, then finally pulled away to win 5–3, taking a 2–0 series lead as the scene shifted to Manhattan.*

At the "new" Madison Square Garden – the latest incarnation of the great sporting palace had opened just the year before – the Rangers asserted themselves in their home crowd, playing with obvious emotion. Early in the game, they began brawling, ganging up on Sanderson, sending a typical hockey message to the Big Bad Bruins that they wouldn't be intimidated. Then, after falling behind 1–0, they rallied back for a 4–3 win – though the result was in doubt until the final buzzer, when Giacomin blocked Orr's last- second wrist shot from the slot. In game four, Orr scored on a slapshot to bring Boston to within a goal at 3–2. But then he made a crucial giveaway behind his own net that set up the clinching goal for the Rangers in what finished as a 4–2 win.

Game five, back at the Boston Garden, would obviously be pivotal, and not shockingly, given the stakes and the high emotion, it kicked off with another series of fights. Orr scored the first goal of the game, finishing off his own end-to-end rush, but was also partly

---

* The game would mark the last appearance in the NHL by Sawchuk, considered by many the greatest goaltender of all time. Fifty-two days later, he died under still-mysterious circumstances following a "playful" wrestling match with his Rangers teammate and roommate, Ron Stewart. The two players, both divorced, rented a house on East Atlantic Beach on Long Island, New York. After coming home from a bar, Sawchuk and Stewart became embroiled in an argument, and then began to scuffle. Sawchuk fell to the ground, in obvious distress. He was taken to hospital, where his gall bladder was removed, and he later underwent another operation to remove blood from a lacerated liver. He died a little more than a month after entering hospital.

responsible for the Rangers' tying goal, when he lost the puck to Gilbert. A little later, after Orr was pulled down in his own end and when no penalty was called, the Rangers moved quickly into transition, with Orland Kurtenbach finally beating Cheevers to put New York up 2–1. Esposito came back to tie the game for the Bruins.

And then the two Boston superstars, different personalities, rivals more than friends, combined their disparate talents as they would so often. Crossing his own blue line on the rush, Orr spotted Esposito cruising through the neutral zone. Esposito, who knew from experience what was coming, suddenly broke toward the Rangers goal, and without even looking in his direction, Orr hit him with a perfect pass just as he was entering the New York zone, on side by half a stride. Using his great strength, Esposito broke free of the last line of defence and then, in the clear, fired the puck past Giacomin. It was the game-winning goal, and in hindsight the score that really won the series. The Bruins had to travel back to New York for what turned out to be the finale, but the Rangers had already given their best. Boston won with relative ease, 4–1.

On now to the conference final – the de facto Stanley Cup final, with only the best of the weak expansion teams left to face the winner. On to Chicago, where the Black Hawks had easily swept away Detroit and were rested and ready with a superstar Bobby of their own. The modern Black Hawks had first emerged as a power in the late 1950s and early 1960s, a period that coincided directly with the arrival of the great Bobby Hull, who received able support from the likes of Stan Mikita. In 1961, they won what seemed destined to be the first of several Stanley Cups. But that early promise dimmed, while the Leafs, and to a lesser degree the Habs, took control. Now the Hawks had fought their way back on top, beginning a run of five seasons in which they were consistently among the very best regular-season teams in the league. Heading into the series against Chicago, Sinden had made a time-honoured strategic choice, declaring that whatever happened, the other team's superstar wasn't going to beat him. He assigned Ed Westfall to be Hull's shadow, to follow him and harass him anytime he was on the ice. That strategy, though not particularly radical when one is faced with a dominant, dangerous forward, still worked exceptionally well. Through Westfall's tireless checking, Hull was effectively neutralized.

The series opened at the Chicago Stadium, arguably a louder and more intimidating place to play than the Boston Garden, and most attention was focused on the magnificent offensive on display for both teams. But the tone of the series would actually be set by goaltending. Phil Esposito's little brother, Tony – named that season the NHL's rookie of the year after setting a single-season shutout record with fifteen – was badly off form, allowing two horrible goals as the Bruins ran to a quick 3–0 lead. At the other end of the ice, Gerry Cheevers, who would start every playoff game for Boston, was exceptionally sharp. The game finished 6–3, Bruins. Orr contributed several of his signature offensive flourishes and also blocked three Chicago shots that seemed headed for the goal. He even stood in front of one of Hull's slapshots, the most fearsome weapon in the history of the game, without flinching.

Orr kicked off game two with a now-familiar end-to-end dash, working a pass-and-return with Stanfield before scoring the game's opening goal. "Orr just killed us," the Chicago coach, Billy Reay, said. "It was futile. We'd shoot the puck into the Boston end, and before one of our guys could get to it, he'd be bringing it back out. That's just another part of the game he's spoiled for everybody."[49] Boston coasted to a 4–1 win, heading home with a decisive 2–0 series lead. The Hawks, understanding the consequences of a third straight loss, picked up their game in Boston, but it still wasn't enough. They led game three 2–1 before finally falling 5–2. Hoping to salvage pride and avoid the sweep in game four, Tony Esposito was back in form, and the Hawks held a 4–3 lead in the third period. But then Ken Hodge scored the tying goal and Johnny McKenzie the winner.

The Boston bench emptied to congratulate "Pie" for that one, knowing that, with the easy path that lay ahead, it had all but certainly guaranteed the Bruins a Stanley Cup. At the final horn, as Phil Esposito patted his brother on the head, the rest of the Bruins gathered for what looked very much like a championship-winning celebration, as the ecstatic Boston fans stood and cheered.

There was one more round to go, one more playoff series to determine which team would actually have its name engraved on the Stanley Cup. But that seemed a mere formality. Through a magnificent regular season, and now through two rounds of play-offs in which he had been the dominant player nearly every moment he was on the ice, Orr was writing the climax to his own heroic tale. He had won the league's regular-season scoring title, the first defenceman ever to accomplish that feat – ever to come close – with thirty-three goals and eighty-seven assists, more assists than any player, in any position, had ever recorded. After the play-offs concluded, he would for the first time be awarded the Hart Trophy winner as the NHL's most valuable player, a selection that stirred no debate. Needless to say, he would also once again win the Norris Trophy as the NHL's top defenceman.

Entering his first Stanley Cup Final, a series that figured to be more coronation than competition, he had only one accolade left. Great athletes, fairly or unfairly, always have their true quality questioned until they lead a team to a championship. It completes the picture of not just a virtuoso talent but one capable of making those around him better. Orr had done that all year long, against the Rangers and the Black Hawks in the playoffs, and now only the St. Louis Blues remained. The NHL was still split between east and west, haves and have-nots, the established teams of the Original Six and the struggling expansion sides, with the playoff victors on either side facing off for the title. (They'd change the format the following season, understanding that the Stanley Cup final had been robbed of its drama by the predetermined mismatch.) The great radical expansion experiment was now three years old, but the feeling in hockey circles was that it might be another decade or more before one of the new teams would catch up and be capable of seriously challenge for the Cup. Still, that imbalance wasn't enough to discourage the governors from cashing two more cheques and allowing Buffalo and Vancouver to join the league for the 1970–71 season.

The St. Louis Blues had represented the expansion forces in the Stanley Cup Final at the end of both of the first two seasons of their existence, and both times had been swept away with little resistance by the Montreal Canadiens. There was no real reason to believe that anything had changed now, that the talent gap had narrowed, especially given the Bruins' dominance in the playoff series with Chicago. (No one outside of Parry Sound would have noticed it, but the Stanley Cup Final would feature all three local heroes playing in the NHL, with Terry Crisp and Gary Sabourin both in the St. Louis lineup.) In hindsight, though, a historic angle emerges to add intrigue to that Boston – St. Louis series. How did one of the greatest coaches, the greatest strategic geniuses in NHL history, attempt to deal with the game's greatest player in his prime? Scotty Bowman had scouted Orr as a boy back in Parry Sound on behalf of the Canadiens. He would be one of the many players, scouts, coaches, general managers to finally get their big break when the league went from six to twelve teams. In 1967, Bowman took over from Lynn Patrick as coach of the Blues early in the franchise's inaugural season and immediately transformed the team into the best of a bad lot. It was in St. Louis that Bowman earned the reputation as a hockey thinker, as an innovator, though his players as often as not came to despise him. The Blues job served as a kind of apprenticeship for the role that was always destined to be his: coach of Les Glorieux in Montreal. There he'd have all the tools at his disposal, and there he'd build a dynasty. Still, in many ways, this was the greater challenge: to take an obviously inferior team into a short series, with a chance – slim, but a chance – to win the Stanley Cup against a team featuring the best player in the world.

Bowman decided that his only course was to attempt to do what no other team had managed that season, to find a way to take Orr off his game. Sure, there were other players on the Bruins who could hurt you, all kinds of them, in fact. But what would happen if you somehow made Orr a little more ordinary? What would happen if you destroyed his rhythm, if you prevented him from winding up on those long rushes, if you made someone else carry the puck and start the play and choreograph the Boston attack? "We just wanted to make sure he wasn't in the mix," Bowman says. "One thing I tried to do, especially in the Boston Garden, was to gear our breakout plays to come up the other wing – up their right wing. You didn't want the puck coming around their left side because he always found a way to keep it in. Where I found him the most dangerous was when you were trying to come out of your end on a breakout play. He invariably made the choice of going to the middle, and he was terrific on the boards. Then all of a sudden you had a turnover. All of that's beside the way he rushed the puck."

To counter that last part, Orr's offensive rushes, Bowman departed from conventional defensive strategy. Often in hockey, forwards had been singled out for special individual attention, as Boston had just done with Bobby Hull. Never a defenceman, though. The risk involved in tying up one of your own forwards deep in other team's zone, or of trying to corral a player who could exploit any room to wander and who routinely made forecheckers look foolish, was considerable. But playing strength against strength, Bowman understood as well as anyone that his Blues didn't have a chance. So he figured it was worth a try. He selected as Orr's designated shadow a player named Jimmy Roberts, a clever defensive specialist who had just completed his seventh NHL season. Bowman had originally known Roberts in the Montreal system and admired both his abilities and his smarts. (Years later, they'd work together as coaches.) Roberts's assignment against Boston was to follow Orr wherever he went, to pressure him when he had the puck, to ignore the other Bruins on the ice and concentrate only on neutralizing that one man. "That was the first time I ever heard of such a thing," Sinden said afterwards. "Nobody has ever shadowed a defenceman before. And that was a pure, unadulterated shadowing job. Nothing else."[50]

The grand strategy worked, and it didn't. "At least he didn't bombard us," Bowman says. When Orr was pressed by Roberts in his own zone, it left a forward open elsewhere and the Blues undermanned. In game one of the finals in St. Louis, Orr certainly wasn't quite as dominant as he had been in the previous two playoff rounds, but the Bruins still won going away. (That said, the game changed most dramatically in the first period, when, with the score tied 1-1, the St. Louis goaltender, Jacques Plante, who had been spectacular to that point, was hit in the face mask by a shot and knocked unconscious. He wouldn't play again in the series, and his replacements, Ernie Wakely and Glenn Hall, couldn't come close to matching his heroics.) "I'm not mad about it," Orr said afterwards of the Blues' innovative checking tactics. "Something like that is part of the game. However, I don't think it worked too well. The score was 6-1, wasn't it?" Yes it was. And the score of game two was 6-2, though Orr broke free in that one long enough to set an all-time points record for a defenceman in the playoffs and to set up a short-handed goal by Ed Westfall at the end of a long rush. The teams were in Boston for the third game, and the story was much the same, with the Bruins winning, this time 4-1, and Bowman still claiming qualified success. "Maybe we didn't execute as well as I had hoped, but it still worked pretty well," he said. "[Orr] didn't run the game like he would have if he wasn't shadowed like that."

And so far in the Stanley Cup Final, Orr hadn't scored a single goal.

Three games. Three rather routine one-sided victories. And now the championship was there for the taking on home ice, at the funky old Garden, in front of the loyal and long-suffering masses, primed for this now, primed to exorcise all of those years of losing, enjoying the buildup to the great celebration, knowing there was no chance that it could all slip away. To their credit, the Blues put up a fight in game four. They were leading 3-2 in the third period when referee Bruce Hood called a faceoff interference penalty – that still sticks in Bowman's craw, all these years later – and Boston tied the score on the power play with less than seven minutes to go in regulation. And thus, on the afternoon of May 10, 1970, the stage was set for a final dramatic set piece.

It wasn't the greatest goal scored in the history of hockey, or the most significant, or Orr's finest, most singular moment of shinny artistry. The outcome of the series was a foregone conclusion, the play was a straightforward give-and-go, and considering all of the magnificent, inspired moments that Orr had conjured up during his professional career, if anything this was a bit anticlimactic, a bit banal. An end-to-end rush through the entire opposing team to score the Stanley Cup – winning goal against, say, the Canadiens: now that would be the stuff of history books. And so would this, not because of the play itself, let alone the opposition, but because of a single, iconic image.

In the first seconds of overtime, the Bruins were pressing for the winning goal, checking the Blues ferociously in their own end. The puck squirted loose, and St. Louis's Larry Keenan got to it first. He chipped at it, trying to slice it off the boards and out of the zone. But there was Orr, taking a huge risk, as he so often did. He moved to block Keenan's clearing attempt, level with the faceoff circle. If the puck had slipped by him, the Blues would have enjoyed at least a two-on-one break, perhaps a three-on-one, with Orr far out of position. Had they had managed to score there and win, the series would have shifted back to St. Louis for game five. And if they had somehow won the next three games . . . Well, forget it, that wasn't going to happen, in any case.

Of course, the puck didn't get by him. Orr blocked it with his body, controlled it with his stick and then fed it to Derek Sanderson in the corner. Instead of retreating to the point, to his defensive position, Bobby Orr headed straight for the goal, knowing that Sanderson would anticipate his move and pass it back. Orr was there to meet the return pass, and with the Blues standing around and watching, he cruised in front of the crease and tucked a shot past Glenn Hall. At that same instant, Noel Picard, the Blues defenceman, finally decided to offer token resistance, tripping Orr, lifting his feet, sending him flying through the air.

In real time, it all goes by in a flash. But that image, frozen in one of the greatest sports photographs ever captured, was singular and spectacular and laden with symbolism. Bobby Orr, taking off. And rather than bracing for the moment when gravity would surely reassert itself, rather than panicking at the sudden loss of control, in mid-air, in mid-flight, he exults, lifting both of his arms to the heavens. Life is suspended, physics defied. What you see in that picture, in that illusion, is magic.

The photographer, Ray Lussier, was working for the now-defunct *Boston Record-American*. He had spent the first three periods shooting from a position in one of the west-end corners of the Garden. But knowing that St. Louis would defend the east goal in the overtime, knowing that the Bruins were bound to press hard for the winner, he left his position and wandered down to the other end of the rink, where he found one of the photographers' stools empty. It was a hot, steamy day, and one of his competitors who had been occupying that spot had gone off in search of a cold beer – later, in telling the story, Lussier would never disclose who the unlucky fellow was. Lussier sat down, planning to leave when the other shooter returned. It was all over in forty seconds.

Back to the scene, to the flash of the red goal light, the horn, the noise, the crowd, the Bruins pouring off the bench and falling together in a crazy, writhing ball of celebration, the realization setting in, the sudden understanding that what had once seemed impossible and more lately inevitable was now absolutely, permanently, unequivocally true: the Boston Bruins had won the Stanley Cup.

"Some people think that Boston began to build this team five or ten years ago," Bowman said afterwards. "They're wrong. Boston began to build this team in 1948, the year Bobby Orr was born." The fans at the Garden understood that all too well. One of the signs in the crowd that Cup-winning day read, "Happy Mother's Day, Mrs. Orr."

The captain, Johnny Bucyk, the Chief, who had held his head high through some awful seasons past, who was always the team's quiet class act, accepted the Stanley Cup from Clarence Campbell at centre ice. Campbell tried to make a speech but couldn't be heard over the din and gave up. Then Bucyk began his ceremonial skate around the ice, doing his best to dodge a crowd of kids who had somehow found their way down and were slipping and sliding along in his wake. At the other end of the rink, Gerry Cheevers waved to the adoring crowd. The public address announcer broke through to bring the news that Bobby Orr had been named winner of the Conn Smythe Trophy, awarded to the most valuable player in the playoffs. (Cheevers, Bucyk and Esposito, the leading scorer during the playoffs, were legitimately in the hunt until the final goal. Orr finished with nine goals and eleven assists in fourteen games.)

The Bruins left the ice soon thereafter and headed for their cramped, dingy dressing room, running a back-patting gauntlet of fans and team employees to get there. The players didn't pause long in the rush to begin the celebration, though Ken Hodge did stop to bear-hug one of the most exultant of the celebrants: Alan Eagleson.

Inside the room, there wasn't an inch of empty space, and the beer flowed even more freely than the champagne. Don Earle, a local sportscaster, set up shop in a corner he hoped would provide some shelter for his cameraman, where one after another, happy, boozy, cigar-smoking hockey players in their underwear stopped to talk about how wonderful it felt, that maybe this was only the beginning, that this might be the birth of a new hockey dynasty.

One of them was Wayne Carleton, who years back, while still a junior, had shared that first *Hockey Night in Canada* interview with a terrified kid from Oshawa who stared at his own feet. "All I can say is it's a great feeling to see Bobby Orr score that goal," Carleton said. "He played a great series. They watched him so close. It was the happiest thing I've ever seen. It's a great thing to be on a Stanley Cup winner. When he scored it, it's even that much greater."

Earle found Orr standing by his locker. He had an arm wrapped around his father's shoulders. Doug was dressed in suit and tie, the look on his face ecstatic and open, like that of a young boy on his birthday. Here was the kid and his proud dad, together in this glorious moment, speaking in a kind of half-literate poetic hockey shorthand, though the sentiment is crystal clear.

"Thanks, Don," Bobby said. "It's so great I don't know what to say. This team. Unbelievable. The guys that were hurt are out yelling for us between periods. They're in the stands. They're fighting for us. The guys that are playing. The goaltending. Put everything together, it's just a great bunch of guys."

"Doug," Earle asked, turning to the proud papa, "how do you feel about it?"

"This is the happiest day of my life," he said. Ever since I" – he paused for a moment, searching for the right word, and in his excitement missed – "accumulated Bobby I've been waiting for this."

"I spent the last five minutes of the third period and the overtime down here with you, Doug, and you were just pacing back and forth," Earle said.

"I wasn't watching, but I was there," he explained. "I want to tell you one thing. My wife is at home and she is crying right now. I just phoned her."

(Bobby wondered aloud whether the CBC was showing this, whether his mom could see it back home in Parry Sound.)

"This is the happiest day of my life," Doug repeated, then said it all over again. "This is the happiest day of my life. I couldn't wish for anything else."

A few hours later, at the victory party, Harry Sinden slipped away for a minute to find a phone, and dialled Wren Blair.

Strangely enough, not everyone was singing hosannas. With every great success story, there has to be someone claiming it isn't quite so, someone to buck conventional wisdom and reveal the emperor's new clothes. Bobby Orr was the greatest hockey player in the world, the greatest player anyone had ever seen, the leader and star of the greatest team in hockey in the here and now. "This is a helluva statement to make, and I'll probably get a lot of flak over it," Sinden said, "but Bobby just may be the greatest athlete who ever lived."[51] And so maybe it was time to knock him down a few pegs, at least from a safe distance. Bowman predicted that the rest of the league would figure Orr out eventually. "In the future I don't think he'll have it as easy. He'll see a lot more of what he saw in the playoffs this year. . . . Of course, there'll be some variations. It's inevitable. The only way to stop Orr is not to let him get started. That's what we tried to do, and I'm convinced other teams will pick up the idea. Another thing, he'll get hit more. He'll be shadowed and hit and agitated, and he'll get frustrated and draw more penalties. That wasn't done in the past. Nobody hit him. They just stood there and watched him like he was God or something. They were awed by him. Everybody was awed by him."[52] The most ferocious debunking, though, came from the pen of Stan Fischler, who just months before had been Orr's confidant and the author of an extremely positive book, *Bobby Orr and the Big Bad Bruins*, in which he expressed few doubts about the young man's abilities or character or anything else. But Orr didn't like the book – or at least he didn't like the fact that any book had been written without his explicit blessing – and there had been a distinct chill in the relationship between the two. Maybe the broadside shouldn't have been quite so surprising, maybe it shouldn't have been a shock that Fischler assumed the familiar journalistic posture of the only guy brave enough to tell it like it really is:

It has become apparent to some insiders that Bobby regards himself as some sort of Messiah who should not be touched, let alone bodychecked. A plentiful supply of bodywork will chip away at his temper and a like supply of verbosity will distract him. So far, though, his opponents, for reasons known only to them, prefer to check Orr as if he is guarded by some invisible shield: thus he is able to roam free. No good!

One who didn't think so was Pat Quinn of the Vancouver Canucks who last year played for the Toronto Maple Leafs. It was Quinn who administered a healthy pasting to Orr during a Boston Garden fight and would have continued to do so if Fred Stanfield of the Bruins hadn't intervened and pulled Quinn away from Bobby.

So it has been amply demonstrated that an ample player such as Quinn can handle, if not manhandle, Orr. It has also been distinctly shown, through the courtesy of instant replay, that Bobby as a defenceman makes a helluva rover.

In the final game of the playoffs he was out of position more times than a palm tree in a hurricane. This is nothing new; it's just that you won't read about it in the papers.

As a defenceman, Orr has been exploited more than people realize. But his offensive sorties smother his defensive flaws. To stop Orr, opponents should exploit his defensive weaknesses. When Bobby's away up ice, the other club should bear in mind that his own end is open and, yes, it is possible to score against him.

As a defenceman, Orr also has a tendency to drop too far back into his own end and to flip-flop to the ice with a drop of a deke. Fake a slap shot and Orr will go flying and the ice will be open. . . .

With the aid of over-adrenalized newsmen, Orr has helped psych out many of his opponents. This is sheer nonsense. The fact that Bobby won the Conn Smythe trophy last spring for playoff MVP is the joke of St. Louis. Players on the Blues confided they thought the prize should have gone to Johnny Bucyk or Gerry Cheevers or Derek Sanderson and then Orr. But the NHL governors, many of whom saw little or no playoff games, voted Orr the Smythe.

But hockey still isn't played in a governor's drawing room, nor on the pages of a daily newspaper. It's played on ice and on ice Bobby Orr can be stopped.[53]

Needless to say, that was a minority opinion.

For Orr, going home to Parry Sound was never quite as simple as the myth spinners would suggest. Over and over again, especially in the early days of his NHL career, Orr told any writer who asked that there was no place on earth better, that someday he hoped to return and raise a family there, far from the corrupting influence of urban America. "I like the slow pace of life up here," he said, "and I like the outdoors. I don't really like the big cities – with all the people rushing around. Some people thrive on it, but it isn't my idea of living. The life in Parry Sound represents Canada to me. What goes on in the city is more American. It is all right if you like it, but it's not for me." Those sentiments are exactly what Canadians longed to hear from their favourite son, temporarily exiled to the United States but pining for fresh air and clean water and good, honest working folks without pretensions.

But by the time the Bruins won the Stanley Cup and Orr was summoned home for his own special day in Parry Sound, he at the very least had a foot in both camps. Boston was his town now. He owned the place, understood its rhythm and its people and could play the hipster, the sophisticate whenever that guise was required. Still, Orr remained a bit insecure about his roots, about his lack of worldliness, all of that represented by the small town in which he'd grown up. If anyone wanted to get on his bad side, which could be a very bad place indeed, all they needed to do was suggest in any way that Orr was a rube, that he was a country hick. Once Boston began to feel more and more like home, he seemed in many ways happy to leave his past behind. And despite those early protestations to the contrary, he'd never again live in Canada, never mind in the town he had left when he was fourteen years old.

On Bobby Orr Day – July 6, 1970 – whatever inner conflict existed certainly wasn't in evidence. Orr returned a conquering hero. They would turn the town upside down for him, and he'd bring a bunch of his famous pals along for the ride. Of course Eagleson was there, as were the flamboyant Toronto sports columnist Dick Beddoes and Milt Schmidt. Terry Crisp and Gary Sabourin, fellow Parry Sound boys made good, were there. Peggy was there, though she and Bobby weren't yet married. In the newspapers, they referred to her as "Bobby's latest." From the Bruins came Tom Johnson and Derek Sanderson and Eddie Johnston. Mike Walton, then a Maple Leaf and Orr's business partner, had a place at the head table, and so did Grandma Elsie Orr, who was still nursing at the local hospital. "Aren't you proud of your grandson?" they'd ask her constantly, and she'd drop the line that Arva had long ago perfected, to send a message about where the Orr family's priorities lay. "Which one? I have three grandsons."

The ragtag parade proceeded down the main drag, with Bobby in an open convertible, reaching out to shake hands, and what seemed like every kid in town trailing behind. They had to find somebody to direct traffic downtown, which didn't happen every day, and they cancelled the Saturday matinee at the Strand Theatre – who was going to the movies on a day so special? The totem pole across from the dock was decked out in an official Bobby Orr sweatshirt: you could buy one just like it at Ronnie's clothing store. Along with a chance to glimpse the guest of honour, the highlight of the show was a forty-foot hockey stick, carried in the parade by a group of strong young men and eventually deposited at the old Orr home on Great North Road, where it would remain for years afterwards, leaning against the outside wall.

The proud Orr parents were naturally cornered by visiting reporters and asked for their thoughts on this marvellous day. Arva worried that her son was "fast becoming a nervous wreck, unable to sit still for a minute." Doug shared her concern but could certainly see the bright side. "In the last couple of weeks he's barely had a minute to himself, let alone for us. No amount of money is worth suffering that kind of existence. Still, he remains great to his family, even though we have lost him a little. He's building us a new house here. Every contract he signs with any company includes a clause to the benefit of the family."

Five hundred people paid ten bucks a head to crowd into the gym at the Parry Sound High School and eat a country dinner of cold cuts, macaroni and cheese, chicken salad, apple pie and strawberry shortcake (and nary a drop of alcohol). All of the proceeds would go toward building a new community centre.

Eagleson made one of the speeches, but the highlight was an address by a Catholic priest from Boston, Father Frank Chase. Bobby wasn't a Catholic, and Boston had long been a town divided along religious (not to mention racial) lines, but obviously Orr had bridged that gap, not just through his hockey talents but through the myriad good deeds he had performed in the community. There were many of those, hospital visits and help for local charities, all done quietly, all far away from the bright lights, none of it in the interest of polishing a public image. Over the years, those who admired Orr the man, and even those who didn't, agreed on that one fact: he gave of himself for many a good cause. ("Okay, I'm lucky, right?" Orr once explained in an interview. "I've been gifted, right? But the world is full of people who have not been gifted. Not only haven't been gifted but have had things taken away from them. . . . I think that compared to those people I'm a very small article. A very small, lucky article." Frosty Forristal, his old roommate, painted this picture: "After he's been to a hospital to see kids – and he does that an awful lot – he can get down in the dumps. He goes and talks with a kid. They have a good conversation. Bobby tells him stories and signs a stick for him and they become good pals. Then Bobby finds out the kid has cancer and it's only a matter of weeks or days. That kills him. He won't be himself for a couple of days, and to make it worse he might go back and see the kid again. But don't write anything about that. He wouldn't want people to know. They would think he's a big shot or something. You know the way he thinks." An anonymous Bruins teammate saw it a little differently: "All that running around to mental hospitals and parishes – it's gonna start showing up in his play.")[54]

"Bobby is the complete hero," Father Chase told the assembly. "By that I mean he's not only a great hockey player but a great person. He has the qualities to be potentially one of the greatest forces for good in our area. . . . So many superstars prove to have feet of clay because they have no one to buttress them. You in Parry Sound are family to Bobby Orr. He needs you, because no one can exist as a superstar without little people like us behind him."[55]

Finally, the guest of honour was called to the podium. He stood in front of an audience who knew him when, who knew his family, who understood where he had come from, how long and unlikely the journey had been. Bobby Orr would never be much of a public speaker. He could get by on few words and plenty of charm, on a wink and a grin and a slap on the back. But this occasion demanded something more, something beyond the dressing room platitudes doled out to keep the reporters at bay, or the smiling commercial endorsements. For just a moment, this would be Bobby Orr unvarnished, unguarded, unprotected, a sight more rare than seeing him stumble on the ice.

"I'm a man now," he said, "and when you're a man you are not supposed to cry. All I know is that there are tears in my eyes."

Chapter Fourteen

THE ALL-AMERICAN CANADIAN HERO

B OBBY ORR WAS AT THE PINNACLE, complete in terms of his on-ice repertoire, transcendent in his celebrity. No hockey player had been in that lofty position before, at least not in the United States. On the ice, fans of the game could look forward to seeing his signature moves: rushing the puck with the grace and power of a figure skater, with the quick lateral shifts that left defenders flatfooted, wondering how he'd slipped by; the slap-shot, as accurate as any in the league and nearly as powerful, set up with a little pause at the top of the backswing, then fired with a snapping release, the puck finding the back of the net with remarkable accuracy; perfectly angled passes, often delivered without even a glance at their intended destination, yet still hitting teammates in open space, in full flight; acts of defensive daring, blocked shots and pucks scooped off the goal line and decisions made that would be crazy risky for anyone else; the pivot spin, the "spinorama," some announcers liked to call it, a hard cut left from a standing position, leaving an opposing checker lost at sea. Some other hockey players did some of that, but none of them could do all of that. Then there were those moments when Orr was killing a penalty, wasting time, when he would seize the puck and just start skating, roaming the ice, breaking all of the rules, heading back deep into his own end and then out again, all at an apparently leisurely pace. *Ragging* it, and somehow no one could touch him, no one on the other side could push him from the meandering path that only he could see. There was the kid on the frozen bay in Parry Sound playing keep-away from the bigger boys. Come and get me. Just try to catch me. Then he's gone again.

That said, it was still hockey, beautiful and astounding for those who had grown up with the sport, but impenetrable to the mass of Americans who knew the game no better than they knew cricket, who would forever have trouble spotting the puck, let alone understanding the game's nuances. Canadians had from their first sentient moments worshipped the icons of their national sport. The Rocket and Gordie Howe and Bobby Hull, all of them were more famous, more beloved than any prime minister. But for so long, hockey had been a regional attraction in the U.S., and even its greatest heroes were local heroes by definition. Unless you lived in New York, Boston, Detroit or Chicago, the whole sport was probably lost on you. Certainly, no hockey player could ever be Mickey Mantle or Wilt Chamberlain or football's Johnny Unitas.

Orr arrived on the scene, and with him came a potent convergence of era and event and fashion and attitude. There was NHL expansion, and there were more national television broadcasts, and there was a kind of awakening, if not to the fine points of the game, or its history, or its culture, at least to the fact that there was a bright young star of stars now at the height of his powers. As would be the case a few years later, in the wake of another NHL invasion, this time of the American sunbelt, when the *idea* of Wayne Gretzky, greatest player ever, became a potent marketing tool, the notion that Orr, this handsome, boyish, unspoiled, self-effacing, generous kid from backwoods Canada, could be better than anyone who had ever played the game was attractive even far beyond the hockey hard core. He looked the part, and he looked of the moment, and he had appeal even to those who previously hadn't given hockey a second thought. He was a star in a way that no hockey player had been a star before. He had broken through to a place where the game that defined him was only part of the story.

In December 1970, with the image of Flying Bobby scoring the Stanley Cup-winning goal still fresh in memory, *Sports Illustrated* named Orr its Sportsman of the Year. He had already won every significant trophy offered by the NHL, but this was an award of a different sort. The weekly bible of sports journalism was the arbiter not just of athletic excellence but also of sports fashion and trend. Being named its top sportsman was a kind of holistic benediction, different from merely being the best player of one game or another. Estimable character was definitely part of the mix, as was a significant cultural status. The magazine was making a statement, elevating a hockey player to that height while knowing that a huge section of its readership had never laced on skates. Since the award was first presented to the great miler Roger Bannister back in 1954, hockey had been completely, happily ignored. (And for *Sports Illustrated*, the truth is that it remains far in the background even now. Only one other hockey player has ever been named Sportsman of the Year: Wayne Gretzky in 1982. The U.S. "Miracle on Ice" Olympic gold medal team from the Lake Placid were given a group honour in 1980.)

Orr had accomplished what Howe and Richard and Hull had never done – he had crossed over in mass consciousness, crossed over with the hockey-indifferent majority of Americans, crossed over into a realm of pure celebrity normally inhabited by movie and television stars. There was his face on the cover of *Sports Illustrated*, dropped into mailboxes, plastered all over newsstands, blue eyes twinkling, a bank of coloured lights behind him. Inside, the accompanying story, written by Jack Olsen, a wonderful magazine journalist and author who would later find fame as one of the inventors of the "true crime" genre of non-fiction, was the most remarkable and complete portrait of the young athlete that would appear during his career. Olsen argued, without qualification, that Orr was the greatest hockey player who had ever lived. He laid on all of the expected superlatives and gave Orr credit for any success the new, expanded NHL had enjoyed in the great wilderness. But it was his impressions of the young man off the ice that broke new biographical ground.

As the parameters of the award required, Olsen emphasized Orr's selflessness and kindness, both as a teammate and as a citizen. Eagleson explained that money didn't matter to his famous client at all, that he didn't even manage to spend the $20,000 in annual allowance he was paid, that he could not have cared less about the fact that he'd soon be a millionaire, that he worried only about how his salary might separate him from his lower-paid fellow Bruins. (That didn't quite jibe with Eagleson's later, no doubt coloured, recollections of Orr as a carefree spendthrift who went through money just as quickly as Al could arrange for him to earn it.) Adding to that character endorsement was the evidence of Orr's charity work.

"He's a bleeding heart and a do-gooder, that's all," Eagleson said. "And most of it's private. He doesn't even tell me about it. He doesn't get receipts. And we lose all kinds of tax deductions because he doesn't make a record of it. Every once in a while he clears out his whole wardrobe and gives it to the priest over at Sacred Heart in Watertown. No, Bobby's no Catholic; he's barely even a Baptist. But he's the most Christian man I've ever known."

Orr didn't want to discuss any of that with Olsen.

"It's very personal with me," he said. "Ask me about broads or booze, anything else."

So Olsen did.

He captured Orr in idle conversation with the omnipresent Frosty Forristall in the Bruins dressing room hours before a game.

"To tell you the truth," Orr said, "I think I've got the perfect number of girlfriends right now."

"How many's that?" Frosty wondered.

"Four," Orr said.

Olsen got this quote from an unnamed "teammate": "Bobby's got this thing about women, see. They all want to mother him and follow him home and do his cooking and everything else, and Bobby's the same as the next guy, right? But then he can't get rid of them. It's not in him to treat women badly. So when he's seen enough of some broad it'll take him four months to let her down gently."

He had Bobby knocking back beers during an interview, one after another. And after a game one night, a tough loss, when Bobby and a woman described as his "late date" and Eagleson and some others gathered at a local watering hole, they become a little too boisterous for the management, who politely asked that they quiet down. Orr summoned the maître d' to his table, then barked at him.

"You listen to me! Don't you ever come to my table and tell me and my friends to be quiet."

So there's the star, there's a bit of attitude, there's a less pristine image, but mostly there's a real flesh-and-blood human being, no saint, but with a good, generous heart, no monk, but with normal, healthy appetites, flawed in the ways we all are, a figure recognizable to readers who couldn't find Parry Sound – couldn't find Canada – on a map. A realistic portrait of the boy wonder, it seemed, with only an unnamed "NHL official" (interesting, given the context, that he would request anonymity) feeling the need to erect a public relations barrier, to try to spin the story off into fairy-tale land: "He brings a new image to the game. He's modest; he's restrained; he's understated. He's the exact opposite of a Joe Namath. Namath reached millionaire status as a kind of mixed-up antihero, but Orr will reach it as a hero in the classic sense. The ones who cultivate the image of the big, bad athlete boozing or chasing broads or blowing their cool, they're the vanishing breed. The Namaths, the Denny McLains. The Bobby Orrs are the incoming breed, and we better be thankful they are around."[56]

Not awfully prescient that, given how sports stardom would evolve in the latter days of the twentieth century, but it could be forgiven in the enthusiasm of the moment and in the excitement that the NHL finally had its own poster boy.

Meanwhile, within the game, there was no real debate about Orr's place, about the magnitude of his accomplishments or the fact that he had single-handedly revolutionized the defenceman's role. Even the ancients agreed with that. It's a normal function of getting on in life to aggrandize the heroes of youth and dismiss, to a degree, their modern equivalents. It was better back then, when the players were tougher, when they weren't in it just for the money. Never mind the numbers. Those are skewed by expansion and technology and a general weakening of moral fibre. That's the familiar geezer's lament. But with Orr, the old-timers seemed more than happy to give him his due and to compare him favourably to anyone who had come before, including the first great offensive defenceman, Boston's Eddie Shore.

Elmer Ferguson, an octogenarian sportswriter in Montreal, had seen Shore up close and in person. He thought Orr was better. "This is because Shore was expected to play defence, while Orr plays both defence and attack and does fine at each."[57] Writing in the Toronto Maple Leafs game program, Red Burnett, a veteran of *The Toronto Daily Star* sports department, was unequivocal in his assessment of Orr's talents. "There has been better hockey and better teams but in my twenty-five years pounding the NHL beat I have never lamped a better or more exciting hockey virtuoso than the towhead from Parry Sound."[58]

Red Kelly, a defenceman with such offensive talent that he was at one point in his storied career converted to forward, spoke of Orr from that unique perspective. "I think Bobby became even more effective, if that's possible, when he changed his approach slightly. He often would play the whole game himself, both forechecking and backchecking on the same play. He took some big risks of injuries, too. In the past two or three years, though, he's altered the style a little. He doesn't rush the puck quite as much but passes it ahead more now. But still, he's always capable of the big rush. He is perhaps more effective now because he makes such good use of the players on the ice with him."[59]

But the greatest benediction may have been the one from the man long considered the greatest player in hockey history, who was already being asked by some to surrender that title to the new kid on the block. "When the other players start watching a kid like Bobby, he must have something," Gordie Howe said. "They used to watch me."[60]

Entering the 1970-71 season as the defending Stanley Cup champions, the Bruins would see changes, but not many. The World Hockey Association wouldn't be in business until the fall of 1972, so NHL players were still tightly restricted in their mobility. Ted Green would come back from his near-fatal head injury, but in truth he'd never be quite the same player he was before the stick-swinging brawl with Wayne Maki. Otherwise, the team returned all but intact, with pretty much the same lineup that had been in place since the big trade that brought Phil Esposito, Fred Stanfield and Ken Hodge from Chicago.

But there would be a significant change at the top. Harry Sinden figured that, given his success building a Stanley Cup-winning team, his employers might want to reward him with a raise. He was earning peanuts, even by the modest standards of NHL coaches at the time. Around Christmas in 1969, with his contract set to expire at the end of the season and the Bruins rolling toward a championship, Sinden asked the Bruins for an $8,000 raise. True to their reputation, Boston wouldn't go any higher than $3,000. Rather than accept the money on the table, Sinden called their bluff. Three days after winning the Cup, he "retired" from hockey and went into private business, working with a home-building outfit in Rochester, New York. "It was obvious to me that what I thought all along was 100 per cent correct," he said in what sure seemed like a bridge-burning article, written under his own name (with assistance from Mark Mulvoy) in *Sports Illustrated*. "The Bruins weren't very interested in Harry Sinden's future. . . . I'll miss hockey. I know that. It was my life for more than twenty years. But I'm leaving a winner – the coach of the Stanley Cup champion – and that is the way to go."[61]

In his place – this, too, would become a hallmark of the Bruins, continuing long after Bobby Orr was gone – the franchise handed the reins of the best team in hockey to one of its long-time employees, Tom Johnson. He had been a very good defence-man for the great Montreal Canadiens teams of the 1950s, winning the Norris Trophy in 1958–59 and the Stanley Cup six times. Johnson finished his playing career with two seasons in Boston and then stuck with the organization in a variety of front office jobs. But he had no coaching experience in the NHL or anywhere else, for that matter. "I've never coached before," Johnson acknowledged, "so I don't know what type of coach I'll be." The price, though, must have been right.

What the players realized soon enough was that, compared with Sinden, Johnson was a soft touch, more than happy to let this exceptionally talented bunch do pretty much as they pleased. Perhaps for a confident, veteran team on the heels of a championship season that wouldn't necessarily be a big problem. There were surely enough leaders among the players in the dressing room to keep things in order.

As a leader, Orr set an example on the ice, while remaining a discreet presence in the dressing room. Though he had long ago shed the reticence from his early years in the league, he was certainly still no rah-rah speechmaker. Don Awrey, who occasionally played defence alongside Orr – but was otherwise socially more likely to be found hanging out with the Phil Esposito crowd – provided one of the more revealing descriptions of his famous teammate from those years. "He's very quiet in the dressing room," Awrey said. "I really haven't got to know him even though I've played with him for three years and sat beside him that amount of time. He's very, very quiet. When he really gets up for a game he doesn't say too much to, really, anybody. I don't think there's one fellow on the hockey team that really, really does know Bobby. I would think he'd have to be one of the team leaders on the ice. Off the ice because he's so quiet I don't think he really expresses his opinions the way he wants to because he is this type of quiet guy."

Orr entered the new season with the same goal as everyone else – to win another championship, as the Bruins were widely favoured to do. But as Eagleson was quick to point out, there were also other challenges awaiting him beyond the horizons of the NHL.

"The immediate target is to win the Stanley Cup again for Boston," the Eagle explained. "Ahead there is the Russians to shoot for. Bobby was only seventeen when he last played against them in Toronto and was the best man on the ice. What he wants now, above everything else, is to play them again – for Canada in world competition."

—

Maybe they weren't laughing *at* the Montreal Canadiens. Maybe it was just the boys sharing a little private joke on the bench. Maybe Espo had said something goofy, or Cash had dropped a funny line, or Pie McKenzie had made a crack about one of the women they'd met in a bar the night before. But in the lore and legend of Montreal hockey – and Lord knows that runs thick and deep – the story persists that, in the second game of the first round of the 1971 Stanley Cup playoffs, the Boston Bruins were sitting on the bench openly mocking Les Glorieux, chuckling away without a care in the world. What could have made the Bruins feel so smug? Oh, a couple of things. They were at home at the Boston Garden, where they hardly ever lost, and they were up 5–1 barely halfway into the game. They had already won the first game of the best-of-seven opening playoff series 3–1, with Orr scoring the winner in the third period. They were the defending Stanley Cup champions, and everything suggested to them that this was but one small bump on what would be a long road to another championship. In the regular season just completed, they had cruised to first place in the Eastern Conference, twelve points ahead of the second-place New York Rangers. Over the course of a 78-game schedule, the Bruins had amassed a record 57 wins, a record 121 points, and scored a record 399 goals, 192 more than they allowed.

Few NHL teams, even the great dynastic champions, had ever been so dominant – and this in the era of league-mandated parity, of the universal amateur draft. Individually, the Bruins stars were charting new ground. Esposito had set a single-season scoring mark with 152 points, scoring 76 goals in 78 games. In fact, the top four scorers in the league all wore Boston uniforms: Esposito, Orr, Johnny Bucyk and Ken Hodge. Orr, it could be argued, had put together a year more statistically remarkable than any of them, though its best measure – the so-called plus/minus number – wasn't widely quoted by hockey fans or scribes in those days. That statistic rated players according to how many goals their team scored while they were on the ice (at even strength or shorthanded) versus how many it allowed (while at even strength or on the power play). Orr, in 1970–71, finished at plus 124 (in other words, the

Bruins scored 124 more goals than they allowed, as defined by the rule, when Orr was playing). No other player had ever been over 100, and only two have passed the century mark since: Larry Robinson, who was plus 120 in 1977, and Bryan Trottier, who was plus 104 in 1979. In his best season, 1985, the most prolific scorer in NHL history, Wayne Gretzky, was plus 98.

In the fun-with-figures world of sports statistics devotees, a number is never just a number. A statistic like plus/minus can be adjusted according to how high-scoring the league is in a particular season, and in every case it in part reflects team performance as well as individual performance. Everything about the NHL in the late 1960s and early 1970s should be viewed in terms of the radical expansion of the league and the subsequent dilution of the talent pool. Big-league professional hockey doubled in size in one season. No other sport had ever attempted anything close to that, and certainly none has done so since. More and more teams were added in quick succession, as the owners hurried to cash cheques from the gullible buyers in non-traditional hockey markets. And this was before the great infusion of European talent that changed the face of the game, and before American-born players began arriving in large numbers. The league was pretty much all Canadian, and since even the great hockey nation could produce only a finite number of great players, Orr spent much of his career competing against many teams that were significantly weaker than those that had come before. That must have inflated his individual numbers and the individual numbers of others. Consider the sudden appearance of hundred-point scorers in the years immediately after the first great expansion.

But the truth is, you can adjust Orr's statistics all you want, you can build in qualifiers, and still he stands alone. (As an exercise, it's sort of like knocking Babe Ruth down a few pegs because he played in an era in which African Americans were barred from the major leagues.) Just measure Orr against his contemporaries. Measure him against all others competing in the same position. There is no comparison – and his 1970–71 season stands alone as the greatest ever played by a defenceman, if not the greatest ever played by anyone in the history of the NHL.

So that's why the Bruins were chuckling, with the top scorer to that point in NHL history in the lineup, with the best defenceman who had ever played the game and with a powerful lineup still very much intact from the season before, when they'd won the Cup. The Bruins had ten players who scored twenty goals or more in 1970–71, a number that had long been a benchmark in hockey. No team had ever enjoyed that depth of talent before. Those laughing players knew they were part of a team for the ages.

There was also the matter of the opposition. The season before, the Montreal Canadiens had missed the playoffs for the first time since 1948, and for the first time ever there was talk of the franchise losing ground to the rival teams in town, the newly arrived Montreal Expos of baseball's National League and even the Montreal Alouettes of the Canadian Football League, who in the fall of 1970 had won the Grey Cup. Toe Blake was gone, Jean Béliveau was contemplating retirement and few other links remained to the glorious past. In the midst of the 1970–71 season, the Canadiens had fired Blake's replacement, Claude Ruel, who was not at all beloved by his players, and replaced him with the very young, inexperienced Al MacNeil, who had been promoted from a minor-league coaching job to act as Ruel's assistant, an innovative concept then. The season also featured a risky blockbuster trade that turned out to be one in a series of master strokes for Montreal's brilliant general manager, Sam Pollock. The Habs sent three bright young prospects to the Detroit Red Wings – Mickey Redmond, Bill Collins and Guy Charron – and in return received Frank Mahovlich, who during his enigmatic career in Toronto and Detroit had been both a dominant scoring winger and a player laid low by his own fragile self-confidence. Certainly there was still talent on the Montreal roster, especially on defence, where J. C. Tremblay remained one of the elite players in his position, and where two rising young stars, Serge Savard and the rookie Guy Lapointe, had impressed everyone in the league. Unfortunately, Savard had broken his leg in five places near the halfway point of the season and certainly wasn't going to be ready for the playoffs. The Canadiens finished third in the east, and during the final week of the regular season lost two games to Boston by scores of 6–3 and 7–2.

The Bruins must have figured they had little to fear. And they would have paid scant attention to the fact that the Canadiens had recently called up a rookie goaltender late in the season from their American Hockey League farm team, the Montreal Voyageurs. Ken Dryden had actually been selected by Boston back in 1964 in the draft of unprotected amateur players (those who hadn't already been locked up by NHL organizations), when he was playing at the Junior B level. Almost immediately afterwards, his rights were traded to Montreal, along with those of Alex Campbell, for the rights to Guy Allen and Paul Reid. (All of those players had been selected in the amateur draft, and none of the other three had ever played in the NHL.) Instead of playing Junior A hockey, Dryden chose to attend Cornell University, then did a stint with Canada's national team. While dabbling in professional hockey with the Voyageurs, he was also a full-time law student at McGill University, shuffling back and forth between practices and classes. That coming summer, he planned to work with the American consumer advocate Ralph Nader's Raiders. Dryden was very tall for a goaltender, at six four; he was quiet and thoughtful and intelligent and, in the opinion of the sportswriters of the time, rather colourless. The Habs weren't thrilled with the goaltending of Rogatien Vachon and his backup, Phil Myre, and so decided to put the big egghead through a short late-season audition, more to assess his future potential than anything else. If he was a real prospect, they didn't want to lose him to another team in the intra-league draft, the mistake they'd made the year before with Tony Esposito.

Dryden started six games that spring and won them all, surrendering only nine goals. He was especially impressive leading the Habs to a 2–1 win over the powerful Chicago Black Hawks. Going into the playoffs against Boston, apparently with little chance of winning and with precious little to lose, the Canadiens coach Al MacNeil gave Dryden the start in the first game at the Boston Garden. He played well enough in the Montreal loss to be given the start again in game two but had surrendered five goals in the first period and a half. And that's when the laughing started.

As the Greeks described it, those prone to hubris always get the wind taken out of their sails in the end. But not so reliably was the great cosmic comeuppance seen in professional sports. There was all kinds of boasting, all kinds of strutting, all kinds of guys who flew right up next to the sun and then landed, unscathed and triumphant. Joe Namath had guaranteed that Super Bowl win just a few months before, and guess what? Muhammad Ali claimed he was the Greatest, and it turned out he was just about right. The champion's swagger goes with the territory. Trash-talking for another generation would become a minor art form. Not so much in hockey, though, a sport in which the athletes were expected to be less demonstrative, more humble, in which a simple raised stick celebrated a goal, in which any display beyond that was considered *de trop.* For a bunch of hockey players, in the middle of a playoff game, in pursuit of the sacred Stanley Cup, to be giggling away to themselves as they put away an overmatched opponent, well, that just wasn't on. And then, as in myth, the tide turned.

Orr himself would provide the symbolic sea change. Skating out of his own zone with the puck, a touch lackadaisical with the game so well in hand, he looked up when he should have looked down and fell victim to a poke check by Henri "the Pocket Rocket" Richard. Richard was greying by then, and had always played in his more famous brother's shadow, even years after Maurice "the Rocket" had retired. He skated around Orr to retrieve the puck, broke in alone and scored. It was only 5–2. The Bruins lead was still secure. But in that moment, some larger shift took place, the Habs finding faith, the Bruins shaken a little. By the time the game was done, by the time Montreal roared all the way back, with John Ferguson scoring the tying goal, and Jacques Lemaire the winner, and Frank Mahovlich adding one for insurance in a 7–5 Habs win, well, it had turned into a real contest. The teams would split the next two games back at the Montreal Forum, and then Boston won decisively at home in game five, 7–3, to take a 3–2 series lead, which figured to shift the emotional balance their way once again. But in game six in Montreal, it was as though the best days had returned. On a blackboard in the Montreal dressing room before the game, somebody had scrawled the words, "Orr can't skate" – not quite true, but at times during the series it had certainly looked as if there was something wrong, as though he was labouring a bit. That was only a small part of the story. Dryden was spectacular. The Canadiens won going away, 8–3. By the game's end, the fans were singing a song that hadn't been heard in the rink for at least fifteen years: "Les Canadiens sont là." It was the tune they used to play on the radio broadcasts every time Montreal scored a goal. The sentiment among the faithful was clear – the Canadiens weren't just "here," they were back in their rightful place on top of the hockey world.

Though the seventh game would be played at the Boston Garden, the pressure had obviously shifted to the home team. The Bruins, bearing the burden of all of those great expectations, were tight and tense, while the Canadiens, just happy to be there, played as though they had nothing to lose. Boston took an early lead, but by the end of the first period, it was 2–1 Montreal, then 3–1 after two. Frank Mahovlich applied the *coup de grâce* early in the third period, scoring on a breakaway to make it 4–1. The Bruins got one back, but that mattered not at all. One of the great upsets in hockey history was in the books.

In the Boston dressing room, those same cocky, laughing play- ers sat silently, in shock, as though a loved one had suddenly, unexpectedly died.

Orr spoke for the team. It seemed as though his eyes were misty. "I want you to do me a favour. Get the guys [reporters] and tell them that our guys played good hockey. It just wasn't good enough. I had a bad series.

"But here's something you've got to know. Tom Johnson isn't to blame for this. He did a helluva job. He made all the right moves. There's nothing he did wrong, and don't let anybody blame him. A lot of people want to blame him. But they can't.

"Tell them to blame me. I made mistakes. Tom didn't. Now do me a favour and tell the guys."

The truth was, Orr's play in the series had been erratic, brilliant one moment, tentative the next. There was talk that the knee was acting up again. He hadn't been skating well at the end of the regular season, and the Bruins had cut back his ice time once they'd cinched first place. Was that the real story? the reporters asked him, looking for something to explain the otherwise inexplicable. Did the knee let you down again?

"My leg is fine," he said. "And if it weren't, I wouldn't be telling you anyway."

It was all becoming a bit predictable now, the Bruins dominating during the regular season, Esposito and Orr battling for the scoring title, the same old gang together one more time – the only question whether they could follow through during the playoffs and win another Stanley Cup. There were subtle changes, though, for the 1971–72 season. Mike Walton, Orr's partner in the kids' summer camp, had joined the team the year before from Toronto, and would play a significant supporting role. Garnet "Ace" Bailey took a regular place on the checking line. And midway through the season, the Bruins made a deal with the California Seals – the worst of the teams from the great NHL expansion – sending Rick Smith west, along with Bob Stewart and a promising young forward named Reggie Leach, who would eventually wind up in Philadelphia. In return, they received Carol Vadnais, a defenceman with considerable offensive skills. At times, Vadnais would be a nightmare in his own end, turning the puck over, surrendering scoring chances. But when he joined in the attack, he could provide a reasonable, though a far less spectacular and reliable, facsimile of the role Orr played.

Boston finished the regular season just two points short of their record-setting total the year before and a full ten points clear of their nearest rival, the New York Rangers, who finished second in the East. Playing all but two games (he had missed only four in the past three seasons), Orr saw his totals drop off slightly: he had thirty-seven goals and eighty assists, for 117 points, enough to leave him second in the scoring race, behind Esposito. He would win another Norris Trophy and eventually go on to win a third consecutive Hart Trophy as the league's MVP, the first player to do so. His problematic left knee acted up mid-season, but Orr played through the pain, and hardly anyone beyond the inner circle understood that he'd been hurt at all.

If the Bruins had learned anything from the upset loss to the Canadiens the spring before, it was that the regular season meant nothing, that the Prince of Wales Trophy, the NHL's award for the team that finished with the most points, was just a great big paperweight. It was all about the playoffs, and this time the Bruins wouldn't let their cockiness get the better of them — though another storied franchise would give them a run for their money in the first round, just as the Habs had the year before. It didn't look like that when all was said and done: Boston eliminated the Toronto Maple Leafs in five games, but the series was far closer than the final tally would suggest. After losing the first game in Boston 5-0, the Leafs fought back to win the second 4-3 in overtime, on Jim Harrison's goal. With the scene shifting to Maple Leaf Gardens, Eddie Johnston was the hero of game three, shutting out the Leafs 2-0. Toronto was in position to tie the series in game four, up 3-1 heading into the third period. But in the final twenty minutes, Johnny McKenzie scored on a breakaway, Esposito tied it, with an assist from Orr, and then Esposito took advantage of a Mike Pelyk giveaway and banked a shot in off Ken Hodge's skate for the winner. Bernie Parent was brilliant for the Leafs in game five, and Toronto scored the first goal of the game. But again Hodge banged in the winner, with referee Bruce Hood waving off a potential tying Toronto goal with thirty seconds left in the game.

The second-round series, against the St. Louis Blues, was the kind of lopsided joke that made people wonder again just how long it would be before an expansion team could possibly win the Stanley Cup. Garry Unger scored the first goal of the first game for the Blues in Boston, and that would prove to be their final hopeful moment. They wound up losing 6-1, lost the next game 10-2 and lost the next one 7-2, with awful goaltending, terrible defensive play and not much offence to speak of. For the Bruins, it looked as if they were coasting through a pre-season scrimmage. The Blues' last-ditch effort in game four, fighting back from a 4–1 deficit to make for a respectable 5–3 finish, couldn't mask the fact that it had been one of the most one-sided playoff series in the long history of the NHL.

The Stanley Cup Finals, though, turned out to be a very different story. For the first time since 1960, the teams with the two best regular-season records were drawn together to decide the championship. In many ways, the New York Rangers were the Bruins' mirror image. But Brad Park and company, it seemed, were always just a step, or a bad bounce, behind Boston. The Rangers hadn't won a Stanley Cup since 1940, but this looked like their best chance since that long-ago triumph. They had knocked off the defending champions, Montreal, in six games, and then swept the first-place team in the West, the Chicago Black Hawks, a far tougher path to the finals than the one Boston had faced.

In the series opener, at the Boston Garden, the Bruins surrendered the first goal and then scored four straight (including two short-handed goals on the same penalty kill) to take a 5–1 lead in the middle of the second period. That, of course, had been the same cushion they had enjoyed against the Canadiens a year earlier, when their overconfidence caught up with them. And for a while, it seemed that history was being repeated – the Rangers came back to tie the game in the third, before Ace Bailey scored the winner for Boston. Orr set up Bucyk for the first goal in game two, a classic spinorama inside the New York blue line, followed by a perfect pass. The Rangers tied the game, but lost, eventually, on Ken Hodge's power play goal.

New York won the first game at Madison Square Garden, 5–2, setting up the pivotal fourth game. In a playoff in which he was dominant most nights, despite the fact that his left knee was becoming more painful with every game, this might have been Orr's finest performance. He scored the game's opening goal, taking a pass from Walton and splitting the New York defence before beating Ed Giacomin with a wrist shot. He scored the Bruins' second goal as well, this time on a power-play slapshot from the point (it was Orr's twenty-first point of the playoffs, breaking his own record for a defenceman). In the second period, with Boston short-handed, he combined with Don Marcotte on a nifty give-and-go, faking a shot before slipping through the pass that put Marcotte in all alone. The Bruins led 3–0, and though the Rangers would eventually battle back, coming within a goal in the final two minutes of the game, Boston now had a stranglehold on the series.

"The way I saw it," Derek Sanderson quipped afterwards, "Bobby controlled the puck for forty minutes and was nice enough to let the other thirty-five players use it for the other twenty. He's not a selfish kid, you know."

Naturally, everything was in place for a victory party as the teams headed back to the Boston Garden for game five. The Cup was in the arena, there was plenty of champagne on ice, the local television crews were all set to film the frenzy, and the Bruins had a private room booked at their favourite neighbourhood bar, the Branding Iron, for the real post-game party. With the home team leading 2–1 heading into the third period, the fans had already begun to celebrate – and perhaps their heroes relaxed just a bit. Bobby Rousseau scored twice for the Rangers, and suddenly the party was off and the series had taken on a different complexion. It was back to New York now, with the Rangers believing they had a shot.

On May 11, 1972, the Bruins would quickly shatter those illusions. They played a clinical, nearly perfect game, with Cheevers shutting out the Rangers and Orr again the star of the show. He scored the first goal, in the first period, shaking Bruce MacGregor with a spin-orama at the New York blue line, and then firing a wrist shot into the corner, past the Rangers goaltender Gilles Villemeure. It didn't have the drama of the overtime winner against St. Louis two years before, and it didn't come with an iconic image like the one captured in Ray Lussier's famous photo, but it was a classic bit of Orr genius nonetheless, and as it turned out his second Stanley Cup-winning goal. In the second period, Cashman tipped in Orr's slap-shot to make it 2–0, and then with time running out in the third period, Esposito sent Cashman in alone to score the cinching goal. Cash danced a little jig after he scored it, his stick high in the air.

As the final seconds ticked off, Hodge sent the puck back to Orr, in the Boston zone. At the horn, he reached down to pick up the souvenir and then leaped into Gerry Cheevers' arms.

Orr finished the playoffs with five goals and nineteen assists, and for the second time was awarded the Conn Smythe Trophy as the post-season MVP, the first time it had been awarded twice to the same player. The Bruins had won their second Stanley Cup in three years, matching the achievement of the franchise's only other multiple championship squad, in 1939 and 1941.

That first Boston Cup run was ended by the Second World War, when so many of the young Canadian men playing the game were forced to leave the hockey life and head overseas. The modern Bruins faced a different set of challenges, most notably the beginning of a rival breakaway league and ownership that was unwilling to pay the price to compete. Though in that moment there seemed no limit to what this group might accomplish, the truth was that, just as had been the case thirty-one years before, the dynasty ended here.

Since they were on the road, since they were in Madison Square Garden, where everyone outside of the merry few in the Bruins dressing room was heartbroken, the celebratory atmosphere afterwards wasn't quite as wild as it had been two years before. That would have to wait for the return to Boston, where during a civic victory celebration the Bruins players would stand on a balcony like South American dictators before a huge, adoring crowd on a sunny afternoon, all of them with a beer in hand, all of them greeted with the kind of hysterical screams and cheers normally reserved for rock stars. Orr's brief introduction – he alone among the players chose to wear a jacket and tie – stirred the loudest ovation from the gathering, with high-pitched teen-idol shrieking layered over the familiar sports-fan howls.

In New York, in the dressing room din, they did their post-game turn for the television cameras – McKenzie and Bucyk and Stanfield, together forever, once again insisting that they be interviewed as a trio (they had just bettered their own record for playoff scoring, combining for fifty-three points). Sanderson swaggered in like the coolest man this side of Namath, puffing away on a cigarette. They asked him about his fight that night with Rod Gilbert. "It was like the mafia. Nothing personal. Strictly business."

And what were the defensive strategies that had worked so well against the Rangers? "I just give the puck to Bobby Orr. Let Bobby do all he can with it."

Orr took his place in front of the camera, with the great silver chalice just off to his right, a baby blue towel draped over his shoulders, partially concealing his pale, hairless torso. A flap of brown hair hung down, sweaty, over his forehead. This time Doug wasn't there to take centre stage, but he wasn't far from Bobby's thoughts.

"Is this going back to Boston?" he asked. "I think my dad and my brother are watching. There's a bunch of guys from Parry Sound there. They'd better be in the hotel room, because I'm coming back to get them."

They had to ask him about the knee. You wouldn't have known it, watching him through the playoffs, watching him take over the final, but there was quiet talk around the Bruins that he was suffering through every game. Orr, though, wasn't going to play the martyr, wasn't going to wreck the moment by dwelling on his own infirmity. That wasn't his style.

"No, it just gets a little sore. Within the next couple of days I'm going to see our doctors and they're going to decide. If they decide they're going to operate they'll do it, I think, around the second week of June."

"It won't be a long, extended time that you're out, will it?" the television guy asked

"Oh no, no, ah . . . I don't really know, to tell you the truth. I don't know anything about it."

The announcers joked about it some more, as though they were all old pals, about how he'd hurt himself earlier in the year in a game against Philadelphia and even they hadn't known it, about how deft Orr had become at hiding the pain and playing on.

"It just gets sore sometimes," Orr said, obviously wanting to put an end to that uncomfortable line of conversation. "That's all it is."

Chapter Fifteen

BYSTANDER

THIS WAS THE EAGLE'S MASTERSTROKE, the triumph of the great impresario. He would do what the custodians of the amateur game had refused to do, what an American could never have done, even in the midst of the first flickerings of détente. He'd deal with godless Commies and he'd deal with the godless capitalists who ran the National Hockey League; he'd convince both sides that there was something in it for them, mostly cold hard cash. He'd persuade the players to go along, though that wasn't so tough since most of them had never had the chance to represent their home and native land. He'd tell them there was something in it for them too, in the short term, in the long term. They'd be proud for now, and down the road they'd be better off. Eagleson wouldn't be the only one responsible for bringing it together, and if you wanted to be churlish, you could suggest not even the main one, but by the time it was over, you'd certainly never know it.

His prize client, though, was still on the shelf, the Stanley Cup celebration now blurred together with that familiar mix of pain, surgery, pain, rehab, pain, then finally the first tentative steps back on the ice. On June 6, Dr. Carter Rowe, the Bruins team physician, did his damnedest to work miracles by cutting away at Orr's left knee. Afterwards, he offered the usual assurances that all was well, that with a little rest and rehab the hinge would be just as good as new, that there was no reason whatsoever to believe that Orr's career would be shortened or imperilled, that his skills would be diminished. Several bits of cartilage were removed, as were bone spurs, and Orr wouldn't be ready to skate again until camp opened in September – when, the doctor suggested, he ought to consider a knee brace. But soon enough, he'd be just fine.

That summer, it was as though Bobby had finally surrendered to the fates, or maybe, finally, he was just fed up with his infirmities. It sounds simple – go home and do your rehab and keep yourself in shape. In truth, it was mind-numbing and uncomfortable and as far from actually playing the game he loved, the game that came naturally, as anything you could imagine. Orr had never been a great patient, largely because of his characteristic impatience. Every time his knee gave way, he wanted to get back to hockey as soon as possible. The exercises, the slow, cautious rebuilding, didn't suit his temperament at all. And now it was as though he'd said to hell with it. He let himself go, gaining an extra twenty pounds. He let his hair grow longer than it had ever been before. Hippie hair – that's what Eagleson called it. His heart wasn't in this reha-bilitation exercise, and there was no way to camouflage it.

The Summit Series between Canada's best professionals and the national team of the Union of Soviet Socialist Republics grew ever closer, and Orr had always said he wanted his crack at the Russians and to play with the maple leaf on his chest. But with camp about to open at Maple Leaf Gardens, there was no pretending that he was ready. He was there for the first workouts, and the cameras captured him skating gingerly (the ice at the storied hockey shrine was always remarkably lousy, so he had to watch his step), like an old man afraid of falling and breaking a hip.

In the pictures he does look heavy, and his hair does look long, but in the context of this group, that's not so unusual. There's no par-ticular sense of urgency among what will be called Team Canada.

Even entering the great unknown, taking on a foe that they have precious little knowledge of, they believe — and nearly everyone in hockey believes right along with them — that the coming series will be a cakewalk. The Russians can't be as tough as the best Canada has to offer, and they can't be as good, and their goalie, the scouts say, is a bit of a sieve. The players don't need summer employment anymore, with salaries on the rise, so they're coming from home and from the cottage, from weeks of off-season idyll, using this as a warm-up for the real games to come. No one's in great shape, and no one is too worked up about it. If this roster can't get by on talent alone, who can? They are Phil Esposito, Yvan Cournoyer, Frank Mahovlich, Ken Dryden and a less celebrated name, a winger from the Toronto Maple Leafs named Paul Henderson, who is more an honest working pro than a superstar. The team is coached by Harry Sinden, who was persuaded by Eagleson to end his short "retirement" from hockey and take his rightful place behind the bench. His Stanley Cup résumé with the Bruins is part of what he brings to the table, but there's also that international experience way back when with the Whitby Dunlops. He's one NHL guy who has actually seen the Russians up close.

Orr's circumstances are different. Were he healthy, he'd be the marquee name on this squad, perhaps its captain, certainly its greatest asset. Instead, he's a marginal presence at the brief training camp, not even a fifth wheel, skating around in slow circles, knowing exactly how the knee feels, telling himself lies about how it will better soon enough, about how he'll fool them all and play now or play when the series shifts to Russia. Except when he's honest with himself, when he must know that can't be true.

A television reporter corners him, and there's no escape, though you can tell from Orr's eyes, from the tightness around his mouth, that he's in no mood for talking, that he doesn't have the energy or the inclination to trot out Aw-Shucks Bobby one more time, that he's pissed off and sore and wants to be somewhere else. So no fake glibness and no disarming smiles this time. Just doing his duty, pure and simple, taking one for the team, one for the cause, one for Al.

"I hope to be in the lineup," he says. "I don't think I'll be in the lineup in Canada but maybe in Russia."

The interviewer is a bit taken aback by that.

"This is sort of against what the Boston Bruins announced a little while ago. Has the knee come along better than you thought or what?"

"Well, the knee has come along great," Orr says. "If I have any intention of playing I should be down here working out the way I am now. I'm working twice a day on the weights. Up in camp, I know I wasn't working out properly. If I have any intention of playing at all, I might as well be down here working out properly. That's the reason I'm here. I don't think the Bruins are going to tell me not to play if I feel I'm ready. They know I'm not going to play if I'm not ready. So I don't think I'll have any trouble from the Bruins if I do decide to play."

"How does it feel?"

"Great." There's the hint of a smile for the first time. "The knee didn't bother me at all. My thigh muscle was a little weak and shaky, but the knee didn't bother me at all."

Orr has become expert at telling that story, explaining that everything will be okay, that the knee will be like new, that he'll be the same player everyone remembers, that no one ought to fret on his behalf. He can sound as though he even believes it.

And so he sits and watches from the sidelines like the rest of us. He sees Espo score the first goal at the Montreal Forum, and figures it will be easy, figures the Russians are nothing, they're paper tigers, they're going to fold up and surrender against these big, strong, supremely talented Canadian boys who play an entirely different kind of game. He sits and watches and by night's end knows their game is different, all right, knows that these guys have an entirely different hockey alphabet, have re-imagined the sport from scratch and turned it on its head and our guys never knew what hit them.

He sits and watches the brief return of equilibrium in game two in Toronto, as though somehow that first embarrassment was merely a fluke, and now the guys have got their legs and measured their opponent and know what to do. He sits and watches and, by the end of the fourth game in Vancouver, knows that's not true, knows that Canada is in trouble, that the guys are a step too slow, that they're confused and not in great shape and there's absolutely nothing he can do about it. Even if he was playing, who's to know if that would have been enough to turn the tide.

He watches as Esposito makes his famous speech to the people of Canada after hearing the boos cascade down, all hair and sweat and big, sad brown eyes and heart-on-the-sleeve passion.

Espo could be a bit much sometimes; he could rub you the wrong way. This emotional patriotic stuff was almost *American,* except that it wasn't, because it had to be forced out of him, because it came out only when we were down and out and apparently defeated, and it seemed that the whole nation had decided to cut and run. It was as though the cliché of the between-periods hockey interview, the guy with the towel around his neck who never says a thing, is exposed for the joke that it is by his honesty. Here was Espo, talking straight to the camera, straight into all of those living rooms, laying the soul of the country bare. Evaporating in that instant were generations of Waspy self-restraint, and deference, and sobriety. Goddammit, he felt something, we all felt something, and every heart beat faster.

Then they got on the plane for Sweden, the intermediate stop on the way to Moscow, and some of the boys looked at Bobby sitting there as though he was part of the team and wondered not so quietly just what the hell he was doing there, what he had contributed, why he was along for the ride if he wasn't going to play. Must have been an Eagleson thing, they figured, though no one was taking Al to task. The fact was, they really needed the Eagle now, heading off to the great unknown. They needed him to protect their food from Commie poison and to make sure there weren't any spies lurking under their beds and to see that they got a fair shake even from those godawful European referees who seemed to have learned the game from a crooked rulebook.

Orr came back home after the series and said the right things because he'd been there. He said, "If we hadn't had a guy like Eagleson, guys like Al and Harry Sinden and John Ferguson, they would have kicked us all over Moscow. Many things happened that haven't even been mentioned and won't be mentioned, but you had to stand up. You had to say, no way, we're not doing this, we're going to do this. Al's the kind of guy who can do that and will do that. If he hadn't been there they would have kicked us all over the country." Us, except there wasn't really an "us" where he was concerned. He skated again when the team practised in Stockholm before heading into Russia. The knee locked up, and it was obvious that flying all that way had been for nought. Orr wasn't leaving, though. He wasn't going to be like those other guys – any good Canadian could name them – the traitorous few who weren't happy not getting ice time and so deserted their brothers in arms in their moment of need. He was sticking around and sticking with Al because that's what teammates did, even if they couldn't play, even if they weren't really part of the team, even if by now most of the folks at home had forgotten they were even there.

Bobby Orr wasn't going to save us. Somehow, that would have to come from within, from the same bunch who had played their way into this predicament. Now, it was all stacked against them. They were the foreigners, they were underdogs. And Jesus, didn't they win. Miracles stacked on miracles. Henderson, an ordinary player who scored an ordinary goal in extraordinary circumstances, saw his life transformed. The symbolism of that jibed with so much of the Canadian hockey mythology: a diligent, honest worker elevated high above even the superstars for that single patriotic act of slamming home a rebound. And there was Espo, the leader, the captain, the heart. And there was Eagleson, escorted across the ice in Moscow by his loyal troops, flipping the bird to the Russians and their scowling cops, defiant, angry, proud, not the meek, deferential Canadian. He was the boss now, the mastermind, the guy who made sure our boys finally got their chance to play the Russians, the guy who would seem as much a part of the victorious team as anyone on skates. He wasn't just a union leader now or an agent. He was a patriot, a Great Canadian, a man who floated above the game and certainly above the business of the game. Because this wasn't about money, certainly. This was about something far more profound.

Time stopped in Canada then. Schools let out. Businesses shut down. Folks gathered around televisions and radios as though war had been declared. It was a point of national demarcation, a history forever divided into the before, the after and the glorious present, the where-were-you-when-it-happened? An exhibition hockey game that the rest of the world hardly acknowledged, that the Russians tried to minimize (if you looked at the total goals in the series, they explained, really they had won). To make a Canadian of a certain age get teary-eyed, just play them the tape of Foster Hewitt: "Henderson scores for Canada!" Works every time.

Bobby Orr sits and watches that and cheers along with the small band of Canadians in the Luznicki Sports Palace; he celebrates afterwards with Al and the boys. There, but not really a part of it. The Bruins still held the Stanley Cup, a second championship in three seasons, and in Boston they still savoured that victory, oblivious to the events across the ocean. They would have Bobby Orr back in uniform for the next season, and maybe they'd do it again. That's what mattered in Beantown.

But in Canada, every schoolchild could rhyme off the names on that Team Canada roster and would still be able to do it more than thirty years later. They'd know who was there, and they'd pretty much forget who wasn't. In Toronto and Montreal, in Parry Sound and Saskatoon, in St. John's and Kelowna and Winnipeg, it was the greatest day of their lives. Bobby Orr sat and watched with the rest of us, and his Canadian heart must have beaten that much faster. He knew what was won, and also, in a different way from anyone else, he knew what was lost.

Back home, back to Boston, back to win another Stanley Cup. Bobby Orr, superstar. But it didn't seem to be quite as much fun anymore. The high-flying days of the early years with the Bruins, the bachelor-pad beach house – all that was history now. Orr had left Little Nahant when the fans started to crowd him, when his privacy was invaded, when his celebrity became oppressive. It's not that he hated stardom, or at least the perks that went with it. He liked having guys around who would take care of his needs and cover his back and devote themselves to him absolutely. But he had never really been a social animal, had never been comfortable in crowds. He could smile and he could shake a bunch of hands if there was a reason for it, if it was an obligation or a paying gig. More often than not, though, he'd make a discreet, early exit. All of a sudden, they'd be looking around, wondering where Bobby had gone. He had perfected the disappearing act.

Orr's life, now, was a series of controlled situations. He'd arrive at the rink ridiculously early on game days, five, six hours before they dropped the puck. Coaches would find him sitting in the dressing room, fiddling with a stick, working on his equipment, walking the halls of the Garden, eager to get back on the ice. "He gets edgy the day of a game," Tom Johnson said. "He eats very little and he'll sleep for maybe a half-hour in the afternoon. Most of the other guys really cork off, but not Bobby. He paces the room, and he'll always be the first guy in the dressing room. He never waits for the team bus because there'd be too many people around at that time. He cabs it. . . . He's relaxed in the dressing room, kidding around with Frosty and the guys. Sometimes that's the only peace he gets." There was still great camaraderie among that group, the characters, the pranks, the wisecracks back and forth, the cooler of Budweiser always full when they came off the ice.

But after games, once the door was opened and the inquiring minds arrived, looking for an instant explanation of that evening's heroics or heartbreaks, Orr had taken to hiding out from the reporters as much as possible, secreting himself away in an off-limits training area, hoping to wait them out, knowing that they'd eventually have to surrender to their deadlines and head back to the press box to file their stories. Some of the beat guys interpreted that rejection most generously: Bobby was tired of being the centre of attention every night, tired of all the plaudits, tired of taking the credit when the Bruins played well. By making himself scarce, he allowed his teammates to share in the glory. Others, though, weren't so kind and wondered how it was that the open, shy, polite kid from Parry Sound could have turned star on them. Who was he to act so aloof? A few wrote about that change, but not many.

In those days it was still considered a journalistic sin to focus on your own working conditions. And since on the ice Orr was impeccable, since he gave his all in every game, played unselfishly, showed no signs of an out-of-control ego, to crap on him for his reluctance to play along with the working press seemed a bit beside the point.

After games, when he had finished with the writers who had hung on to the bitter end, waiting for their quote, when he'd slipped past the fans who waited outside the Garden, hoping for a handshake and an autograph – and if you signed one, you had to sign a hundred, or hear about the poor hero-worshipping kid you turned down – Orr retreated behind closed doors at his new digs in the high-rise Prudential Tower. There was a doorman there, and security, and anyone who showed up hoping to see Bobby Orr had better be prepared to run that gauntlet. On the inside, it still seemed like a comfortable place. Orr himself had matured, was more secure in himself and in his place in the game, in the big city. Before he married, there were plenty of parties at the apartment and, as always, the girls came and went. After Peggy arrived on the scene and they began living together in the months before their wedding in Parry Sound, Orr's life settled into a more domestic pattern. Any trip outside, for shopping, for dinner, to a bar, was problematic now, and mostly not worth the effort. Everything he needed was inside that cocoon – right down to the jigsaw puzzles, his long-time hobby, which he could solve quicker than anyone. As long as he was there behind closed doors, there was nothing to worry about. (The bonds of fame held him even when he retreated to Parry Sound in the summer. At least, that's how Doug saw it. "Every June Bobby and I go to Moon River for a traditional fishing trip. Father and son just relaxing and talking together. It was something we valued, but this year it got fouled up. We'd be fishing quietly and the boats would come out and bump into us. Hey, Bobby – give us your autograph. He was good and signed. He's always good. I would have told 'em to go to hell.") Not quite Elvis hiding out in Graceland, but that kind of famous, at least in Boston, and that kind of a prisoner of celebrity. Leo Monaghan, the long-time hockey writer for *The Boston Globe,* who first met Orr as a fifteen-year-old, told his readers that the young star had become "a recluse." Orr's circle of true, trusted friends was narrow, and they soon learned that any perceived breach of trust, any hint of disloyalty, and they'd be cut out, absolutely. To be Orr's friend, it helped to be a bit of a sycophant. But there were plenty happy to play that role, just for the chance to be in his presence. That inner circle was small, and its makeup shifted over time, but there was that consistent streak of dependency. Anyone who wasn't there for Bobby wasn't there for long.

Staying at the top wouldn't prove so easy. The Boston Bruins had the makings of a dynasty, two championships in three seasons, a third lost to a hot goalie, which happens to the best of them sometimes. But keeping the old gang together proved problematic, especially for an organization that, Orr's own contracts aside, was loath to spend money on player salaries. With the World Hockey Association now offering players the chance, finally, to cash in, the era of indentured servitude was coming to an end. They had options, had the chance to head for far-flung teams with funny names and secure a financial future for their families. That chipped away at the old gang. And the NHL continued to add franchises at a reckless pace – Buffalo and Vancouver in 1970, the New York Islanders and Atlanta in 1972 and, coming up, Washington and Kansas City in 1974. Each new round brought another expansion draft, which meant losing a veteran player or two off the roster. The stars remained, but key role players like Ed Westfall (drafted by the Islanders, he would last long enough to become part of another Stanley Cup dynasty there) were gone, and had become more difficult to replace, since the amateur talent pool had been further subdivided. The Bruins didn't help themselves by trading away some of their better young prospects, who would eventually come back to haunt them wearing other uniforms – players like the slick Philadelphia forwards Rick MacLeish and Reggie Leach.

The Bruins were also struggling with their organizational direction. Sinden returned to the franchise after his triumphant coaching stint with Team Canada, succeeding Milt Schmidt as the general manager. But Tom Johnson, not even a full season removed from winning the Stanley Cup, was fired fifty-two games into the 1972–73 season and replaced by Bep Guidolin, who had coached Orr during his final season with the Oshawa Generals. The Adams family, who had owned the team since its inception, sold it to television people in 1973, severing that ancient connection. Forever after, Boston fans would be asking themselves whether the owners of their favourite team cared as much about winning as they did – and whether they'd spend the money to do it. Sinden, who had originally bolted from his job as the head coach because he didn't think he was being paid a fair wage, would as a general manager earn a reputation for counting every one of his bosses' pennies.

Meanwhile, a new hockey power was rising in an unexpected locale, a team the likes of which had never been seen before. The Philadelphia Flyers had entered the league as part of the great expansion of 1967–68 and among those weak-sister franchises had done little to distinguish themselves. But management there had been assembling a core of players, many, as it turned out, with roots in the Boston organization (MacLeish, Joe Watson, Gary Dornhoefer, Leach, Bernie Parent). The two keys, though, were the drafting of Bobby Clarke, a scrappy, skilled forward from Flin Flon, Manitoba, who would become the team's captain, its brains and heart, and the hiring of Fred "the Fog" Shero as the Flyers head coach. Shero was an odd duck with a long minor-league pedigree, a brilliant strategist but also a bit of flake. Even his own players had trouble understanding his marching orders. Really, though, it wasn't hard to see the template from which he was working. Shero had noted the rise of the Bruins in the late 1960s and early 1970s, saw how the combination of toughness bordering on belligerence and plenty of talent could dominate in the NHL. He wondered what might happen if you took it up a notch – the belligerence part, that is. Shero didn't have a Bobby Orr – nor did anyone else. But he would eventually assemble a group that could certainly play the game but would make those rough, tough Boston teams look like a band of pacifists by comparison.

In the three seasons between 1969 and 1972 that would mark the peak of the Big Bad Bruins, consider that the team's individual penalty leaders totalled 125, 132 and 141 minutes respectively. And these were the league's most feared intimidators, despised by opponents for their rough, dirty play, called out by sensitive sports-writers for despoiling the beautiful game of their youth. Then consider that in 1972–73, a previously obscure left winger from Saskatchewan named Dave Schultz racked up 259 penalty minutes for the Flyers to lead the league, with three other members of that team each topping 200 minutes (Schultz, at the peak of his goon-ery, would have a 472-penalty-minute season). The Flyers would intimidate, but they could also play with an underappreciated finesse. Clarke, who had been a star of the Summit Series (though he would be best remembered for the slash that broke the ankle of the Russians' best player, Valeri Kharlamov), would become the first member of an expansion team to win the Hart Trophy. He was joined by other highly skilled players like Bill Barber and Leach. But that talent seemed secondary, especially in the public imagina-tion, to the fact that these Flyers behaved like street thugs. They'd fight at the drop of a hat. They would happily beat more faint-hearted opponents into submission, referees be damned. Whatever the referees allowed, they'd get away with, and then a bit more than that. For Philadelphia fans, who loved every minute of it, the proof was in the results. The Flyers weren't quite ready to take con-trol in 1972–73. That year, Scotty Bowman's high-flying Montreal team was the class of the league, defeating Chicago in the Stanley Cup finals. But the barbarians were at the gates.

Boston's season ended with a meek five-game first-round playoff loss to the New York Rangers. Esposito won another scoring title, and Orr another Norris Trophy, but for a host of reasons – including the WHA defections and having Esposito blow out his knee in the first playoff game against New York – they weren't the same team that had won the Stanley Cup. The next season, 1973–74, brought a return to form. Boston was 52–17–9 during the regular season, thirteen points ahead of the second-place Montreal Canadiens in the much stronger NHL Eastern Division. (Orr's contribution was another statistically magnificent season: he scored thirty-two goals and recorded ninety assists.) They then roared through the first two rounds of the playoffs, sweeping the Toronto Maple Leafs and beating the Chicago Black Hawks in six games. Boston entered the Stanley Cup Finals against the Flyers (who had won a tough seven-game series over the Rangers to get there) as prohibitive favourites. That feeling was in part based on the knowledge that no expansion team had ever won – or come close to winning – the Cup.

Shero went into the finals just as Scotty Bowman had in 1970, when he was coaching St. Louis, intent on finding a strategy to neutralize Orr, to minimize his ability to control the game. Accomplish that, he figured, and everything else would take care of itself. And maybe because Orr was one or two steps slower, maybe because the knee injuries had robbed him of some of his explosiveness, maybe because the Flyers were more talented and more dogged and more committed to the task than the St. Louis team had been, Shero's troops came much closer to accomplishing their mission. But there was also an essential difference between Bowman's approach and Shero's. The Blues had been instructed to dump the puck into the Boston zone on the opposite side from where Orr played, to try to keep it away from him as much as possible. The Flyers were told to do just the opposite – shoot it into his corner and then jump on him, forechecking. "We knew that keeping some sort of halter on Bobby was an absolute must if we were to beat the Bruins," said the Flyers' "Cowboy" Bill Flett. "We gave him the puck and made him work with it. Then we put as many men in his path as we could and didn't give him enough room to get started. It seemed that the other teams always were reluctant to commit men deep in the Bruin zone to forecheck him because he'd burst out and trap them. The Flyer view was that if he had the puck and we had men between him and our goal, we'd be safe temporarily. You see, many times Orr is most dangerous when he hasn't got the puck because he's free to turn on all the speed, find a hole and then get the puck back when he's on the fly. We felt we were safer with him in front of us with the puck than moving behind us without it."[62] Clarke, in particular, was Orr's nemesis. Whenever Orr picked up the puck in his own end, Clarke seemed to be there, and even if he escaped to begin the rush up ice, Clarke was there a half-step behind, hooking a little, holding a little, doing anything he could to slow Orr down. "I told them . . . we'd shoot the puck at Orr, make him work," Shero said. "Except we never mention Orr and Esposito by name in our dressing room. But they know who we mean when I say shoot it in on the left side. They listened because of Clarke. All year he's told them to shut up and do whatever I say, that Fred'll explain it later."

And being the Flyers, the Broad Street Bullies, they also put a licking on Orr. If there was a chance to pound him into the boards, or knock him to the ice, they'd take advantage every time. "They had Orr and he can do an awful lot," Shero would explain later. "But we've got seventeen good hockey players and every one of them put out. It was seventeen against one."

The tone of the final was set in game two, or at least that was the first time that the possibility of the Flyers winning the Cup seemed real. The series had started at the Boston Garden, and Philadelphia, which had beaten the Bruins only four times during the seven-year existence of the franchise, had won there only once – the first game they ever played there, back in 1967. Predictably, the Bruins took the first game 3–2, with Orr scoring the winner in the final minute of the third period, and they were cruising through the second. The home team had taken a 2–0 lead in the first period (a frame also notable for a brawl between Schultz and Terry O'Reilly, in which the Flyer hit O'Reilly square in the face with a head butt) and was up 2–1 late in the third period, on the verge of seizing a 2–0 lead in the series. In the final minute, with goaltender Bernie Parent removed for an extra skater, Orr was pressured in the corner, couldn't clear the puck and then was unable to tie up MacLeish, who threw a blind backhand pass into the slot. André "Moose" Dupont was the unlikely recipient. His tying goal with fifty-two seconds to play is remembered by Flyers fans as one of the biggest in the team's history.

Philly won that game in overtime, and won the next two at home to take a 3–1 lead in the series. Back in Boston, the team facing elimination, Orr played his best game of the series, scoring two goals and assisting on another in a 5–1 Bruins win. "You can have all the Bobby Clarkes in the world," Sinden said afterwards. "I'll take one game like that from Orr. He made thirty moves no one has ever seen before." Returning to the Philadelphia Spectrum for game six, the Flyers hauled out their secret weapon. As a change from the usual playing of "The Star-Spangled Banner" before games, the team had taken to occasionally substituting a recording of Kate Smith singing Irving Berlin's patriotic hymn, "God Bless America." It had become a talisman for the team – they won almost every time the tune was played. Now, they'd have Smith there in the flesh, singing in the Spectrum at centre ice. After she'd finished the song and began walking off along the red carpet that had been stretched out to centre ice, Orr and Esposito both skated forward to shake her hand – Espo, always wildly superstitious, must have been hoping that somehow the mojo might rub off. But the Kate Smith spell held, and the Flyers would triumph, 1–0. The only score came on a first-period goal by MacLeish, who tipped in Dupont's shot, but in truth the victory came almost entirely thanks to Parent's brilliant goaltending – which as much as the anti-Orr strategy was the story of the series. It was the first time all season long that the Bruins had been shut out. (Parent's great play would be acknowledged when he was awarded the Conn Smythe Trophy. A year later, he would become the first player ever to win it two years in a row.) For Boston fans, the lingering image of the series must have come from the final three minutes of the game. Clarke seemed to have been sprung on a breakaway, but Orr, in pursuit, caught up to him before he could shoot and spun him around, off the puck. Referee Art Skov, making one of the gutsier calls in playoff history, whistled Orr for holding with 2:22 left in regulation. Orr was enraged and skated at Skov, screaming. When he was finally led to the penalty box by his teammates, he sat with his head hanging down, unwilling to watch what might transpire. That penalty killed any chance of a last-ditch Bruins comeback. Orr got out of the box just in time to pick up a loose puck in his own end and float a long wrist shot toward Parent as time expired and the wild celebration began.

For the first time, an expansion team had won the Stanley Cup. More new teams were coming into the league the next season. The traditional NHL powers couldn't take anything for granted anymore.

And a team that hung on too long to past glories would surely find itself in trouble. That was the case even if the best player in the game was still in the lineup.

What the hockey world had just witnessed was how that player, though he certainly wasn't eliminated as a factor in the series, had been denied the opportunity to dominate. The rest of the league of course took note. For the first time, a team had set out specifically to neutralize Orr, and to a large degree had succeeded. There was a blueprint now that every other club was sure to follow.

After the game, Orr slipped quietly into the Flyers victory party, looking for his old rookie roommate, Joe Watson.

"Congratulations, Joe," he said, in Watson's recollection. "You guys really earned it."

"Jesus, thanks," Watson said. "It's sure great, ain't it? Here, have some champagne."

Orr wouldn't let him pour it.

"No thanks," he said. "I don't deserve it."

"Can you believe it?" Watson said later. "If anybody deserved anything, it was him. My goodness gracious, he's their leader. He was carrying the puck into our end all afternoon. He doesn't have to be dejected the way he played. My goodness gracious, whatta player!"

Chapter Sixteen

BETRAYAL

IT IS THE HOCKEY JUDAS STORY. How golden Bobby Orr, nearly crippled now, approaching the inevitable end of his magnificent, star-crossed career, sacrificing the last bit of life in his bad knee in the aid of his country, was fucked, yes, fucked, by Al Eagleson, in whom he had placed his blind and absolute faith. There was one last negotiation, one last contract to sign. The Boston Bruins, for whom Orr had done so much, had won two Stanley Cups, had made everyone involved with the team wealthier and happier, were willing to go to extraordinary lengths to look after his future well-being. It was the least they could do, the right thing, the fair and honourable thing. They knew he wouldn't play much longer, if he played longer at all. They knew he'd missed almost the entire season before. Never mind his skating, he now even walked like a hobbled old man. The owner, Jeremy Jacobs, though he was from Buffalo, not Boston, though he hadn't been part of those past glories, though he had no connection with the old days, with the Weston Adams family, with the ghosts of the Boston Garden, was willing to hand over a portion of his team – 18.6 per cent of it! – to secure Bobby Orr's present and future. Such an offer was unheard of in any professional sport. With franchise values about to skyrocket, it would have set Orr up financially for life. And there would be some poetry in the gesture, giving him back something tangible, giving him, literally, a piece of what he had done so much to create. Not a fair trade, perhaps, for what hockey had done to his body, but at least he'd walk away with something real.

But Orr never even knew the offer was on the table. Eagleson kept that from him, told him the Bruins weren't interested, that they weren't willing to pay him much of anything if he couldn't pass a physical. After all those years, they were just putting him down like an old, infirm family pet. Eagleson told Orr that, unlike the Bruins' new owners, his pal Bill Wirtz and his old buddy Bobby Pulford were true humanitarians, that they were willing to guarantee Bobby's salary if he joined their Chicago Black Hawks, no matter what the risk. And so poor, blind Bobby left Boston angry and broken-hearted, donned a uniform in which he never looked right, never felt comfortable, and played but a few painful games at the pathetic end of his career none the wiser. It was only years later, long after he and Eagleson had parted company, after his personal finances had gone south, that he learned the terrible truth.

As the hockey world would eventually come to understand, Eagleson committed plenty of sins, one of which briefly landed him in jail. Wearing all of those hats, consolidating all of that power, he was a very big frog in what for professional sports was still a rather small pond. At his peak he represented more than 150 players as their agent, and he represented all of them as their union leader. He was the broker and fixer and wheeler-dealer for Canada's re-entry into international hockey, he had an extremely cozy relationship with NHL owners, and he made money at every stop. The players made money too, at least more than they had in the bad old days, before the formation of the Players' Association, before expansion and the brief existence of the World Hockey Association gave them access to at least a limited free market. But it was Al who made out better than any of them, and eventually the players came to understand that. They came to understand, as well, that promises made about their pension money weren't worth a damn.

The fans, their eyes finally opened by the work of crusading journalists and Carl Brewer's persistent inquiries, were infuriated by that. They saw how the heroes of their youth had been ruthlessly exploited by the hockey owners, and how a more contemporary generation had been bullied and played for suckers. Eagleson became the focus for that anger, and there was no underlying sentiment or affection to cushion his fall. He was just a lawyer, after all. He didn't play the game. But what really cut to the hearts of hockey lovers, what made Eagleson the sport's greatest pariah, was that single act of betrayal around Bobby Orr's last contract. When they were told that Eagleson had pulled a fast one, that the Bruins' good-faith offer at the end had never been delivered, they knew where to find those forty pieces of silver. A lot of the rest of what Eagleson did . . . well, that was business, and business can be dirty and cold and immoral. What he did to Orr, though, the rock on whom he had built his empire, was something else again. That was personal, and it was evil, and that they could never, ever forgive. It was all there in black and white.

Now, into history, and into a world considerably more grey. The 1973–74 and 1974–75 seasons had statistically been close to Orr's finest, as he recorded first 122, then 135 points, just a notch below his record-setting 1970–71 campaign, winning a second scoring title in 1974–75. Even if a little of the youthful flash was gone, even if he wasn't quite so lightning quick, his maturing powers, his knowledge of the game, his absolute confidence allowed him to dominate, to score goals and pile up assists to a degree previously unimagined for a defenceman. Nearly as significant was his durability: over that period, Orr played in 154 regular-season games, plus another 19 in the playoffs. The pattern of injury-shortened seasons during the early years of his NHL career seemed but a bad, distant memory.

The Boston Bruins, though, a team now very different from the one that had won two championships in three years, no longer had the stuff to ride his coattails. Following the playoff loss in the Stanley Cup Final to the Flyers in 1974, the Bruins fired coach Bep

Guidolin and replaced him with a colourful career minor leaguer named Don Cherry, whose NHL playing career had consisted of one playoff game with the Bruins in 1955. (Cherry would become the greatest keeper of the Bobby Orr flame long after the player's retirement, long after Cherry had given up coaching for the more lucrative world of broadcasting, where he became not just Canada's most famous ex-coach, but its most famous person.) In Cherry's rookie season as an NHL head coach, 1974–75, Boston finished behind Montreal, Philadelphia and a rising young team in Buffalo. Facing Chicago in the first round of the playoffs, a club that had ended the season with a record just over .500, the Bruins won the first game 8–2, then dropped the next two to lose the best of three series.

Sadly, Orr's healthy run was illusory. He was, in fact, on the clock. Based on what doctors had said in private, not their happy public proclamations following every operation that Orr was healed, he had known, and Eagleson had known since at least 1972, that there was a time limit on his left knee, that it would only get worse. The joint would fail eventually, permanently, and it was highly unlikely he would be playing the game long into his thirties. While that was the hard truth, for obvious reasons it wasn't part of Eagleson's opening address as he entered into negotiations with the Boston management on Orr's last NHL contract. The team had been lucky enough to employ the best player in the NHL, to win two Stanley Cups – and everyone knew that it could have been, perhaps should have been, three or four. The fans filled the building every night, the Bruins were the most popular team in a big-league sports town, and so once again Orr's compensation ought to have set a new standard for what a hockey player might earn.

In August 1975, the Bruins were sold by Storer Broadcasting Co. (the company that had bought the team from the Weston Adams family in 1973) to three brothers from Buffalo: Jeremy, Max and Lawrence Jacobs, who operated under the corporate name Sportsystems. As one of the conditions of having the sale approved by the league's governors, Jeremy Jacobs, who took the lead in the ownership group, promised that Bobby Orr would be signed to a new contract with the Bruins. That was significant, because for the past few months, Eagleson had been telling anyone who would listen that his most famous client was entertaining astronomical offers from the Minnesota Fighting Saints of the WHA, a ten-year deal worth as much as $6.5 million. There was a full season remaining on Orr's Boston contract, but if the Bruins didn't ante up, Orr would have no choice but to jump to the rival league, following in the steps of former teammates like Johnny McKenzie, Gerry Cheevers and, briefly, Derek Sanderson, all of whom had fled the penurious Bruins. ("If the Bruins hadn't been sold, I think he'd be signed with the Fighting Saints tomorrow," Minnesota's team president, Wayne Belisle, said at the time.) When those reports began to circulate, some Boston fans, for the very first time, vented their displeasure at Orr himself, as though he was the greedy party. They even went so far as to boo him – in small numbers, mind you, and a bit timidly – at the Boston Garden. But soon enough, the focus shifted to the new Bruins ownership, and the consensus grew that the Jacobses were too cheap to pay their greatest player his true market value, an impression Eagleson wasn't in any hurry to correct. He spent much of the summer of 1975 negotiating directly with Jeremy Jacobs – Harry Sinden had been cut out of the loop because Jacobs thought he might be too sentimental when it came to Orr – and by early September they had verbally agreed on the framework of a new deal. One of its provisions, revolutionary at the time, was that Orr would eventually receive an 18.6 per cent stake in the team, or alternatively $925,000 (the Jacobses had paid $10 million for the franchise), in addition to an annual salary of $350,000 a year for the next five years. The very idea was unusual enough that the Jacobses wanted to run it by their tax people, and Eagleson wanted to run it by his own tax advisers as well as the NHL president, Clarence Campbell. After the fact, Eagleson maintained that Campbell didn't have to think twice: the league wouldn't permit it, he said. An active player couldn't own part of a franchise, or hold an option to buy part of a franchise – it would violate NHL bylaws. So when Eagleson returned to the table, the terms of the negotiation shifted, with Orr's annual salary increased to between $500,000 and $600,000, and the contract length set at either five or six years. That was in line with a contract Eagleson had just negotiated for Marcel Dionne with the Los Angeles Kings: five years at $300,000.*

The negotiations with the Bruins were moving along swimmingly, and a happy conclusion seemed certain until September 20, 1975, the day Orr surrendered to the chronic pain in his left knee and went under the knife for the fourth time, with Dr. Carter Rowe in Boston again handling the operation. It was described as a minor procedure, but it was major enough to change the entire tone of the talks between Eagleson and the Bruins. Immediately, the Jacobses brought in an outside lawyer and also consulted the insurance firm Lloyd's of London, which refused to underwrite the proposed deal because of understandable doubts about Orr's knee.

Eagleson advised Orr not to step on the ice again until they had something on paper with the Bruins – which was going to be tough, since Jacobs was now hearing medical opinions, including from one of his brothers, an orthopedic surgeon by trade, that Orr's knee was so bad that there was no way he could play much longer. But Orr, determined and stubborn as ever, was driven to return as soon as possible, to help the team and to prove that he could still compete, ignoring all advice to the contrary. Asked about the stalled contract negotiations, he told a reporter, "Things aren't going as smoothly as they had been. I hope this snag isn't because of the knee. The knee is coming along nicely, and the doctor is very happy about it."

---

* Reports of the Orr contract talks were among the biggest NHL stories heading into the 1975–76 season. Eagleson, as was his normal practice, made sure that the boys on the beat always had plenty of grist for the mill. At the same time, another small hockey news item was all but lost in the shuffle. After a final season as a player-coach with the San Diego Mariners of the WHA, Harry Howell announced his retirement. He had said back in 1967, when he won the Norris Trophy as the NHL's best defenceman, that he was happy to be honoured then, because the Norris would surely be Bobby Orr's for the foreseeable future. Orr won the Norris in each of the next eight seasons.

Orr was back with the Bruins on November 8, playing in a 4–2 loss at Vancouver. The timing couldn't have been more dramatic. The day before, with the team off to what was for them a stumbling start, Sinden pulled the trigger on a trade that would live long in infamy for many a Boston fan. Trying to change the culture of the dressing room as well as the balance of talent, he dealt Phil Esposito and defenceman Carol Vadnais to the Bruins' hated traditional rival, the New York Rangers, in exchange for Jean Ratelle, Brad Park and Joe Zanussi. (Cherry was called on to break the news to Esposito, and he took Orr along as insurance, figuring that Espo wouldn't go berserk or attack him or jump out the window of his hotel room if Bobby was there.) With that one transaction, Sinden signalled the end of the old Big Bad Bruins. They had already been broken up to some degree by age and by defections to the WHA. But removing Esposito from the dressing room permanently severed a link with the glorious past. (Not that the team wouldn't play well afterwards. Under Cherry, they would remain Stanley Cup contenders for several years, losing twice in the finals.) The Bruins' immediate response to the deal and, just as significantly, to Orr's return, was to play their best hockey of the season. After losing to Vancouver in a game in which Orr was held off the score sheet, they won six and tied three in their next nine games. In his ten games back, Orr had five goals and thirteen assists. Then, on November 28, the team assembled at Boston's Logan Airport for a flight to Chicago, where they would play the Black Hawks the next night. Before the plane took off, Orr went to Cherry and delivered the bad news. His knee had locked up as he was climbing out of his car in the airport parking lot. He knew from his long, sad experience that there was something wrong. The pain was terrible. He didn't think he could play that night. "As soon as he spoke to me," Cherry said, "I told him the wisest thing would be to stay in Boston and have the knee checked by Dr. Rowe. It's nothing serious – just a precaution."

It was plenty serious. The next day, Dr. Rowe operated again, what would be the fifth surgery on the knee. The first report had Orr out for seven to eight weeks, which would have represented

a significant chunk of the season. It turned out to be far worse than that. Three months in, the leg still wasn't responding to therapy. By the following spring, Orr allowed himself to be placed on the disabled list so that the Bruins could add an extra player to their roster for the playoffs. Then he escaped temporarily to Parry Sound. Those ten games were all he would play in 1975–76 and, as it turned out, the last he would play for Boston.

Needless to say, if the Bruins were hesitant to make a deal after the first operation, their feet became considerably colder after the second. There were continuing talks between Eagleson and the lawyer who was now speaking for the Jacobses. Orr sat in on some of the sessions but not all of them. Leaving one of those, at the airport in Toronto he turned to Eagleson and said, "Geez, Al, I guess if I was a horse the Bruins would shoot me and collect the insurance."

It was time to change their strategy. The WHA was looking shakier by the moment, and in any case Orr wanted to stay in the NHL. Though he was still under contract to the Bruins, Eagleson made it clear that other teams ought to feel free to express their interest. At one point, he claimed there were ten or twelve NHL clubs in the hunt for Orr's services – and naturally and correctly Harry Sinden complained about tampering. Los Angeles and Detroit were in the mix, and St. Louis and Los Angeles. Even the horrible expansion team in Kansas City. Speaking to his trusted friend, the reporter Russ Conway, Orr was forthright about what those teams would be buying. "All I'm doing is telling any owner in advance who wants to have me that they are purchasing damaged goods," he said. "I don't want any owner to think that I'm in perfect condition. My knee seems fine, but I'm going to have it checked out again. Some owners might want to wait till I pass a medical, and they're entitled to that. Some clubs have told me it doesn't really matter what shape my knee is in, and those are the people Mr. Eagleson will talk to."

Feeling the heat from their fans, worried about a looming public relations disaster, the Bruins tendered one final offer in the spring of 1976. They proposed a five-year deal, at $600,000 a season – but required Orr to pass a physical heading into each training camp,

where it would be determined whether he could play at the level he had in 1974–75. Only the first year of the contract was guaranteed. If he failed the physical, the rest of the money was gone. Eagleson's public response cut to the chase. "There is only one way that Bobby Orr will ever be back with the Bruins. And that's if Jerry Jacobs asks him for another meeting and straightens out the whole situation. Otherwise he's gone. After June 1, we'll listen to all offers, but he wants to play in the National Hockey League."

Now the auction was on, though a strange one. Step right up for a chance to bid on the finest player of his generation, still only twenty-eight years old, just months removed from two of the greatest statistical seasons in NHL history, a proven winner, a two-time champion, a blue-chipper. All of that, and he's played only ten games in the last hockey year, he's had two more knee operations, he's not healthy by any means, and there are real questions about how fit he'll ever be. Still, there were takers. By June 1, when Orr officially became a free agent, the bidding remained active. "I talked to Bobby Saturday," Eagleson said, "and we narrowed it down to five cities – Chicago, St. Louis, Los Angeles, Kansas City and Philadelphia. 'Let's cut it down some more,' he told me. 'I don't want to go to Los Angeles because it's too far away and involves too much travelling. I don't want to go to Kansas City because I think it would be tough to try to help that bad a team. I don't want to go to Philadelphia because I think they're good enough without me.'"

So it was down to St. Louis, where Orr would be asked to play saviour for a franchise in dire financial straits, and Chicago, where Eagleson enjoyed an exceptionally warm and trusting relationship with the owner, Bill Wirtz. The Blues made their pitch, but were worried about what player Boston might demand in compensation (as the free agency rules of the NHL then required). The Black Hawks had no such qualms and were willing to guarantee Orr a five-year contract, even if the knee made it impossible for him to play that long. Eagleson said that it was a moral gesture on Wirtz's part. Wirtz was the one to whom Jacobs had pledged that he'd sign Orr and keep him away from the WHA, and according to Eagleson, when that didn't happen he felt pangs of responsibility.

"Bobby was completely stunned by the humanistic approach Wirtz took," Eagleson said, "and that in itself had Bobby convinced Chicago was the place to play hockey."

On June 8, 1976, Bobby Orr became a member of the Chicago Black Hawks, and a great hockey city mourned. "He knew his days with Boston were numbered," Eagleson said. "He went there in 1966 out of an Ontario town and only eighteen. The ties he has developed in that city are unbelievable. It was rough, but now it's over and Bobby is relieved." Relieved, perhaps, but more hurt and angry, especially at Jacobs and Harry Sinden.

Many years later, the fallout from that contract signing would continue to reverberate. In 1990, in a famous story written by Ellie Tesher and published in *The Toronto Star,* Orr went public for the first time about the financial setbacks he had suffered after retiring from hockey, all of which in one way or another he laid at Eagleson's feet. The subject of the Bruins offer of an 18.6 per cent share of the franchise came up. "Orr," Tesher wrote, "recently learned from insiders that, during the unsuccessful 1976 contract negotiations with the Bruins, he had been offered a share – more than 10 per cent – of the team. But Eagleson did not tell him of that offer during negotiations or after, Orr said."[63]

Well, maybe they were "insiders." And maybe Eagleson wasn't being straight when he claimed the offer was off the table long before they made the deal with Chicago. And maybe Orr somehow didn't know because he was oblivious; because he told Eagleson to take care of it for him, he didn't want to bother with the details and wasn't paying attention – which is how he handled so much of his other business. Maybe Al advised him against taking the Bruins offer because he planned to deliver him to his pal Bill Wirtz. Maybe years later someone was given access to all of Orr's correspondence and, picking through the papers, found a reference to the 18.6 per cent and asked Bobby about it. It sure seemed to have been news to him.

But back in 1976, immediately after the signing with Chicago was announced, it was all there in black and white. In *The Toronto Star* on June 7, 1976, the veteran hockey writer Frank Orr wrote in a story that ran on the front of the sports section, "Eagleson revealed that on Sept. 15, 1975, he had reached a deal with the Bruins which would have paid Orr a total of $4-million for ten years. But when Orr's knee required surgery before the season opened, the deal changed considerably. 'Then they offered a five-year deal at $295,000 or 18.6 per cent ownership of the club in 1980. I didn't think it would be wise for him to be a player-owner.'" In *The Globe and Mail,* on June 9, similar information ran under the byline of Donald Ramsay. "The Bruins offer, which Eagleson termed 'ridiculous,' was a five-year offer for $295,000 a year. In addition Orr was to receive $925,000 in cash payable in June 1980. That was to be a cash payment or involve Orr's receiving 18.6 per cent of the Bruins' stock." Variations on that story appeared in other newspapers in Canada and in Boston.

Bobby Orr says he didn't know any of that, and who's to say that isn't true? But if someone was trying to hide it from him, someone didn't want him to know what the Bruins had put on the table, this was a mighty strange way of doing it, blabbing to a bunch of reporters. It was certainly no secret.

Shortly after Orr signed with Chicago, the sports sections were filled with more off-season hockey news. Canada had named its team for a brand new international tournament scheduled to go ahead the following September. Modelled on soccer's World Cup, it would bring together the six leading hockey nations – the Soviet Union, Czechoslovakia, Finland, Sweden, the United States and Canada – for the first time with no restrictions. Everyone was eligible to play, amateurs and pros, NHL players and WHA players. It would be the best against the best. And, of course, Eagleson was right in the middle of it, as the organizer, entrepreneur and guiding light.

It seemed a natural evolution. The '72 Summit Series between Canada and the U.S.S.R. had been followed two years later with an all-star team from the breakaway WHA trying, unsuccessfully, to recapture the same magic in an eight-game exhibition against the Soviets. The novelty there was that Bobby Hull would be allowed to play – he'd been barred by the big thinkers of the NHL two

years earlier because he had disloyally decided to work for someone who would pay him much, much more, deserting Chicago for
Winnipeg. And Gordie Howe, lured out of retirement for the
chance to play alongside his sons, would also be part of the mix.
Briefly, there was speculation that Orr might also play, having
been denied his opportunity by injury in 1972. There were stories
floating around suggesting that Eagleson was trying to leverage a
television deal by dangling Orr as a star attraction. It never went
further than that, and in any case it's hard to imagine that even
Eagleson could have persuaded the NHL governors to go along
with having their biggest star suit up with players from a rival league.

A year later, two powerful Soviet club teams, the Central Red
Army and the Soviet Wings, came to North America to play a
series of exhibitions against NHL sides. That series produced both
the classic New Year's Eve match at the Montreal Forum between
the Habs and Red Army, regarded by many as the greatest game
ever played, and the infamous matchup at the Philadelphia
Spectrum in which the Flyers' goon tactics caused the Red Army
team to temporarily walk off the ice. The Bruins lost their game
against the Red Army at the Garden, but Orr was hurt and missed
yet another chance to test himself against the Russians.

What Eagleson was working toward now was something much
grander. The notion of NHL players participating in the Olympic
Games remained out of the question, since the International
Olympic Committee and the International Ice Hockey Federation
were still clinging desperately to their ideal of amateurism – oblivious to the fact that the Eastern Bloc players were professionals in all
but name. But hockey didn't necessarily need the Olympic imprint.
If the money was there, the Russians and Czechs would certainly be
willing to play along, as would the NHL. And given the increasingly
international character of the league itself – and the obvious need, as
it continued to expand, to tap into the European talent base – it was
in everyone's interest to be part of the show.

The new tournament, dubbed the Canada Cup, would go ahead
just before NHL training camps opened and feature what many
believe was the greatest Canadian hockey team ever assembled.

When the squad was named in June, Orr was part of a defensive corps that would include the big three from the Montreal Canadiens, Larry Robinson, Guy Lapointe and Serge Savard, and a young player from the New York Islanders who seemed like the first of Orr's stylistic heirs, Denis Potvin. That said, even Eagleson believed it was at best a fifty-fifty proposition that Orr would be ready to play. The same week he signed with the Chicago Black Hawks, Orr had his left knee examined once again, this time through a relatively new, far less invasive procedure called arthroscopy. Dr. John Palmer at Toronto General Hospital was in charge, and afterwards he passed on the good news. "Except for a couple of problems, the knee is perfect," he said. "As things stand right now, I'm sure Bobby will be able to play again. We're just being careful."

All that was left now was rest and rehab, and the question of whether Orr would be able to tolerate the pain involved in stepping back on the ice. The Black Hawks, who might have objected, given their huge investment in "damaged goods," gave him permission to play in the Canada Cup if he felt well enough. That was Wirtz's gesture of good faith toward Orr and perhaps a nod to his good pal Eagleson. There was no question that Orr desperately wanted to finally be part of a representative Canadian team and to play against the Russians for the first time since his all-star appearance as a junior. After sitting out in '72, and missing the Red Army game with Boston, he understood that this would almost certainly be his last shot.

The Russians in 1976 were still exotic. The cross-pollination that would come in later years, the borrowing back and forth between the Soviet method of hockey, pioneered by Anatoly Tarasov, and the traditional Canadian game had yet to take place. Instead, here were two absolutely separate, unique ways of interpreting the same sport that had evolved in isolation over the decades. The Canadian team in 1972 had been flummoxed by the alien style at first, before persevering through guts and grit and not a small amount of good luck. Watching the Soviets play, the Canadians saw that their rivals' style was so much less linear, less straight ahead than the familiar Canadian game, their patterns more elliptical, circles within circles.

Even watching them practise, using strange drills that were treated as a punchline until the smartest North American coaches decided to copy them, was like being dropped into a parallel shinny universe. Whether it was better or worse was a debate you didn't hear in Canada much, given how tightly national identity and pride were wrapped around what we considered in every way our game. But it sure was different, it was fast, and it emphasized skill and precision. It was a beautiful thing to watch.

What no one had yet seen was how the Russians would cope with the greatest creative genius ever produced by the Canadian game. How Bobby Orr, who had seen hockey differently from anyone who came before, who played defence in a style beyond traditional definition, might match up against this foreign variant. He was the one Canadian player you could imagine stepping into the Soviet lineup and not looking at all out of place, picking up that alternative interpretation, matching his own rushes to their rhythm, hitting those marvellously skilled forwards with breakaway passes. But how would they cope with him? It had become an article of faith in Canada that had Orr been in the lineup at what was the peak of his powers, the '72 series wouldn't have been nearly so close.

Four years later, Canada wouldn't be surprised by what the Soviets offered. They wouldn't underestimate the calibre of their opposition. They were as familiar with the greatest Russian players as they were with the stars of the NHL. They'd enter a tournament with all of their best talent on the ice, regardless of which league they had chosen as their professional home. They would have a serious training camp, without shortcuts. The rest of the world would be there as well, turning it into a true world championship. "This is a big thing, all right," Orr said. "I'm anxious to play against them. I've been wanting to do it for a long time."

By August, that fifty-fifty shot was looking far more like a sure thing. Interviewed at the Orr-Walton camp in Orillia, Bobby delivered the unexpectedly good news. "Two months ago, there was no way that I thought I would play. But in the last month, the knee has felt just super." Super for him was different from super for anyone else, and after what he had endured during the past calendar year, the lost season, the multiple surgeries, the departure from Boston, he fully understood the possible consequences. Every time he stepped onto the ice, there was a chance it might be the last time. But this was Al's baby, and this was Canada, and this, finally, was the chance to play the Russians. He could save himself for the NHL, for his debut in Chicago, but after watching from the sidelines four years earlier, watching in Moscow as a heroic victory was won, Orr understood that, really, it was no choice at all. He had to play.

For Canadians who were looking on then, with the fear and exhilaration and joy of '72 still fresh in memory, their team invested with that absolute *need* to win, to beat the Reds, to show them whose game this really was, the first Canada Cup was one of the great hockey experiences of a lifetime, the finest team ever assembled, wearing the national colours, utterly dominant – with just a hint of drama, a bit of danger in the mix, and that from an unexpected source. Looking back thirty years later, we can see that those same games seem almost anticlimactic. Canada's march to the championship has a sense of inevitability beyond knowing the final score, beyond remembering how it all played out. You look at that team, coached by Scotty Bowman, with eleven future Hall of Famers in the lineup, you look at the Soviet side, obviously in the midst of a generational transition, soon to be remade into another powerhouse but for the time being nothing special, and the outcome seems predetermined. But for the heroics of an unheralded, thirty-four-year-old, distinctly roly-poly Czech goalie named Vladimir Dzurilla, Canada would have cruised unchallenged to victory. As it was, they lost once in the round robin competition, from which the top two teams would emerge to play a best-of-three final, dropping a 1–0 decision to Dzurilla and the Czechs, the defending amateur world champions. But because Czechoslovakia had in turn lost to the Swedes and tied the Americans, they certainly didn't seem to be a threat on the level of the 1972 Big Red Machine, and a hot goalie could carry them only so far. (One of the worries heading into the tournament was whether the Americans would embarrass themselves, whether they would be even remotely competitive with the other five teams. They didn't have any future Hall of Famers in their lineup, though they did have two future NHL general managers, Craig Patrick and Mike Milbury. As it turned out, they acquitted themselves very well. Four years later, a different U.S. team would do much more than that at the Olympics in Lake Placid.)

Canada entered its final game of the round robin tournament against the Soviets at Maple Leaf Gardens knowing that only a tie was required to advance to the final. This was the glamour matchup – Prime Minister Pierre Trudeau was among those in attendance – with fans anticipating some of the drama and rivalry of '72, or of the New Year's Eve classic between the Red Army and the Habs. Instead, the crowd in Toronto saw their heroes win a relatively easy 3–1 victory, with only the goaltending of Vladislav Tretiak keeping it that close. For Canadians, in addition to demonstrating clear, albeit temporary, superiority over the Russians, the tournament had become a showcase for a new generation of stars: Gilbert Perreault and Rick Martin of the Buffalo Sabres, Darryl Sittler of the Maple Leafs and Denis Potvin of the New York Islanders, who would finish the tournament tied with Orr for the scoring lead. Perhaps the greatest realization, though, at least for the fans of the Maple Leafs was that their stalwart defenceman Borje Salming, playing in the tournament for Sweden, might have been at that moment as good as any player in the world. When the tournament all-star team was named, he deservedly claimed one of the two spots on defence.

The other went to Orr, who had been in turn steady and spectacular for Canada, a great player among great players, still masterful in his ability to control the pace of the game, even though he hadn't been able to practise with the team once during the tournament because of the pain in his knee. He wasn't a one-man show by any means, and as the team headed into the first game of the best-two-out-of-three final, there were certainly other members who might have laid claim to being its most valuable player. But on the night of September 13 at Maple Leaf Gardens, Orr produced a virtuoso performance, reminiscent of his best days in Boston, the last truly great game he would ever play. Nearly every shift was vintage Orr. He scored twice, once with four Czech players helpless to stop him, calmly flipping a backhand over Dzurilla's shoulder, once on a slapshot from the point; he set up another goal and was easily the best player on the ice. Canada won 6–0, chasing Dzurilla early on from the net, where he was replaced by Jiri Holecek. That left them with only one victory over an apparently overmatched opponent remaining before they claimed for the first time the true, unfettered championship of hockey.

The second game of the final, with the action shifted two nights later to the Montreal Forum, seemed at the start as though it would be another rout, a triumphal march to the Cup. Canada got early goals from Perreault and Esposito, and again the Czech goaltenders switched places, Holecek heading for the bench and Dzurilla back in net. That move seemed to restore their equilibrium. Czechoslovakia pulled back to within a goal on the power play – Orr was on the ice working to kill the penalty. They tied it when Orr, facing down a Czech forward one-on-one as he crossed the blue line, watched helplessly as a slapshot zipped past him and past Rogatien Vachon in the Canadian goal. Not long before Canada took a 3–2 lead, Orr crossed the Czech blue line on a rush and was flattened from behind by a cross-check, taking a hard shot to the left knee on his way down. No penalty was called. Czechoslovakia tied the score again, again on the power play, and again Orr was on the ice for the goal against. The visitors briefly pulled ahead 4–3 when Orr dropped to block Peter Stastny's slapshot, was hurt on the play, and the rebound was fired home as he lay prone on the ice.

He had been on for all four Czech goals, which wasn't quite as bad as it might have seemed, given his overall ice time, and especially given the penalty-killing minutes he was logging. But it was obvious that Orr was slowing down, that he was having difficulty moving, that he seemed stiff and when caught out of position was very slow to react. Afterwards, he told confidants that had the final gone to a third game, he probably wouldn't have been able to play at all.

Orr was in the middle of a shift, far behind the play, when Sittler scored the overtime winner, streaking down the left wing, faking a slapshot and then neatly skating around Dzurilla and flipping the puck behind him. With the Paul Henderson goal that preceded it, with the Mario Lemieux goal that would follow in the Canada Cup of 1987, it took its place among the great clutch Canadian hockey moments.

Though perhaps it had never really been in doubt, the victory celebration had much of the same patriotic emotion that followed Canada's famous win in Moscow four years earlier. In the mob scene at centre ice, Eagleson, wearing his bright blue Canada Cup blazer, rushed in among the players and emerged carrying Sittler's stick, which he held high like a trophy for the cheering crowd at the Forum to see. The Montreal fans warmly applauded the Czech players and seemed especially fond of Dzurilla, who, after removing his mask, showed off a magnificent pair of bushy black sideburns. In a gesture familiar to soccer fans but alien to Canadians, who had grown up watching only hockey, the Czech players offered to exchange jerseys, and the joyous Canadians quickly accepted the offer. Orr found himself wearing the red number 4 of Oldrich Machac, a veteran defenceman with the Czechoslovakian team, long regarded as one of the best at his position in Europe.

Before the Canada Cup itself was handed out, a long series of individual awards was presented, first by Maurice and Henri Richard and then by Trudeau. The most valuable Canadian player for the game was named (goaltender Vachon, who had inherited the job before the tournament began, when Ken Dryden was injured), as was the most valuable Canadian for the entire tournament (Vachon, again). Finally, and somewhat confusingly, given all of the awards that had preceded it, the famous voice of the Forum's Claude Mouton announced the most valuable player of the tournament, period: Bobby Orr.

A sentimental choice? Perhaps, but who would argue it? (Well,

Potvin, for one, who thought the trophy ought to have been his.) An insider deal orchestrated by Eagleson? Maybe. But who would begrudge him that, especially had they known that it would be the last sustained, significant hockey Bobby Orr would play in his life.

Trudeau presented Orr with an Inuit sculpture. Though that seemed the natural, final warm-up act before the presentation of the Canada Cup itself, there was in fact another award to be doled out. This one, another sculpture from Baffin Island, went to Eagleson for making all of this possible. He looked in every way like a man on top of the world. Only then, finally, did the team's captain, Bobby Clarke, stripped to his pads and minus his false front teeth, accept the Canada Cup from the prime minister, though no one dared actually lift the trophy, since it weighed 150 pounds. The Canadian players skated off to the dressing room for the celebration, with the crowd still standing and cheering.

"How's the cripple?" Eagleson shouted at Orr in the midst of the dressing room cacophony, drawing a laugh.

Orr grabbed Eagleson in a bear hug, took a piece of white athletic tape and plastered it across his mouth.

Training camp would start soon enough. They would go their separate ways in the NHL, in the WHA. Back to business as usual. Eagleson would start planning the next tournament. Following on this great success, it would have to become a regular event. The fans in Canada would demand it. And so would the hockey business. It was a money-maker for the league, for Hockey Canada, for the players. For Al.

And now Bobby Orr would leave for a new city, a new team, a new uniform, his fourth stop as a hockey player: Parry Sound, Oshawa, Boston, Chicago. He didn't know how it would be there, how it would feel to be surrounded by new teammates, to play for a new coach, to be cheered in a new building. All he knew was that this had been one sweet, poetic triumph. And that his knee was killing him.

Not so long after the Canada Cup ended, Eagleson was invited to appear on *90 Minutes Live,* a late-night talk show on CBC television that was conceived as a Canadian counterpart to Johnny Carson's *Tonight Show*. (That it couldn't possibly be anything of the kind, that Peter Gzowski, the nonpareil radio broadcaster, was utterly ill-suited to playing the glib, glad-handing role, was obvious to pretty much everyone outside the CBC from the first minute of the first show.)* Eagleson was always a terrific talk-show guest – funny, quick, a charmer by nature. Gzowski naturally asked him about his star client, about what the future held in store for Bobby Orr.

The Canada Cup may well have finished him, Eagleson admitted. The wear and tear of those games had finally destroyed what remained of his left knee. And beyond hockey, he had probably lost another $2 million in off-ice income because he could no longer play the game the way he once had. It was tragic, really. He was still a young man.

"That's why I like him so much," Eagleson said. "He gave his career for his country."

---

* Peter Gzowski (1934–2002) was famously uncomfortable as a television host, his warm, low-key, folksy style wildly unsuited to the medium. The program *90 Minutes Live* lasted just two seasons. In addition to being the most beloved radio host in Canadian history from his stints on *This Country in the Morning*, and especially *Morningside*, Gzowski also wrote what is rightly considered one of the few masterworks on hockey and Canadian culture, *The Game of Our Lives*. Following the brilliant young Edmonton Oilers team through the 1980–81 season, Gzowski's best, most original writing came in his attempts to describe and define the genius of Wayne Gretzky.

Epilogue

O N THE DAY THE EAGLE WENT DOWN, old players filled most of the public seats in the Boston courtroom, row upon row of hockey-card faces attached to lumpy, unfamiliar bodies, fatter, greyer, deep lines cutting across old-hide Florida tans. They had gathered to bear witness, to feel and revel in Alan Eagleson's pain, to see him humbled, to get something of themselves back, though not all those desires would be satisfied in the end.

Holding centre stage, the American prosecutor was a handsome, blown-dry self-promoter, a politician revelling in the spotlight as though this was his personal moment of triumph, as though he himself had brought the foreign shyster to justice. Truth was, the case in the United States, part of a carefully bargained cross-border deal, was a cheap little consolation prize. The Eagle would be in and out of jail in a few months; he'd be back living the life, splitting his time between Canada and England, secure in the knowledge that even as they were bringing him down, yanking his plaque out of the Hockey Hall of Fame, taking back his Order of Canada, his powerful friends had remained his powerful friends, that he hadn't been made a pariah after all.

Al being Al, even in this dark moment, he couldn't help quietly schmoozing with the reporters in the crowd before the legal ceremonies began. These were the boys who had once loved him best because he'd taken them around the world and treated them like kings and shown them one hell of a time. Al didn't have quite the same bluster, or the same retinue. Back in the glory days, he'd arrive with a full entourage of sycophants shuffling behind in his wake, he'd own the room, he'd be overflowing with smiling, profane, fuck-you confidence. Quieter now, some small talk, a few harmless jokes, just to make some human contact, just to convince himself that the old boy still had it, that eventually all of this would pass.

How Bobby Orr slipped into the courtroom like a spectre is one of those little mysteries – though it figured that if you were Bobby Orr in Boston, even long after the heroic nights at the Garden had passed into memory, no back door was barred, no entrance was off limits, no one would dare say no, even in the hallowed halls of justice. The bailiff intoned, "All rise," the judge walked to the bench, and suddenly there in the last row was the blond mop, the boy's mug, unmistakable. He was three months short of fifty years old now, but to look at him you would never have guessed it, at least without seeing him try to walk on his old man's knees, and there was comfort in that: if number 4 wasn't aging, maybe the rest of us weren't aging either.

Orr was, as always, perfectly turned out, neat, tidy, like a model in a department store catalogue. Years back, Earl McRae, who wrote profiles of sports figures as well as anyone ever has, did a piece about Bobby for the old *Today* magazine, which found it too hot to handle and so passed it on to a more brave, now equally defunct Canadian periodical called *Quest*.[64] It was what would later be recognized as a genre exercise, a story about trying to pin down a star who refuses to be interviewed, the narrative tracing the futile chase, the pursuit itself taking the place of the traditional biographical sketch. Orr's reluctance to play along seemed odd at first glance, since McRae had written plenty about him during his hockey-playing past, all of it glowing. But less comfortable in retirement, less sure of himself than he'd ever been carrying the puck,

Bobby put the writer off and deked him and told him to go fuck himself and then, finally, sitting in a hotel room, half-dressed, gave him a few perfunctory minutes, which became the climax of the piece. Later, Orr read the story, and he hated McRae ever after – turned off writers in general, so rumour had it, though maybe he'd never really loved them all that much in the first place. An extremely sympathetic reader might be right there with him, since the story, though understanding and affectionate, was one of the first to cast any kind of shadow on the legend, suggesting an uneasy, unhappy, perhaps cash-poor life after hockey. But that's not why Bobby detested the story, and detested McRae for writing it. What ate away at him was a single detail, a throwaway line, a fleeting image. While sitting reluctantly for the uncomfortable interview in the hotel room, he had, McRae noted, a hole in his sock. Bobby Orr – who had taught himself how to dress like a sophisticate after moving to Boston, who loved buying clothes, who liked to see himself as a hipster, a style maker in a great big city, who understood the power of the right wardrobe, who had happily left his north-country-rube past far behind – with a hole in his sock. It made him sound like a hick, he told his friends, and what could be worse than that?

Orr's falling-out with Al Eagleson became public knowledge only after they changed the name of a sports injury clinic at York University in Toronto that Orr's dollars were supposed to have endowed. Bobby balked as things went sour, so Al ended up writing the cheque instead, and then he got the place of honour on the marquee. Years before that, before their official parting, the balance of the relationship, of mutual need and mutual benefit, had already dramatically shifted. Orr couldn't settle into a role after his playing career ended following a few sad, painful games with the Black Hawks in which it was clear he could barely skate. He tried working as an assistant coach, but the players came to hate him, and he tried working in the front office, but that didn't suit his skills or temperament either. He was lost. He had been a hockey player and only a hockey player for just about his entire life, only to have that calling torn away from him too young. And Eagleson didn't really need him anymore. His position as the most powerful man in the game was secure, whatever happened to his first, most famous client. The Bobby Orr business that had once been his ticket was only a sideline now. Sitting in Al's office one day, a fellow lawyer heard the secretary tell Al that Bobby was on the line from Chicago, that it was something important, that he really needed to talk. "Take a message," Eagleson said. He'd thrown him over. It was personal. It wasn't just business. It was a matter of the heart every bit as much as it was of the balance sheet. The kid had loved and trusted him unconditionally, without reservation, and now the man would make him pay for his betrayal.

After the split hit the headlines, follow-up stories featured duelling versions of the truth, but mass sentiment obviously came down hard on the side of the beloved, hobbled hockey star rather than on the side of the powerful lawyer and agent and union leader. Orr really let fly with his feelings only once, in a long feature that appeared in *The Toronto Star* under the byline of Ellie Tesher, who later went on to become the paper's answer to Dear Abby. Orr cast himself there in pathetic terms, as the poor, innocent, simple dupe, as the naive victim who just didn't bother himself with the details, who trusted too much.[65]

That wasn't quite the beginning of the end for Eagleson, but soon thereafter, emboldened by the appearance of the first cracks in his armour, the journalistic probing began, at the forefront a dogged investigative reporter named Russ Conway who worked for a paper just outside of Boston called *The Lawrence Eagle Tribune*. Who knows what the confused readers must have thought about it. Year after year, the local rag brought them crime stories and happy features about hero Boy Scouts and tales of small-town political intrigue, along with thousands upon thousands of words about the inner workings of the National Hockey League Players' Association, about some Canadian lawyer named Al Eagleson, his business dealings, his web of relationships, his seeming conflicts of interest within the sport of professional hockey. The newspaper's editors, apparently unique in the craft, just let Conway run with it.

Bobby Orr was at most a peripheral figure in the stories. He was never identified as a source. But he was hardly peripheral to

Conway. They were close friends, and the reporter was something of an acolyte. Eagleson, under attack, always put two and two together, and he assumed Orr was driving the inquisition, was working full-time behind the scenes to bring him down. There were others who put their names right out front, including that other one-time Eagleson client Carl Brewer, who was smart enough and eccentric enough and dogged enough not to give a damn what anybody thought. Most of the great scoops are the combined product of hard work and righteous motivation and dumb luck and discreet sources with axes to grind who help the process along: each reporter has his own Deep Throats. Whether Orr was indeed one of those in the matter of Alan Eagleson, the world may never officially know for sure.

In public, Orr certainly wouldn't rise to the bait. As the walls were crashing down around Eagleson, he maintained a distance while doing his best to keep the Bobby business up and running. On the first day that Eagleson stood up under oath and testified in his own defence, Orr was making one his endorsement appearances, this time for a credit card company. The gimmick was that a few lucky sods would win the chance to play table hockey against their hero. Orr would look the part and slap the lucky winners on the back and share whatever hockey memories they might bring up. It was well within his comfort zone. When asked that day about Al, Bobby refused to address the subject. He politely demurred and offered only a little joke about the unfortunate timing. Only when asked what kind of advice he gave to young hockey players just approaching the professional ranks did Orr slip the dagger in. "I tell them all about my experiences," he said. "I encourage the kids to stay involved in their affairs. Pay attention to what's going on."

Orr's professional huckster persona would later be further distilled in a series of television commercials for a car company in which he would hardly speak at all. Just smile the smile and be Bobby Orr and maybe fool around with a bunch of hockey-playing kids at the local rink. Real modern kids had pretty much lost track of who he was, who he had been, and the National Hockey League never really understood the art of celebrating its ancient stars.

Even the archival record was spotty. So many of Orr's greatest games had been lost forever, erased or taped over at television networks to save a few bucks. But the parents, the ones buying those cars and using those credit cards – they surely knew.

His other business ventures hadn't worked out quite so well – at least until he became a player agent, until he could show up in the kitchen of a teenage prospect and make the parents' knees shake just by being there, the irony of his moving into the profession Eagleson had all but invented lost on no one. The greatest hockey player of all time was never cut out to spend eight hours a day sitting behind a desk, or to hold a meaningless ceremonial post with the NHL. But he needed the endorsements, and later the agent work, to pay the bills. He was embarrassed about the financial problems, which began with a huge, ugly tax bill and were magnified because the day that he and the Eagle parted ways the cash flow stopped pretty much dead. He hadn't paid attention to what was going on. He hadn't been involved in his own affairs.

Orr lived quietly, privately. His wife and sons were never pushed to the forefront. He had layers of friends and acquaintances; like a Russian doll, there were circles within circles within circles, the last, the most intimate, the smallest. At any sign of disloyalty, any lack of discretion, expulsion as a friend of Bobby Orr's was instant and final. He kept his good deeds quiet too – the hospital visits, the charity stuff, the favours for old friends back in Parry Sound, where he returned in summer to visit his family, where they still talked about him like he was a man turned god. He played some golf until his knees would no longer allow it, until he was forced to have both joints replaced just so that he could walk without pain. And, always, he loved to fish. In later years, he stopped drinking cold turkey, maybe because, as so many hockey stories had it, the booze made him dark and angry. But he kept the newfound teetotalling quiet. Thought that the hockey guys might look at him funny if they knew he'd gone dry.

Always, carefully, he picked his spots. He picked this spot, in the Boston courthouse, to finally, publicly join his aggrieved hockey brethren. He knew that Eagleson would know he was there. He knew that Eagleson would feel the stare, would cast a sideways glance, would understand that the circle was now complete. Orr looked on as Eagleson stood for sentencing, as the lawyers' deal was made official. Guilty pleas on three counts of mail fraud. A million-dollar fine and eighteen months in jail, to be served in a relatively comfy Canadian prison. Nothing more. Not really even much of a slap on the wrist. More a kiss – though Eagleson and his friends argued and argue still that he could have won unconditionally if he'd chosen to fight the legal fight to the bitter end, but that it would have cost him years and millions and he wanted to spare his family all that.

When the verdict was delivered, a voice rang out in the back of the courtroom. Not Orr's, of course.

"Thank God for the United States of America," Carl Brewer hollered, "because this never would have occurred in Canada!"

The other players kept their thoughts to themselves, except for the few who muttered loudly enough: "Son of a bitch." All rose once more as the judge left the bench, then all eyes turned to the back of the room, especially the eyes of reporters, who had noticed the late arrival, who wanted desperately to know, in this defining moment for him, for hockey, what was on his mind.

But Bobby Orr was gone.

Acknowledgments

THIS IS NOT an "AUTHORIZED" BIOGRAPHY of Bobby Orr, and it is not a traditional sports biography in any case. When it comes to Orr, sadly there has never really been one of those (Mark Mulvoy's *Bobby Orr: My Game from 1974* is the closest thing to it, and more than half of that book is devoted to hockey instruction) and it seems unlikely that there ever will be. When I met with Bobby Orr to discuss this project, in the company of our mutual friend, *The Globe and Mail*'s fine hockey writer Tim Wharnsby, he talked about the possibility of writing his own book after he was retired from the business of being a sports agent, perhaps in five years. In the end, he chose not to participate in this book, and asked that I refrain from approaching members of his immediate family. I honoured his wishes.

The research for this book included original interviews, the use of secondary sources and contemporary interviews, and extensive examination of the video record of Bobby Orr's playing career.

Because the book was not explicitly blessed by Bobby Orr, some doors were closed to me – friends, acquaintances and former team-mates, understanding that Orr has tended to cut out from his life those he deemed disloyal, were unwilling to risk that. Other doors, though, were opened by those who understood that this would be a fair-minded, admiring but independent project. Not all of them chose to be identified either in the text or in these acknowledgments, but I would like to thank them here – they know who they are – for their invaluable assistance in telling this important story.

Among those who spoke to me and were willing to be acknowledged, I would like to thank Wren Blair, Scotty Bowman, Babe Brown, Bob Cardy, Brian Conacher, Gretl Feller, Fran Rosa, Dick Irvin, Ken Johnson, Mike Kolisnek, Shawn Lackie, Joe Lapointe, Bill Little, Bill McMurtry, Earl McRae, Joe Watson, Cora Wild, Howard Willett, Doug Williams and Ian Young. I was also warmly welcomed at the Bobby Orr Hockey Hall of Fame in Parry Sound, where one day I happened to cross paths with the very genial Doug Orr.

Phil Pritchard and the rest of the gang at the Hockey Hall of Fame in Toronto were, as always, generous with their time and assistance.

This book would not have been possible without the work of two first-class researchers. I have had the pleasure of working with Elizabeth Klinck on two books and a documentary film. She has no peer when it comes to tracking down interview subjects and persuading them to talk. As many people in the hockey world know well, Paul Patskou possesses what may be the finest film collection on the planet. He gave me full access to his library, was always available to answer questions, and fact-checked the manuscript. The exceptional collection of photographs in this book was tracked down by Damián Tarnopolsky, and the copy-editing was handled, with a deft touch, by Alison Reid and Deirdre Molina. Thanks also to John Koslowski for sharing some material from his personal hockey library.

My employers at *The Globe and Mail*, most notably sports editor Steve McAllister, have always allowed me the freedom to grow professionally by pursuing outside projects.

I feel very fortunate for having been able to work with the wonderful, encouraging crew at Knopf Canada for my last three books. This project was enthusiastically supported by Brad Martin and Matthew Sibiga, who were willing to wait patiently while I decided what form the book would take. I have received great emotional and practical support, as always, from my chum Scott Sellers. And I feel particularly blessed to have Diane Martin as a friend, as an editor and as a summertime neighbour in Newfoundland.

Finally, I would like to thank my family, my wife, Jeanie MacFarlane, and my children, Nathaniel, Jacob and Holly, who have come to understand over the years that their husband and father might have to disappear from time to time in aid of his unpredictable, sometimes maddening, but ultimately rewarding work. Without their patience and support, none of this would be possible.

Notes

CHAPTER ONE

1. *Toronto Telegram*, July 6, 1970.

CHAPTER TWO

2. Jim Proudfoot, *Toronto Star*, December 27, 1988.
3. Ibid.
4. *Toronto Star*, June 12, 1945.
5. Norman MacLean, *Inside Hockey*, 1969–1970.
6. Milt Dunnell, *Toronto Star*, July 6, 1970.
7. Ibid.

CHAPTER THREE

8. As quoted by Howard Berger, *The Globe and Mail*, April 15, 1998.

CHAPTER FOUR

9. Stan Fischler, *Hockey News*, May 1962.
10. Jim Proudfoot, *Hockey News*, October 8, 1960.
11. Ibid.
12. Ibid.
13. Ibid.
14. Ken McKenzie, *Hockey News*, March 20, 1965.

CHAPTER FIVE

15. Mike Lamey, *Hockey Pictorial*, March 1968.
16. Hal Bock, *Dynamite on Ice: The Bobby Orr Story*, Associated Features, 1972.
17. Trent Frayne, *Maclean's*, February 19, 1965.
18. Ibid.
19. Ibid.
20. Ibid.

CHAPTER SIX

21. Mike Lamey, *Hockey Pictorial*, March 1968.
22. Milt Dunnell, *Toronto Star*, July 6, 1970.

CHAPTER SEVEN

23. Red Fisher, *Sport Magazine*, October 1968.
24. Ibid.
25. Ibid.
26. Jim Proudfoot, *Hockey World*, November 1968.
27. Bud Wilkens, *Pro Hockey's Sports Review*, 1970–71.

CHAPTER EIGHT

28. Sam Goldaper, *Inside Hockey*, 1967–68.
29. Norman MacLean, *Inside Hockey*, 1969–1970.
30. Ibid.
31. Ibid.
32. John Ahern, *Boston Globe*, 1970.
33. Paul Rimstead, *Canadian Magazine*, April 11, 1970.
34. Ibid.
35. Keitha McLean, *Montreal Star*, April 2, 1971.

CHAPTER NINE

36. As quoted in Stan Fischler, *Bobby Orr and the Big, Bad Bruins*, Dell Publishing, 1969.

CHAPTER TEN

37. Stan Fischler, *Bobby Orr and the Big, Bad Bruins*, Dell Publishing, 1969.
38. From *The Mighty Quinn*, documentary produced for Leafs TV by Mark Askin, Toronto, 2005.
39. Ibid.
40. Bobby Orr with Mark Mulvoy, *Bobby Orr: My Game*, Little, Brown and Company, 1974.

CHAPTER TWELVE

41. Stan Fischler, *Bobby Orr and the Big, Bad Bruins*, Dell Publishing, 1969.
42. John Ahern, *Boston Sunday Globe*, April 5, 1970.
43. Earl McRae, *Weekend Magazine*, March 18, 1978.
44. Ahern, *Boston Sunday Globe*, April 5, 1970.
45. *Sporting News*, September 15, 1970.
46. Paul Rimstead, *Weekend Magazine*, April 11, 1970.
47. Ibid.
48. *Sporting News*, September 15, 1970.

CHAPTER THIRTEEN

49. John Brogan, *Hockey Sports Stars of 1971*, Winter 1971.

50. Ibid.

51. Ibid.

52. Ibid.

53. Stan Fischler, *Hockey Illustrated*, November 1970.

54. Jack Olsen, *Sports Illustrated*, December 21, 1970.

55. Bob Pennington, *Toronto Telegram*, July 6, 1970.

CHAPTER FOURTEEN

56. Jack Olsen, *Sports Illustrated*, December 21, 1970.

57. Norman MacLean, *Hockey World*, April 1970.

58. Red Burnett, *Maple Leafs Game Program*, December 4, 1971.

59. Frank Orr, *Hockey Pictorial*, 1975.

60. Nick Donner, *Hockey Magazine*, December 1970.

61. Harry Sinden as told to Mark Mulvoy, *Sports Illustrated*, October 19, 1970.

CHAPTER FIFTEEN

62. Frank Orr, *Hockey Pictorial*, 1975.

CHAPTER SIXTEEN

63. Ellie Tesher, *Toronto Star*, August 5, 1990.

EPILOGUE

64. Earl McRae, *Quest*, October 1982.

65. Ellie Tesher, *Toronto Star*, August 5, 1990.

Selected Bibliography

BOOKS

Blair, Wren, with Ron Brown and Jill Blair. *The Bird: The Life and Times of Hockey Legend Wren Blair*. Etobicoke, ON: Quarry Heritage Books, 2002.

Bock, Hal. *Dynamite on Ice: The Bobby Orr Story*. Toronto: Scholastic Book Services, 1972.

Clayton, Deidra. *Eagle: The Life and Times of R. Alan Eagleson*. Toronto: Lester & Orpen Dennys, 1982.

Conway, Russ. *Game Misconduct*. Toronto: Macfarlane, Walter and Ross, 1995.

Cruise, David, and Alison Griffiths. *Net Worth: Exploding the Myths of Pro Hockey*. Toronto: Viking Penguin, 1991.

Devaney, John. *The Bobby Orr Story*. New York: Random House, 1973.

Eagleson, R. Alan, and Scott Young. *Power Play: The Memoirs of Hockey Czar Alan Eagleson*. Toronto: McClelland and Stewart, 1991.

Esposito, Phil, with Peter Golenbock. *Thunder and Lightning: A No-B.S. Hockey Memoir*. Toronto: McClelland and Stewart, 2003.

Fischler, Stan. *Bobby Orr and the Big Bad Bruins*. New York: Dell Publishing, 1969.

Jackson, Robert B. *Here Comes Bobby Orr*. New York: Henry Z. Walck Inc., 1971.

MacInnis, Craig (editor). *Remembering Bobby Orr*. Toronto: Stoddart, 1999.

Orr, Bobby, with Dick Grace. *Orr on Ice*. New York: Grosset and Dunlap, 1970.

Orr, Bobby, with Mark Mulvoy. *Bobby Orr: My Game*. New York: Little, Brown and Company, 1974.

Plimpton, George. *Open Net: The Professional Amateur in the World of Big-Time Hockey*. New York: W.W. Norton and Company, 1985.

MAGAZINES

Brogan, John. "The Secret Strategy to Stop Bobby Orr." *Hockey Sports Stars of 1971*, Winter 1971.

Donner, Nick. "Is Bobby Orr the Greatest of All Time?" *Sports Special Hockey*, Fall 1970.

Fischler, Stan. "A Primer on Stopping Bobby Orr." *Hockey Illustrated*, November 1970.

Goldaper, Sam. "Bobby Orr: Superstar of Tomorrow." *Inside Hockey*, Winter 1967–68.

Halpin, Charlie. "Young Boston Hockey Giant Pick of NHL's Rookie Crop." *Hockey World*, November 1966.

Jackson, Keith. "Super Bruin Bobby Orr." *Hockey World*, May 1970.

Lamey, Mike. "Few Men Know Bobby Orr So Well." *Hockey Pictorial*, March 1968.

MacLean, Norman. "Bobby Orr's 'Book' on the Top NHL Forwards." *Inside Hockey*, Winter 1970–71.

MacLean, Norman. "The Real Bobby Orr." *Inside Hockey*, 1969–70.

MacLean, Norman, "Super Boy Bobby Orr." *Hockey World*, April 1970.

McCarthy, Jack. "The Bruins Hoping to Do It to 'Em Again." *Hockey Illustrated*, May 1971.

McRae, Earl. "Poor Bobby." *Quest*, October 1982.

Monahan, Tom. "Bruins Strike Rich Orr." *Hockey Pictorial*, December 1966.

Olsen, Jack. "Sportsman of the Year." *Sports Illustrated*, December 21, 1970.

Orr, Frank. "Bobby Orr: The Boy of Winter." *Hockey Pictorial*, January 1975.

Phelan, Jack. "Bobby Orr: Superstar for Boston?" *Hockey Illustrated*, February 1968.

Rhodes, Paul. "Can Bobby Orr Beat His Jinx?" *Pro Hockey*, Winter 1969–70.

Wilkens, Bud. "Bobby Orr: Bargain Basement Super Star." *Pro Hockey's Sports Review*, 1970–71.

VIDEO

Canada Cup 1976. Executive producer Jonathan Gross. Toronto: Video Service Corporation, 2005.

Permissions

Grateful acknowledgment is made to the following for the permission to reprint previously published material:

Quotations on page 153, 160 and 190 are from *Bobby Orr and the Big, Bad Bruins*. Copyright © 1969 Stan Fischler. Reprinted by permission of Dell Publishing, a division of Random House, Inc.

The quotation on page 170 is from *Bobby Orr: My Game*. Copyright © 1974 Bobby Orr and Mark Mulvoy. Reprinted by permission of Little, Brown and Company, a division of Hachette Book Group USA.

The quotation on page 135 is from the *Boston Globe*. Reprinted by permission.

Quotations on page 197 and 198 are from the *Boston Sunday Globe*. Reprinted by permission.

Quotations on page 135 are from *Canadian Magazine*.

The quotation on page 79 is from *Dynamite on Ice: The Bobby Orr Story*. Copyright © 1972 Hal Bock. Reprinted by permission.

The quotation from page 45 is from *The Globe and Mail*. Reprinted by permission.

The quotation from page 27 is from the Hockey Hall of Fame website. Reprinted by permission.

The quotation on page 218 is from *Hockey Illustrated*. Reprinted by permission.

The quotation from page 227 is from *Hockey Magazine*. Reprinted by permission.

Quotations on page 66, 67 and 68 are from *The Hockey News*. Reprinted by permission.

Quotations on page 77, 107, 227 and 254 are from *Hockey Pictorial*.

Quotations on page 208, 211, 216 and 217 are from *Hockey Sports Stars of 1971*.

Quotations on page 125 and 227 are from *Hockey World*.

Quotations from page 32, 132 and 134 are from *Inside Hockey*. Reprinted by permission.

Quotations on page 83, 85 and 86 are from *Maclean's*. Reprinted by permission.

The quotation on page 227 is from *Maple Leafs Game Program*. Reprinted by permission.

Quotations on page 164 and 166 are from *The Mighty Quinn*. Copyright © 2005 Mark Askin. Reprinted by permission.

The quotation on page 135 is from the *Montreal Star*.

The quotation on page 125 is from *Pro Hockey's Sports Review*.

Quotations on page 120, 123 and 124 are from *Sport Magazine*.

Quotations on page 201 and 202 are from *Sporting News*. Reprinted by permission.

Quotations on page 221, 226 and 228 are from *Sports Illustrated*. Reprinted by permission.

The quotation on page 145 is from the *St. Paul Dispatch*. Reprinted by permission.

Quotations from page 25, 26, 33, 34, 107, 263 and 281 are from the *Toronto Star*. Reprinted by permission.

Quotations from page 20 and 221 are from the *Toronto Telegram*.

Quotations on pages 197 and 201 are from *Weekend Magazine*.

The quotation on page 267 is from *Quest*.

Every effort has been made to contact the copyright holders; in the event of an inadvertent omission or error, please notify the publisher.

STEPHEN BRUNT, a columnist at *The Globe and Mail*, is Canada's premier sportswriter and commentator. He is the author of *The Way It Looks from Here: Contemporary Canadian Writing on Sports*; *Facing Ali: The Opposition Weighs In*; *Mean Business: The Rise and Fall of Shawn O'Sullivan*; *Second to None: The Roberto Alomar Story* and *Diamond Dreams: 20 Years of Blue Jays Baseball*. He lives in Hamilton, Ontario and in Winterhouse Brook, Newfoundland.